Society and the Absurd

A Sociology of Conflictual Encounters

T0338971

Society and the Absurd

A Sociology of Conflictual Encounters

SHLOMO GIORA SHOHAM

SECOND REVISED EDITION

sussex
ACADEMIC
PRESS

BRIGHTON • PORTLAND

2 4 6 8 10 9 7 5 3 1

First published 1974 by Basil Blackwell, Oxford; this second, revised and expanded edition published 2006 in Great Britain by
SUSSEX ACADEMIC PRESS
PO Box 2950
Brighton BN2 5SP

and in the United States of America by
SUSSEX ACADEMIC PRESS
920 NE 58th Ave   Suite 300
Portland, Oregon 97213-3786

British Library Cataloguing in Publication Data
A CIP catalogue record for this book is available from the British Library.

Library of Congress Cataloging-in-Publication Data
Shoham, S. Giora, 1929–
    Society and the absurd : a sociology of conflictual encounters /
    by Shlomo Giora Shoham.— 2nd rev. ed.
    p. cm.
    Includes bibliographical references and index.
    ISBN 1-84519-067-X (pb : alk. paper)
    1. Social norms. 2. Social interaction. 3. Alienation (Social psychology) 4. Deviant behavior. 5. Conformity. I. Title.

HM676.S46 2006
302.5′44—dc22

2005037864

Typeset and designed by G&G Editorial, Brighton & Eastbourne
Printed by TJ International, Padstow, Cornwall
This book is printed on acid-free paper.

Contents

Acknowledgments

The author wishes to warmly acknowledge the generosity of the Zegla Institute at the Buchman Faculty of Law, Tel Aviv University, as well as The College of Management at Rishon LeZion and the Gordon College for Education. I also wish to thank my assistant Dara Barnat, whose devoted and intelligent editorial work shaped the manuscript. Martin Kett should be thanked for the index. And Editorial Director at Sussex Academic Press, Anthony Grahame, has as usual facilitated publication of the book.

Introduction
The Breakdown of Meaningful Interaction

This volume sets out to study the breakdown in meaningful interaction among human beings. As we will discuss in greater detail, any meaning or knowledge of self, objects and others is bound to be normative. Norms are created by human beings for human beings, by groups for individuals and vice versa. They are born through conflict or interaction. The Absurd, therefore, is a breaking down of norms, or a series of grave disharmonies within them, as perceived by the individual. The self-concept is not inherited, but *built* by absorbing transmitted patterns of culture on an inherited biological potential. Similarly, objects are meaningless if not structured cognitively and cathected through the normative transmission of the relevant others. The latter are also presented to the self inside a value-laden normative envelope, and the synthesis of these influences is implied by the title of this work. Anglo-American sociology is notoriously value-skewed and adjustment-centered. Theoretically, this stems from Durkheimian premises, still very influential for many American sociologists, where "everything which is a source of solidarity is moral, and morality is as solid as these ties are numerous and strong".[1] Durkheim regarded non-conformity to group values not only as deviating behavior, but also as *bad* behavior.

Value-judgment is one of the recognized anathemas of social science. However, even sociologists have doubted the possibility of a value-free sociology.[2] There are, of course, some wide social phenomena, which may be studied with a certain degree of cold rational disinterestedness, although never with the lack of involvement a mathematician displays while analyzing a quadratic equation.

Such disinterestedness is hardly possible with the study of social deviation. Semantically, deviation is an aberration, a turning from the right course, obliquity of conduct. Language is not merely a symbolic tool of communication, but by describing someone as *deviant* we express an attitude, we morally brand him and stigmatize him with our value-judgment. Social deviation, like crime, is a social ill or a "social problem". The ultimate aim of the study of the etiology and pressures leading to crime and deviation (although Utopist) is to devise better ways and means to combat and prevent them. This stems from a clear-cut value-involvement. A physician studying the etiology of trachoma and syphilis is clearly *against* blindness and disintegrating limbs.

The original Durkheimian conception of deviance, which still reigns supreme in American sociology, regards the unadjusted, the pariah and the outsider as being detrimental to the interests of the group by definition, and their faulty solidarity invariably injures the group itself. Consequently, one of the vital norms of every group is that the individuals comprising it should "adjust" to its normative system and values. The term "adjustment" is imme-diately associated with the use of power and pressure to chip off the corners of the square peg so that it fits into the round hole. In statistical terms, "to adjust" signifies not to deviate from the modal value of the normal curve, say, one stan-dard deviation. Philosophically, it might have its roots in the Greek *meden agan* (nothing in excess) engraved on the temple of Apollo at Delphi. Actually, "adjustment" is a virtue prescribed by the group whose interest (i.e. solidarity) it serves, and which has the power to enforce it and apply sanctions to those who are maladjusted. The analysis of the processes leading to deviation in the Durkheimian tradition is necessarily based on an axiomatic value judgment that group cohesion, solidarity and conformity are "functional", social (as opposed to anti-social) and *good*.

"Adjustment" literature in the socio-psychological, psychiatric and educa-tional fields is based on this axiomatic premise. The image of a balanced personality, one that "plays according to the rules of the game", is a direct corol-lary of this premise. Of course, "adjustment" involves compliance with harsh and cruel standards of competition and overcoming status and class barriers, but the alternative is worse: social ostracism, economic hardship and the scorn of peers and associates. The Durkheimian system of analyzing conformity and deviation excludes the possibility that a society, although cohesive and conspic-uous for the solidarity of its members, might be anti-social, deviant and bad. G. Nettler once remarked, "The possibility that a society may be 'organized' on antisocial or unethical principles has been voiced by novelists – a possibility which Durkheim would have regarded as a contradiction in terms".[3] The prag-matic base for the adjustment-centered American sociology is its service involvement with bureaucracy, industry, commercialized culture and enter-tainment.

The "cult of adjustment" deepens and widens with increasing urbanization and standardization of production, consumption and the mass media. This process has been recorded on many levels, from the novels of Budd Schulberg and Nathaniel West, through the semi-sociological and sociological accounts of Vance Packard, David Reisman and William H. Whyte, to the philosophical expositions of Ortega y Gasset. The gist of these expositions is related to the standardized needs of a "mass-society", the necessity to cater for the statistical average. Of all distributions, the normal curve is the most cherished one. The cult of mediocrity is linked to the needs of mass production and standardized tastes in goods and services. The mode, the mean and the median are the idols of modern society, and its dreads and anxieties are measured by the number of standard deviations from the modal values. This leveling process creates an image of the social situation whose edges have been blurred and whose focal points unduly accentuated. The mass is intolerant of ambiguity. It wants a conspicuous image. It is also insensitive to finesse, where in order to be effective, a stimulus should hit it bluntly on the head. Their high priests feed sophisticated computers with the relevant or irrelevant data on the prevailing tastes of egg yolks, the colors of cars, and the vital statistics of the latest sex idol. Frequently, the prophecies of the electronic brains do not coincide with the interests of the high priests and their sponsors, and so enter the image-makers. Pohl and Kornbluth, the science fiction writers, conjured in their numerous books an image of a society run by Madison Avenue and its counterparts in other cultures. But their work is neither science nor fiction; it reflects today's reality. Modern society is towed by image-makers towards conspicuous consumption. Presidential hopefuls and *Encyclopedia Britannica*, whatever their merits, owe their popularity to the same technique which sells Kellogg's Corn Flakes and Carnation Milk. More than ever before, production goods, services and entertainment, cater to and promote the average and standardized need and taste. This ensures a wider market and better sales. Even "the special", "the exclusive", "the top people", "men who lead" and "people who decide the destiny of the world", are standardized images to ensure wider markets for artificially scarce products. In the realm of social images, quantity is synonymous with quality.

The demand can also be "promoted" to raise these modal values and, as the promoters and image-makers would stress, to augment, illuminate and glorify the widest common denominator of consumption. The catering of some American sociologists to the adjustment needs of production and Talcott Parsons and his disciples mainly characterize consumption. Tiryakian, in his article on existential phenomenology and the sociological tradition, calls the Parsonian sociology "rational optimism". He further claims that this school, because of its inherent value bias, "gives very little attention to social problems as reflections of an underlying crisis".[4] This seems to indicate that he is unaware of the saliency of social conflict as a problematic structural feature of modern society. The "equilibrium" model suggests that the ship of American society can be kept on its main course mechanically by means of an automatic pilot. Parsons's stance is, no doubt, based on Durkheim's value judgment that the maladjusted injure the group by slackening its solidarity. The deviance from the normative group cohesion is, therefore, by definition anti-social and bad. Parsonian sociology has a pre-conceived attitude towards normative phenomena and behavior. It tends to disregard some of their most salient features, particularly those we have stressed relating to normative disjunctions and normative disengagements. The lacuna in Parsonian sociology is not surprising. A Euclidian Geometry based on Euclidian axioms cannot possibly take into account the non-Euclidian Geometry based (from the Euclidian point of view) on nonsensical axioms. A total disregard of the existentialist social expositions would automatically be implied for sociologists orientated to adjustment. (The only attempt known to the author to compare American sociology and existentialism is Tiryakian's).[5] They would be conceptually incapable of dealing with the existentialist premises.

For Sartre, adjustment is the stereotyped "us object". The mass and the crowd follow images and slogans thrown at them by "the third" as leader. The crowd may also "rush into servitude and ask to be treated as an object"[6] by the image-maker, the *Das Man*. Each of the individuals "then forms the project of losing himself in this object-ness".[7]

In his early existentialist writings, Sartre emphasizes "being-for-itself" as the sole authentically existing entity. Any collectivity *by definition* hampers, injures, and twists this "being-for-itself". The images created by the impersonal collectivity are, therefore, inevitably objectifying instruments robbing the individual further of any authentic existence he may still possess. Sartre demonstrates that social images created by the "generalized others" of the social institutions cannot be grasped and comprehended subjectively by the individual. The image remains an abstract force, which drives, moves, and navigates him. He cannot perceive or experience the image as a meaningful part of himself; it remains only a lifeless vector – an unauthentic objectified driving force. To Sartre, the only human reality in existence is the subjective consciousness and conception of the self. This is the only source of transcendence ("If God is dead Man is God"), as well as the only basis of values.[8] Ego can never be subjectively conscious of the subjectivity of others, because he is a mere object (*en soi*) to their subjective consciousness, just as they remain mere objects for him. Ego's presence limits and obstructs alter's freedom and self-consciousness and vice versa. The result of this multiphasic limitation and obstruction is that most of the interaction and interrelation among human beings is initiated and terminated by fear, shame, pride and vanity. Social life is characterized according to Sartre by an endless and agonizing conflict. The truly existing entity is the individual. Others at best are nauseating, and social solidarity (if it exists at all) is based on amorphous, vague and negative values (from the individual's point of view). Other existentialists have similarly endorsed the individual as against society. Kierkegaard saw in the collectivity, in solidarity, mere ambiguity, indifference, anonymity and non-authentic existence. Heidegger's *Das Man*, the average, the commonplace, is the unauthentic superficial state of fallenness.

For Berdyaev, the authentic knowledge of things and therefore of existence is through affective attachment, an impossibility when applied to the collective impersonality. Jaspers visualizes the collectivity as always bringing out "the most superficial, the most trivial and the most indifferent of human possibilities",[9] and Marcel sees society as the most detrimental to the authentic existence of the individual. This literature and perspective has never been seriously scrutinized by adjustment-centered sociology.

In this work we have tried to begin a sociological analysis of such existentialist concepts as choice and estrangement, involvement and despair. Adjustment-centred sociology cannot deal with these themes. Can adjustment-centered sociologists comprehend anger of such intensity as Simmons and Winograd in *It's Happening*?

> Look at you, brainwashing a whole generation of kids into getting a revolving charge account and buying your junk. (Who's a junkie?) Look at you, needing a couple of stiff drinks before you have the guts to talk with another human being. Look at you, making it with your neighbor's wife just to prove that you're really alive. Look at you, screwing up the land and the water and the air for profit, and calling this nowhere scene the Great Society! And you're gonna tell us how to live? C'mon, man, you've got to be kidding.[10]

The rebels on the campuses of the United States were fighting against the war in Vietnam and for civil rights, not because social justice was good and the war served the interest of Big Money, but because "it's all a lie". The war in Vietnam was phony and racial discrimination was meaningless. The current trends might culminate, therefore, in a political non-ideology to supplement the anti-novel, the non-theatre, the atonal-music and the latest "minimal" school of the plastic arts. Man embraces the Absurd!

The Absurd is a breakdown of value-involvement, a disengagement both resulting from and leading to a breakdown in human interaction; this is why our sociology deals with the Absurd. The mixing of the two is no doubt a difficult task, riddled by conceptual pitfalls. However, the no-man's-land between sociology and existentialism has been very scantily explored. If our exploration of this neglected but intriguing labyrinth is but a beginning, we have at least begun.

Accidia and the Absurd
A Conceptual Discussion

Accidia is Not Anomie

We propose a conceptual revival of "accidia" ("acedy" or "accidie") to denote an individual's breakdown of involvement with social norms and values, just as "anomie" ("anomy" or "anomia") has been resurrected from a sixteenth-century usage to denote normative disintegration in society. The need for a distinct and specific concept of accidia stems from the fact that anomie was conceived by all its exponents, from Durkheim to Merton and beyond, as an attribute of groups and not individuals. For Durkheim, anomie was a collective hangover from a social (mainly economic) shock. One of its manifestations was the breakdown of controls over man's aspirations:

> Whatever class has been especially favored by the disturbances (of affluence) is no longer disposed to its former self-restraint, and, as a repercussion, the sight of its enhanced fortune awakens in the groups below it every manner of covetousness. Thus the appetites of men, unrestrained now by a public opinion which has become bewildered and disorientated, no longer know where the bounds are before which they ought to come to a halt . . . Because prosperity has increased desires are inflamed . . . The state of rulelessness or anomie is further heightened by the fact that human desires are less disciplined at the very moment when they would need a stronger discipline.[1]

Durkheim is speaking of a normative rupture of society. The effect of this on individuals is almost taken for granted, and the normative enclosure has burst open. Containment by the bumper effects of boundaries and limits has suddenly disintegrated. Individuals are exposed to the disrupting effects of limitless desires and boundless aspirations. Merton, Durkheim's contemporary apostle, also stresses the societal nature of anomie. This might come as a surprise to some students of human alienation, because in his now classic exposition of *Social Structure and Anomie*,[2] Merton expressly deals with *individual* modes of (mal)adaptations. However, the crux of Merton's analysis rests on the group, on the disjuncture between the social structure and the cultural system, between social goals and the normative avenues to achieve them. The individuals in

Merton's paradigm are affected by these social disjunctions but his units of analysis are still *societies* and not *individuals*. He expressly excludes mental processes, which cannot be anchored on the social and cultural levels of analysis from his study, and explicitly states, "Anomie refers to a property of a social system . . . Anomie, then is a condition of the social surroundings, not a condition of particular people . . . to prevent conceptual confusion different terms are required to distinguish between the anomic state of the social system".[3] This conception of anomie is focused, therefore, on a societal state and the individual's confrontation with it is secondary. The individual is left in the shade and his or her subjective state of mind is entirely disregarded. Merton realizes, no doubt, that the socially focused conceptualization of anomie leaves a lacuna and calls for a separate personal concept of anomie. He refers us, therefore, to *anomia,* a term coined by Srole to describe the anomic state of the individual. Still, accidia is more of a personal subjective state of mind than anomia.[4] The latter, as measured by the five variables in Srole's scale,[5] is again a confrontation of an individual to some societal states and not a description of individuals as such. Srole implies, thereby, that anomie as a property of society may be measured by the distribution of anomia as a property of individuals and vice versa. This assumes, quite unwarrantably, that objective social properties are always accurately reflected in objective individual properties, as if individuals' subjective perceptions – phenomenologically their experience of their society – were irrelevant and made no difference. This is, to our mind, untenable because any acute state of social anomie must be subjectively perceived as such by individuals, otherwise it would not necessarily be correlated with anomia as an objective property of individuals. This may be likened to the common sociological and Marxist fallacy, which is at best a crude simplification, of regarding an objective state of economic need, measured by a low standard of living, as a predisposing factor to crime and delinquency. Perhaps the most ultimate and objective human deprivation is the threat of starvation. But most human beings would not regard this as a sufficient justification for cannibalism. Hindus would not regard it as an incentive to slaughter sacred cows, nor would many orthodox Jews resort to eating pork no matter how available it was. On the other hand, some individuals might subjectively define the lack of funds to buy a mink coat for a new mistress as a need potent enough to induce them to embezzle money from their employers. The relationship (or the lack of it) between anomie and anomia seems to be rather similar to the problematic correlation, asserted by crude versions of Marxism, between economic need as objectively measured in society and economic need as subjectively conceived by individuals.

Melvin Seeman, in a well-known paper, identifies five types of alienation.[6] The first three, powerlessness, meaninglessness and normlessness (anomie), are clearly attributes of society. The other two, isolation and self-estrangement, are subjective states of mind but they do not cover the same ground as accidia, for reasons which we shall specify later. We shall note here that powerlessness was the mode of alienation imputed originally by Marx in his early writings to capitalist society. He conceived this as a state in society where the worker does not have any means of control and decision over the processes of his work and its outcome.[7] A subsequent conceptualization in the Marxist tradition led to the term "fetishization", which was coined by George Lukács to denote the estrangement of man's creations from himself, his reification into a mere object in a surrounding world populated by an increasing number of thing–objects and people–objects.[8] These have lost their normative or affective meaning and have turned into neuter, dead weights in his cognition. However, "fetishization" still relates primarily to ego's surroundings; it is a condition of his environment and not of his subjective self. Although the comparison would be vehemently disputed and abhorred by Lukács, this is in some ways similar to Heidegger's *Das Man,* which also refers to the meaningless reification of things and persons. The existentialist counterpart to our conceptualization of accidia as a property of individuals consists of their conceptualization of the situation where a person becomes reified and objectified *to himself.* We may think here of Sartre's estranged consciousnesses of *être en soi* when applied to ego's self-image as perceived by ego himself.[9] We will say, then, that the objectification of ego's self as subjectively perceived by him is the core of our conceptualization of accidia as an attribute of individuals and not of social structures.

Accidia is Phenomenological, Not Behavioral

The second justification for the separate conceptualization of accidia stems from the fact that most, if not all, exponents of disorganization, anomie and alienation – from Durkheim, through Merton, Parsons, to Seeman and others – deal with value deviation (that is, *experienced* disengagement, the *consciousness* of detachment and withdrawal), and deviant *behavior* as one entity. At most, they regard value deviation as a predisposing factor to deviant behavior. Accidie, however, pertains to value deviation alone, which may not have any overt behavioral manifestations.

The fourth cardinal sin of acedy was the spirit of not caring. "The fourth heed of the beast of hell is slath [sloth], whyche is callyd of clerkys accidy".[10] This is the state of mind of heedlessness associated with depressive detachment, passivity and sadness. Indeed, the treatment of value deviation as predisposition to deviant behavior is bound to differ from the analysis of value deviation as an end product *per se.* Accidie, as a state of mind, might draw some of its conceptual contents from the Absurd as expounded by Camus. He sees it as a *mood.* His subjective definition of the absurd is inherent in his statement that, "there can be no absurd outside the human mind".[11] The Marxists would, no doubt, condemn this phenomenological conception of alienation, as a subjective state of mind, as an idealistic fallacy. However Lukács, in his now disowned early writings, aptly phrased the conceptual background for the Absurd as a state of mind when he dealt with subjectivity as a self-contained entity, which struggles irrationally to express itself and is confronted with an alien and hostile reality.

Accidia is Dynamic, Not Static[12]

Our concept of accidia, then, denotes value deviation, to be distinguished from anomie as a societal state and from other modes of deviant behavior. This would apparently have Merton's blessing. However, the latter's exposition of anomie and deviation, as well as Parsons and Seeman's, is more of a static description, taxonomy or typology. We, however, conceive accidia as a dynamic process, as indeed may be gleaned from the following original exposition of the term:

> The church appeared as old because your spirit was aged and already faded, and powerless from your ailings and doubts. For as the aged, having no hope any more to renew their youth, expect nothing but their last sleep; so ye, being weakened by worldly affairs, yielded yourself up to accidies and cast not your cares upon the Lord, but your spirit was broken, and you were worn out with your griefs.[13]

The dynamism of our conception of accidia rests in its being the final link in a triadic chain. First, there occurs an initial normative gap between previously internalized norms and newly transmitted ones. Secondly, there is congruity-motivated involvement by the subject to bridge this gap. And finally, if this involvement-effort fails, there is a value-breakdown, a disengagement – or to use current slang, the subject mentally "cops out". Our dynamic conception of accidia is anchored on the congruity principle, which is a basic ego defense mechanism – motivating human beings to resolve their normative conflicts and thus to re-establish their otherwise threatened cognitive balance and consonance. We shall deal at length in chapter 2 with the nature and functions of this congruity principle. However, only when the latter has failed to operate, only when ego has failed to regain normative homeostasis, is the way paved for the subsequent value breakdown. Here we might even risk an analogy with social control theorists such as Tannenbaum[14] and Lemert.[15] They claim that the very existence of norms and laws (together with their application and enforcement) *creates* crime and deviance. Analogously, the very existence of the congruity principle creates value deviations. That is to say, the fact of the subject's motivation to solve normative conflicts creates the possibility of failure, and thus creates its consequence, varying degrees of value breakdown and disengagement. The processes leading to accidia are dynamic in another sense, where they invariably entail a learning process quite similar to the learning of criminal behavior as hypothesized by Sutherland – one that is existential and not abstract.[16] Nobody becomes accidic by proxy, so to speak, as a mere spectator.

Identification with the normative conflict of fictional heroes and personalities in novels, films or television shows is abstract and insufficient. Only direct experience of normative incongruities, which do not lend themselves to patching up or to bridging, can produce the depressing depths off accidic states of mind. As against this, the current exposition of alienation is quite demonstrably static. Merton, in *Social Structure and Anomie*, did not intend to present more than a paradigmatic scheme of types at given coordinates of disjunction between cultural goals and the means to achieve them. He did not preclude the movement of an individual from one type to another but he did not try to represent his movement schematically. Rather, his presentation was a facsimile of an individual's deviant adaptation at a *given time*. Seeman's types are also a description of *states of alienation,* and Srole's items in his anomia scale seem to be a curious end-of-the-road despair. "It's hardly fair to bring children into the world the way things look for the future", or clichéd party small-talk, "these days a person doesn't really know whom he can count on", etc.

Accidia, as a dynamic process, also differs from the existentialist concepts of *Nausea and The Absurd.* Sartre's Roquentin suddenly gets an attack of Nausea, an utter disgust with existence, and he feels himself disconnected from his surroundings. "The Nausea is not inside me", Roquentin sums up his introspection, "I feel it out there in the wall, in the (waiter's) suspenders, everywhere around me. It makes itself one with the café, I am the one who is within it".[17] These fits of nausea are rather temporary and, as conceived by Sartre, not unlike periodic attacks of migraine.

The Absurd, as expounded by Camus, is "the confrontation of this irrational world and the wild longing for clarity whose call echoes in the human heart".[18] Here is a disjunction, which, at least outwardly, reminds us of Merton's dissonance between goals and the means to achieve them. With Camus, however, the basic disjunction is between the human need for congruity and clarity, and the lack of it in reality. The Absurd also resembles Merton's exposition in its rather static nature. Meursault (Camus' *Outsider*) epitomizes, no doubt, the absurd existence by the senselessness of his work, his lovemaking, the murder he commits, his trial and his death. But Meursault too is an end product. Camus does not divulge to the reader how this Absurd existence came into being. Men do not come into the world with an Absurd state of mind; some cognitive processes lead them to perceive the dissonance between their passion for clarity and the engulfing meaninglessness of their surroundings, or in Camus' own words, the confrontation of man's "urge toward unity and the clear vision he may have of the walls enclosing him".[19] Precisely these chains of processes are lacking in Camus' presentation of *the state* of the Absurd. But, apart from its being less dynamic, Camus' concept is the nearest in content to our concept of accidia, and to our analysis.

Accidia is a Disengagement, Not a Negation

Medieval sources state:

> Acedy, the besetting sin of the monk, was of two kinds: it sent him to sleep in his cell, or drove him out of it. The same vices attack all men, but not all in the same manner and order. Through Acedy . . . through not caring the monk is remiss at his task, and finds it wearisome to listen to the voice of the reader. The monk becomes finally disconnected with his surroundings.[20]

Precisely this disconnectedness of a person value-wise from his surroundings is the core of our concept of accidia. The point we wish to make is that the current expositions of alienation do not disconnect it from the cultural system of society. Alienation is conceptualized as opposing or negating that system not disengaging from it. We conceive of accidia, however, as a disengagement, which implies nothing necessarily about opposition or negation. Lemert once remarked, "Conformity and deviation are complementary aspects of the same phenomena".[21] And this certainly applies to the concept of deviation and alienation expounded by both American and Marxist sociologists. They situate alienation and deviance within the same cultural continuum as adjustment and conformity. We situate accidia, by contrast, outside this continuum altogether. The complementarity of conformity and deviation is obvious in the case of groups selling drugs, prostitutes and gambling to the public; this is a symbiotic relationship of supply and demand. Furthermore, membership of criminal or other deviant groups involves conformity to these groups' normative systems, and this is equivalent, for purposes of our present analysis, to conformity to the dominant normative system of the society. Other discrepancies, more subtle but not less basic, may be observed between accidia, and some of Merton and Seeman's conceptualizations. Merton's very use of the title *Individual Adaptations* for his typology connotes integration within the cultural system. These adaptations might push the individuals some standard deviations away from the mean, but it would not push them off the normal curve. In Merton's typology, "ritualism" is not a deviation either statistically or in terms of content. "Innovation" and "rebellion", *if successful,* don't merely endorse norms, they set them up. "Retreatism", however, is the nearest in content to accidia. Of course, this comparison is subject to our previous reservation that all Merton's types deal with static descriptions of societal states which entail overt behavior, whereas accidia is a dynamic process leading to a subjective state of mind of value-breakdown and disengagement.

As a matter of fact, Merton equates retreatism with accidie.[22] However the former, as he describes it, can result from "sour grapes" rejection of the normative system. Thus, retreatism would consist of an attitude of resentment directed at the cultural system. This would be a negative rationalized *attachment to* the "sour grapes" and completely distinct from the apathetic detachment of accidia. Indeed Merton characterizes retreatism as follows:

> [Accidia] is manifested in nostalgia for the past and apathy in the present . . . From the standpoint of its sources in the social structure this mode of adaptation is most likely to occur when both the culture goals and the institutional practices have been thoroughly assimilated by the individual and imbued with effect and high value, but accessible institutional avenues are not productive of success. There results a twofold conflict: the interiorized moral obligation for adopting institutional means conflicts with pressures to resort to illicit means (which may attain the goal) and the individual is shut off from means which are both legitimate and effective. The competitive order is maintained but the frustrated and handicapped individual who cannot cope with this order drops out. Defeatism, quietism and resignation are manifested in escape mechanisms, which ultimately lead him to escape from the requirements of the society . . . this process occurring while the supreme value of the success-goal has not yet been renounced.[23]

The goals are rejected not because an individual feels a value-disengagement and divorce from them, but because he failed to achieve them. Almost by definition this is a state of resentment. This is explaining away a failure to achieve a goal while still coveting it. In our terms, and for our analytical purposes, retreatism as a resenting negation is still an involvement. The "sour grapes" attitude, towards goals and values is not even ambivalence; it is a gluttonous affinity with the cultural system and the social structure. The involuntary rejection of goals is a superficial one full of self-pity. The moment the opportunity occurs, the retreatist-*cum*-resenter will grab the cultural goals he was barred from attaining, with hungry eyes and greedy hands. The accidic, on the other hand, is an "outsider" who is completely detached from both the "positive" and "negative" sides of the value continuum. He is Camus' Meursault, for whom killing or not killing amounts to the same thing,[24] who realizes cognitively that he has killed a man but who cannot comprehend his being declared a murderer.[25] He is also Camus' Judge-penitent in *The Fall*, whose most serious acts seemed to him to be those in which he was the least involved.[26] Meursault, being completely detached from the accepted value system, had to anchor himself on formal cues of behavior in order to make any headway in his daily dealings with people.[27] He could not rely on the *contents* of peoples' interactions because these entail value judgments and as such are completely alien to him. Merton's classification of retreatism includes psychotics, autists, pariahs, outcasts, vagrants, vagabonds, tramps, chronic drunkards and drug addicts.[28] Some of these are the resenting "sour grapes" negators, while others are "over-indulgers" and "sinners". Negation is still an involvement on the same continuum, albeit on the wrong side of it. There is probably no better portrayal of the theme that puritans and sinners are complementary aspects of the same phenomenon than Fellini's films. The debaucher in *La Dolce Vita* is a renegade ascetic. Both the nuns who stage Jullietta's burning at the stake and the characters at the house of pleasure are obsessed with hedonism. Dieticians tell us that both the obese gluttons and emaciated fasters are obsessed with food. In criminology we teach that very often there is a subterranean affinity between the underworld and its official prosecutors.[29]

The accidiac outsider, on the other hand, sees himself hovering above, drifting under, but never *on* the conventional normative continuum. He permits himself everything not through a rabid reaction-formation of eating pork on Yom Kippur, but because he cannot see how the accepted norms and values apply to him. The Judge-penitent even tells us in *The Fall* that he could grasp morals *in abstracto*, but when confronted with human beings they crumbled into mockery or vanity.[30] Meursault went to the movies after his mother's funeral.[31] He made love promiscuously by going mechanically through the act without any emotional involvement. Love was an awkward word to him.[32] Friendship was alien to him and his only reaction to a marriage proposal was, "why not".[33]

Pious saints like the Talmudic Reish-Lakish and the Catholic Augustine were notorious lechers in their youth. The switch from a "life of sin" to a life of religious fanaticism and apostasy is quite common. The accidiac, however, would tend to agree with Sartre that, "it seems that Man is incapable of producing more than an impotent God".[34] Similarly, when the examining magistrate brandishes a crucifix at Meursault, his natural reaction is in fact barely to react at all. Existential man is anaesthetized to *all* value-systems and commitments, particularly religious ones (including *committed* atheism). Similarly, accidiacs, to use the Judge-penitent's simile, would be like some of Dante's angels who were neutral in the fight between God and Satan.[35]

An individualistic counterpart of Durkheim, Merton and Parson's conceptualization of anomie and alienation has indeed been attempted by Karen Horney. She imputes to competitiveness the central stature given by Durkheim and Weber to the achievement motive, which is semantically different but similar in content. She continues:

> The influence on human relations of this competitiveness lies in the fact that it creates easily aroused envy towards the stronger ones, contempt for the weaker, distrust towards everyone. In consequence of all these potentially hostile tensions, the satisfaction and reassurance, which one can get out of human relations, are limited and the individual becomes more or less emotionally isolated.[36]

However, engagement in a cutthroat obstacle course towards the "room at the top", or towards scarce commodities, is hardly an accidiac disengagement, a breakdown of involvement. The achievement-oriented competitor might be motivated by asceticism (the Protestant Ethic preaching success as a sign of God's grace), or by hedonism (the belief that the spire of the social pyramid houses plenty of wine, women and song). He might end up on top with physical illness, fatigue and neuroses to be sold over to a fashionable psychiatrist, or he may lie broken at the base of the pyramid drunk with self-pity, "sour grapes" resentment or alcohol. More likely he would be somewhere in the middle huddled in a niche or hanging on with tooth and nail to the rough and slippery sharkskin surface of the pyramid. These, however, are the extremes of any individual's integration into a competitive social system. Emotional isolation might perhaps be a mild precursor to accidiac disengagement, but not when a person still regards himself as within the normative system of the group. The vain boredom of those at the top is the temporary fatigue of the mountain climber who has reached one peak. His feeling of aimlessness is an *effect* of achievement, and is usually an intermediate phase. The climber accustoms himself to the rarefied air and looks for another peak. Those at the top might be full of vanity and pride, but mostly they prefer to be so while retaining their expedient positions up there. The resentment of those in the gutters is also a proof of their value *attachment* to, not *detachment* from, the culturally approved goals. The isolation of the proud winners and the isolation of the bitter losers are both more physical than cultural. They are two different types of attachment to the same coveted cultural goals. By contrast, our conception of value-breakdown as accidiac disengagement places the value-deviant completely outside of the achievement pyramid. Accidia is a Camusian Fall. The Judge-penitent voluntarily relinquishes the heights of success, but does not succumb to the skid row of the waterfront at Amsterdam. Value breakdown is an esoteric stance *outside* the orbit of cultural goals and *away* from the swinging pendulums of normative continua. It is also, "quite solitary and very exhausting. No champagne, no friends raising their glasses, alone in a forbidding room".[37] Accidia goes with loneliness.

Stole's anomia items[38] are also indicative of a more structured alienation than accidia. His despair items are more of the involvement, of a movement towards the other extreme of the same continuum. The accidiac, on the other hand, is not structured. The powerless, the victims, even the martyrs are part of the social and normative structure, but the accidiacs are not. They stem from the social system but they came out of it and their links with society and its institutions are fragmentary and ethereal, like the smoke coming out of the engine and then hovering in diffusion over the passing train.

Among the types of alienation presented by Seernan, the nearest to our present exposition is "self-estrangement". The latter is quite in line with our conceptualization in so far as it relates to Fromms' description of "a mode of experience in which the person experiences himself as an alien and has become estranged from himself".[39] This is similar to the element of self-objectification, which we have identified as one of the components of accidia. However, Seeman relies considerably on an other-directedness element in his conceptualization of self-estrangement. The former, as expounded by Ortega y Gasset and Riesman, is a very common personality trait among individuals comprising "the mass society" and "the lonely crowd".

Other-directedness makes for "joyful obedience", and contentedness of the late Dale Carnegie brand. But for the accidiac, other-directedness is non-existent. Camus' Meursault regards the judge who is trying him for murder, the courtroom and its audience as having hardly anything to do with him. At most his trial appears to him as a game.[40] He assumes the spectator and not the participant role, and feels at times quite interested in the proceedings because it is his first time at a criminal trial. He sometimes even feels *de trop* in his own trial.[41] The Judge-penitent in *The Fall* is also "playing at doing things, and not doing, being and not being there".[42] The accidiac regards his environment as an arena where games are staged incessantly, but where he is a watcher not a player. To him, man is a game-player dabbling in semi-serious games, but the accidiac himself is not one of the players.

Existentialist Despair versus Sociologistic Adjustment

In a sense, our conception of accidia is the ultimate in despair, whereas many instances of anomie as Merton, Parsons and others describe them, are primary goals, means of activity, passivity dissonances. But this is *only the initial normative gap,* prior to ego's involvement, his effort to bridge it. Moreover, Merton and Parson's modes of anomic or alienative "adaptations" may be regarded paradoxically as "success-stories". Ritualism, for instance, is the "adaptation" or "adjustment" most coveted by employers the world over. The ritualist employee on the assembly line, or behind a desk in the Kafkaesque halls of the mammoth impersonal bureaucracy, is an asset. His ability to ruse means to the level of ends in themselves makes him an "ideal worker", a "perfectly adjusted individual" and "an integrated team worker", in the jargon of the industrial psychologist. The adjustment-centered sociologists might regard ritualism, therefore, as, at least, a semi-commendable mode of adaptation. We, however, may regard it as the epitome of value-deviation, not unlike Camus' argument that the Absurd is more likely to be experienced in the midst of daily routines.

These diametrically opposed conceptions of ritualism epitomize the differences between the adjustment-centered sociologists and the existentialists. To the former, the ritualist (a modern Sisyphus) is the modal condition of the assembly line and punch card community. And in the last analysis, this is as it should be. For Camus, Sisyphus is the hero of the Absurd:

> Sisyphus returning toward his rock, in that slight pivoting he contemplates that series of unrelated actions which becomes his fate, created by him, combined under his memory's eye and soon scaled by his death. Thus convinced of the wholly human origin of all that is human, a blind man eager to see knows that the night has no end, he is still on the go. The rock is still rolling.[43]

Parsons, more than others, represents the sociologists' value judgment as legitimizing adjustment. His statement, "action generally is teleologically oriented to the attainment of goals and to conformity with norms",[44] would fill Heidegger with abhorrence. For Parsons, the existentialist cry that the majority is always wrong would be a contradiction in terms. It would sound to him as the Absurd incarnate. The following definition of anomie characterizes his line of thought:

> Anomie . . . is a state where large numbers of individuals are to a serious degree lacking in the kind of integration with stable institutional patterns, which is essential to their own personal stability and to the smooth functioning of the social system.[45]

Parsons conceives the social system as moving in pulsating rhythms of interaction through streamlined modulations of change towards a shared system of value-orientation.[46] The catastrophe of anomie disrupts both the smooth flowing social structure and the peace of mind of individuals, which is anchored on conformity to the prevailing normative system. Alienation is not only "bad" for society but is also "the subjective tone of self destructive experience",[47] damned both by the dogmas of the Holy Ecclesia and the secular religions of social solidarity. Social psychologists such as Newcomb explicitly endorse social solidarity. Newcomb postulates that the more and the stronger the interpersonal interaction in a group, the less the antagonistic relationships among the individuals comprising it. Sartre, who regards meaningful communications among human beings as an ontic impossibility, would no doubt reject this kind of social solidarity orientation. To him, antagonism is the inevitable form of interaction between ego and his surrounding alters.

Merton does indeed follow Durkheim's conception of the "functionality" of value consensus. His advocacy of social cohesion is less outspoken than Durkheim's equation of solidarity with morality. But deviance is still generated, according to Merton, by a disjunction between the social and cultural structures, whereas the "functional" (i.e. *good*) state of affairs is when "cultural goals and institutionalized norms operate jointly to shape prevailing practices".[48] These expositions of alienation, while advocating (overtly or by implication) value-consensus, provide an easy dichotomy of "ins" and "outs". By contrast the accidiac, in line with some existentialist premises, refutes the feasibility of value-consensus and dismisses the notions of solidarity as a delusion. The despair of the accidiac constitutes, no doubt, a value judgment. But the sociologistic advocacy of cohesion and consensus is equally a value judgment. This is apparently inevitable, as Morris Cohen aptly states:

> This effort to look upon human actions with the same ethical neutrality with which we view geometric figures is advisable. But the questions of human value are inescapable, and those who banish them at the front door, admit them unavoidably and therefore uncritically at the back door.[49]

The existentialist value judgment implies, rather bluntly, that the adjustment of an individual to the normative system of the group is both undesirable and impossible.

Heidegger's *Dasein* – man's being-in-the-world – is at the same time being-with-others (*Mitsein*). Whereas *Dasein*, through introspection, may lead to a quest for meaning and the authentic understanding (*Verstehen*), the inevitable being-with-others subjects the *Dasein* to the generalized-other (*Das Man*). Heidegger, unlike Mead, sees in this generalized-other the root of all evil. Because of its objectified nature, *Das Man* is an amorphic identical image of "They", or "Anyman", who is mainly characterized by blurred features, ambiguity and mediocrity. Man's relationship with *Das Man* can only be based on clichés coined by the channels of public opinion (*Offentlichkeit*). Intercourse with *Das Man* cannot be through mutual and authentic understanding, but is always by means of trivial small talk (*Miteinanderreden*). For *Dasein*, Man's authentic being-in-the-world, to "adjust" to the generalized-other, would be to undergo an existential lobotomy. Only then in a vegetative state after the frontal lobes have been severed, can one bear the diffusion (*Dispersio*) and anxiety (*Angst*) generated by the interaction with *Das Man*. Man's being-with-others, the highly coveted sociologistic "adjustment", is for Heidegger a state of fallenness (*Verfallen*),[50] not from eternal grace but from authentic existence.

Sartre's chapter on "bad faith" (*mauvais foi*) in *Being and Nothingness* is well summarized. "My reactions to the extent that I project myself toward the other, are no longer for myself but are rather mere presentations . . . consciousness of another is as not being; its being-in-itself of 'now' and of 'here' is not to be. To be conscious of another means to be conscious of what one is not".[51] Ego as subject, as *Dasein*, as being-for-itself, is the center and source of existence. The leveling down of this authentic uniqueness of ego to the rank of the generalized-other is a decapitation. The advocates of social "integration" and "adjustment" call for cohabitation between *Dasein* and *Das Man*. This is impossible because the subjectivity of ego cannot interact with alter. When *Dasein* is exposed to the generalized-other and becomes part of it, it loses its authenticity and becomes an entirely different entity. It has changed. The adjusted person is a socialized zombie.

In social psychology, dissonance theorists postulate that experience of failure poses new and greater challenges. One is induced to rationalize that "one learns through experience", "one is hardened by life", "one is made tough by dangerous exploits", etc. The existentialists, however, would disagree. To them, the ordeals of ego's encounter with society and its institutions weaken and numb him. He is softened and becomes spent in the process. For the existentialists, adjustment is degradation, falsification and hell on earth. It is the fall from the pedestal of the center of existence to become a speck of dust in the shifting sand dunes of collectivity.

Heidegger and Sartre aimed high. Their premises completely undercut, among other things, the theoretical bases of adjustment-centred sociology. This is not unlike the way Kant and Nietzsche completely undercut God-based metaphysics. Many contemporaries such as D. H. Lawrence, George Orwell, Kafka and Camus, as expounded by the existentialists, have voiced the impossibility of adjustment. All eulogized the incompatibility between the music of their hearts, the high snowy mountains reached after a long and lonely journey into their inner space, and the sorry state of things "out there" as managed by the dilapidated "generalized-other". Orwell tried more than Lawrence to come to terms with alter, but both conceded defeat. Lawrence became immersed in his subjective modulations of sex, as real as chariots in the evening clouds, while Orwell, down and out, contemplated the glittering soap-bubble of socialist Utopia destined to burst, leaving only the pigsty of *Animal Farm*.

Perhaps a clown has carried out the keenest exposition of the existentialist fallenness. Henry Miller writes:

> If you stop still and look at things . . . I say look, not think, not criticize . . . the world looks absolutely crazy to you. And it is crazy, by God! It's just as crazy when things are normal and peaceful as in times of war or revolution. The evils are insane evils, and the panaceas are insane panaceas. Because we're all driven like dogs. We're running away. From what? We don't know. From a million nameless things. It's a rout, a panic. There's no ultimate place to retreat to – unless, as I say, you stand stock still. If you can do that, and not lose your balance, not be swept away in the rush, you may be able to get a grip on yourself . . . able to act, if you know what I mean. You know what I'm driving at . . . From the time you wake up until the moment you go to bed it's all a lie, all a sham and a swindle. Everybody knows it, and everybody collaborates in the perpetuation of the hoax. That's why it's so easy to trump up a war, or a pogrom, or a vice crusade, or any damned thing you like. It's always easier to give in, to bash somebody's puss in, because what we all pray for is to get done in proper and come back. If we could still believe in God, we'd make him a God of Vengeance. We'd surrender to him with a full heart the task of cleaning things up. It's too late for us to pretend to clean up the mess. We're in it up to the eyes. We don't want a new world . . . we want an end to the mess we've made. At sixteen you can believe in a new world . . . you can believe in anything, in fact . . . but at twenty you're doomed, and you know it. At twenty you're well in harness, and the most you can hope for is to get off with arms and legs intact. It isn't a question of fading hope . . . Hope is a baneful sign; it means impotence. Courage is no use either: everybody can muster courage – for the wrong thing.[52]

Meaninglessness and nothingness are embodied in death, *Thanatos*. Miller's account of man's fallenness is complemented by existentialist philosophers' emphasis on death. Jaspers, for instance, regards human existence as a prelude to death, with the ultimate teleological dominance of the latter. Apart from the bio-social processes inherent in this fatal progress, it is accompanied by a slow, or in some cases quick, rape of innocence. On our way to *Thanatos* we shed our childhood dreams one by one. With the last vestiges of our *naïveté*, we sever whatever has remained of the umbilical cord, which tied us to sweet pre-natal suspended animation. The blunting of sensitivities and an opaque-eyed déjà vu thus marks the end of the race. A combination of Celine's long *Journey into the Night* and Beckett's couple in *Happy Days* slowly sinking into their heap of mud. Our limited span of existence, which for Heidegger is more primordial than man himself, generates a continuous *angst,* which is the basic mood of human existence. Moreover, there seems to be nothing in our cognition of the world, except some transcendental delusions or temporary sensual narcotics, which can alleviate this underlying anguish. We have no choice, apparently, but to join Camus' Sisyphus in recognizing, "the ridiculous character of the habit (of living). The absence of any profound reason for living, the insane character of that daily agitation and the uselessness of suffering".[53]

Let us assume that our cognition of the world becomes meaningful only within an ethical context. The existentialists assert the impossibility of *social* ethics, of social responsibility and of an ethical context in general. This makes our cognition a mere mechanical perception and never meaningful knowledge. The existentialists deprive us of the comforts of our delusions of meaningfulness at the very outset. Furthermore, they hold that our efforts to combat *Thanatos* by *Eros* are doomed to fail. Sartre extends his position as to the impossibility of meaningful relationships between ego and alter to the ontic absence of love. There cannot be an effective link on an equal basis between a *pour soi* and an *en soi.* Emotional attachment between individuals is a dyad of victors and vanquished; love is subjugation. Love clogs the smooth operation of social organizations, and of the depersonalized "units" running them. A properly impersonal unit can replace any "faulty" unit. The liberal Bibikov in Malamud's *The Fixer* hangs himself, and Gletkin, whose streamlined efficiency is not stultified by pity or any other altruistic affects, replaces Koestler's humane Ivanov. The dialectics of *Eros* and *Thanathos* have indeed been a basic tenet of psychoanalysis since Freud's exposition of these two "cosmic" instincts as unevenly dominating Man's life. *Eros* constantly loses to *Thanathos* until the latter "at length succeeds in doing the individual to death".[54] Freud, however, conceived this dichotomy as a struggle within the individual of libidinal forces and aggression. The existentialist view transcends ego's psyche, it sees the authentic being of ego seared, singed and smothered by its constant clashes with the social structure and institutions. These clashes are meaningless and absurd precisely because we cannot even guess their purpose. Whatever the latter, sinister or righteous, the authentic existence of an individual, his *Dasein,* is stripped of its *Eros* by *Thanathos* in the guise of the social system. Man becomes a reified zombie, an objectified entity of clichés and routines. If death is depersonalization, then the social system is death.

Enforced Freedom

Heidegger's bizarre use of the word "freedom" is rather misleading. What he actually means is that man is thrown into this world, and he is propelled in free fall towards an ontic certainty – his death. It is the freedom of one galloping down a steep road. One falls towards one's end without the cushions of comforts and illusory purposes because there aren't any. What remains, then, is a thrownness (*Geworfenheit*) propelled towards annihilation with the accompanying moods of anxiety and despair. Heidegger expounds this grim freedom with characteristic teutonic heaviness:

> Anticipation reveals to Dasein its lostness in the they–self, and brings it face to face with the possibility of Being–Itself, primarily unsupported by concernful solicitude, but of Being–Itself, rather in an impassioned Freedom towards Death – a freedom which has been released from the illusions of the 'they' and which is factical, certain of itself and anxious.[55]

On the other hand, Sartre's conception of freedom is muddled and rather hard to follow. The first impression one may gather from the chapter on Freedom in *Being and Nothingness*, is that he postulates nothing more than a serpentine version of classic indeterminism.[56] If this was his message, he no doubt renounces it in his political play, *Les Sequestrés d'Altona*. The main character, the Butcher of Smolensk was not a free agent. His blood and soil upbringing, his Krupplike industrialist father and Prussian militarism made his performance in the SS virtually predestined.

However, the following passage on the condemnation to freedom is not unlike Heidegger's being-thrown-to-freedom. Sartre says:

> If negation comes into the world through human reality, the latter must be a being who can realize annihilating rupture with the world and with himself . . . the permanent possibility of this rupture is the same as freedom . . . I am condemned to exist forever beyond my essence, beyond the causes and motives of my act, I am condemned to be free . . . Freedom is precisely the nothingness which is made-to-be at the heart of man and which forces human reality to make itself instead of to be.[57]

Sartre appears to be saying that through action man struggles towards an authentic existence, but is fated to acquire an inauthentic essence. It is as though the characters from the Brothers Grimm or *The Arabian Nights,* through contagion, draw a curse upon themselves and turn gradually to stone. Man is condemned to action and interaction because, as Being-for-itself, he is surrounded on all sides by inanimate objects, by being-in-itself. Therefore he is under a life sentence to freedom, which is also the means by which the conscious Being-for-itself can be continually annihilated and lost into being-in-itself.

Camus' Meursault exemplifies this fated freedom, this freedom to lose one's self and to relinquish one's subjectivity and responsibility, when he does not have the faintest idea why he killed a man, and goes through the motions of his own trial as if he was not there at all. Sisyphus is faced with the freedom of thrown-ness (*Geworfenheit*). "In a universe suddenly divested of illusions and lights, man feels alien, a stranger. His exile is without remedy since he is deprived of the memory of a lost home or the hope of a promised land".[58] Indeed, a possible link between existence and essence is that the latter is the channel through which we grasp the present without the necessity ever to anchor on the past or the future. The existentialists raised the present from its rather low stature. Most of the "isms" faced the future, "for a new world", "for a greater society", "for the blooming of a million flowers and a thousand suns". The romantics eulogized the present by making love and singing love songs to the past. With an exclusive focus on the present we create some more vantage ground for despair. No challenges of the hills beyond and no bittersweet remembrance of things past. Being-for-itself is an encounter with the stark-naked moment with no comforting shades to soften the glare.

Transcendence and Despair

Heidegger claims that the chronic meddling of metaphysics in the affairs of *Dasein* created the illusion that only transcendental premises may infuse meanings to Being. When these fail to deliver the goods, man slumps into a mood of forsakenness.[59] Forsakenness is the price for imputing to transcendence powers that it does not have. When asking questions which have no answers from someone who *cannot* answer them one gets only echoes of one's own anguished queries boomeranging from the void.

Sartre, too, deplores the metaphysical adventures of the being-for-itself, its incessant search for reincarnations, its dreams of resurrection and prime movers. Being-in-itself has chronic megalomania – it wants to be God. Well, the latter is an ontic impossibility and being-for-itself, by its transcendental meanderings, becomes a useless passion.[60]

Kierkegaard traces Man's despair to his constant failure to relate the individual's truth with everything else, which is the untruth. "If life is despair as Kierkegaard stipulates", says Camus, "existentialism is philosophical suicide because by it thought negates itself and tends to transcend itself in its very negation . . . In the absurd world the value of a notion or of a life is measured by its sterility".[61] Accidia is the confrontation with this sterility.

Accidia: Summary and Definition

As a concluding summary of this chapter we present the following schematic description of Accidia as distinct from the sociologistic expositions of Anomie and Alienation:

Accidia	Anomie and Alienation
Property of Individuals	Property of Groups
State of Mind	Overt Behavior
Dynamic Process	Statified Description
Detachment from the Social Structure	Institutionalized Negation
Self-Disconnectedness	Adjustment Centered

We are now in a position to put forward a working definition of the Absurd, which stems from our previous analysis.

Albert Camus sees the Absurd as the confrontation of the irrational world and "the wild longing for clarity whose call echoes in the human heart".[62] In crude epistemology this would mean that the Absurd is a disjuncture between one's own ideal image of what things should be and what they are now.

The insight of intellectual Olympians must, alas, be broken down in order to be palatable to us mortals. We may reformulate Camus' statement as meaning that the Absurd is a state of mind; a breakdown of value-involvement, disengagement. Any individual is prompted by the congruity motive to bridge whatever normative disjunctures may arise between his previously internalized norms and new normative transmissions. But if he fails in his efforts he is faced with the Absurd. This definition contains, no doubt, many concepts that call for further elucidation and relationships that need clarification.

Our definition divides into two basic themes. The first is the *initial disjuncture* between the norms previously internalized by an individual and the new normative transmissions to which he is exposed. The second is the *breakdown of involvement*, the disengagement experienced by an individual following his unsuccessful attempts to bridge this normative disjunction. A dynamic process is inherent in our definition and we may note five consecutive developmental stages of this process:

1. Previous normative internalization
2. Novel normative transmission
3. Initial disjunction
4. Congruity-motivated involvement
5. Absurd breakdown

The first theme consists of stages 1–3, while the second theme consists of stages

4 and 5. These five stages also contain the key concepts of our definition. We will analyze them in detail, one by one, in Chapter 3. But first we must turn to a discussion of the general picture of man as motivated by the congruity principle; a picture which has underlain ancient philosophy, as well as modern sociology, religion as well as science, adjusted man as well as forsaken man.

The Congruity Principle

In Chapter 1 we defined the absurd as a breakdown of congruity-motivated involvement. In Chapter 3 we will attempt a precise theoretical analysis and explication of this breakdown and disengagement process. But first, in this chapter, we will try to get some idea of the main features of this process by briefly surveying and discussing the broad manifestations of the congruity principle in the history of philosophical, psychological and sociological thought. Later in the chapter we will look, in a comparable way, at the literature relating to the actual efforts men undertake to render the incongruous congruous. This will introduce us to the processes involved in men's attempts to bridge over whatever disjunctions may happen to arise between them and newly transmitted normative expectations, requiring different behavior and perhaps even a different way of life from them. It is men's failure to bridge this gap, having first made the effort to do so, which leads to the absurd and accidic states of mind, discussed in Chapter 1.

Feature and Functions of Congruity

Homo Conveniens

The human longing for unity has been stressed and relied on by many – from the pre-Socratic Parmenides through the European-Jewish Freud, to the Mediterranean Camus. The latter regarded the congruity motive as a supreme implement and necessity:

> To understand is above all to unify . . . if thought discovered in the shimmering mirrors of phenomena eternal relations capable of summing them up and summing themselves up in a single principle, then would be seen an intellectual joy of which the myth of the blessed would be but a ridiculous imitation. That nostalgia for unity, that appetite for the absolute illustrates the essential impulse of the human drama.[1]

Camus places the congruity principle above everything else as a characteristic of human effort. From monotheism to $E = mc^2$, the grand triumphs of unification to the myriads of monistic "nothing-but" theories in specific fields attempt to squeeze the relevant phenomena into one generalized blanket: Historical Necessity, The Will to Power, Dialectical Materialism, Functional Analysis, Conflict Theory, Operant Conditioning, *L'Uomo Delinquente*, and Differential Association. By *reductio ad absurdum* we may even take Camus' own insistence on the primacy of the passion for unity as a tautological demonstration of the plenipotency of the congruity motive. Man is, therefore, not so much a *Homo Sapien*, a *Homo Faber* or a *Homo Ludens* but a *Homo Conveniens* – the harmony-seeker, the one who strives for unity and congruity.

The initial gap between a receiving self and new (and possibly very different) normative transmission tends to be narrowed, as demonstrated by Alfred Kuhn, his associates and pupils,[2] by a *subjectivistic bias*. The new normative transmissions are twisted to fit previously internalized ones. Consider, as the apogee of such subjectivism, Kazantzakis' advice to his fellow humans. "Greetings man, you little two-legged plucked cock! It's really true (don't listen to what others say). If you don't crow in the morning, the sun does not come up". On the other hand, the congruity motive also produces a *tendency to conform*, as demonstrated by Sheriff, Asch, Crutchfield and others.[3] This moves the individual's former norm stance towards the new normative transmissions sanctioned by his membership or reference groups. The reliance on the congruity principle is indeed universal. As we shall see in the following survey, it has been taken for granted in philosophy and theology from time immemorial. In some of the social and behavioral sciences it has been treated as an axiomatic starting point for elaborate theoretical models and in social psychology it has been at the base of the Balance and Dissonance theories. However, we may observe that these were either axiomatic uses of the congruity principle or its phenomenal description. There were hardly any attempts to deal with the functional reasons as to why should there be such a unifying principle at all.

Let us take a brief look at how *Homo Conveniens* and the congruity principle have presented themselves in the history of philosophical thought. Apart from Parmenides, who based his philosophy almost exclusively on the central unity of things, most of the other pre-Socratic philosophers, notably Pythagoras and Anaxagoras, also incorporated into their teaching the harmonious congruity of the universe. The latter even postulated that the Black Furies, the cosmic watchdogs, will chase any planet back into orbit that breaks the congruity of the universe by deviating from its course. For Plato, justice is synonymous with order and evil with disharmony. The systems of morals and ethics equate the good with wholeness and unity.

In the Far East we find the *Rig-Veda* proclaiming Unity as underlying all creation. "One breathed breathlessly by itself. Other than it there has been nothing since".[4] Everything that is not incorporated into this unifying reality is an illusion and although the "One" may be obscured by human verbosity it is still the core of essence. "Priests and poets with words make into many the hidden reality which is One".[5] The Buddhist Nirvana, as well as the Union with the Divine postulated by Lao-Tsu, are transcendental counterparts of the individual's craving to immerse his separate entity into a primeval unity. Indeed, the *Book of Tao* conceives the whole of Creation as tied with umbilical cords to Unity that gives it life and form. The ancient things that hold the Unity are Heaven, which by Unity is bright and pure, and Earth, which thus is firm and sure.

The congruity principle in Jewish mysticism is rather more elaborate. It is achieved through the individual's partaking in the all-embracing and engulfing Torah. This mystical union is conceived by the Kabbalists not as an intellectual activity, but as a means of a fusion with Divinity. "In union", says a fourteenth-century Kabbalist, "there is redemption".[6] This is rather similar to the "participation mystique" imputed by Lévy-Bruhl to the primitive mentality.[7] However, the similarities between these two conceptions of congruity are in their forms and dynamics. Content-wise, the congruity of Jewish mysticism is with the Torah, which is an elaborate normative system, whereas the congruity of the individual through the "participation mystique" is with creation at large. This, again, is hardly new. The pantheism of Spinoza postulates, "The greatest good is the knowledge of the union which the mind has with the whole nature".[8] The congruity principle thus becomes the foundation of all ethics.

In later Western philosophy, Kant stresses the use of the congruity principle in logic and science but not in metaphysics. Hegel's dialectical movement of opposites towards the unifying synthesis is another instance of congruity. Nietzsche elucidates the congruity principle in flowery language:

> We have no right to be disconnected; we must neither err "disconnectedly" nor strike the truth "disconnectedly". Rather with the necessity with which a tree bears its fruit, so do our thoughts, our values, our yes's and no's and ifs and whethers, grow connected and inter-related, mutual witnesses of one will, one health, one kingdom, one sun".[9]

Finally, Bergson takes as axiomatic the unifying function of the intellect. "It seeks unification simply because it has need of unifying".[10]

The behavioral and social sciences also deal mostly with the "hows" of the congruity principle and not with its "whys". Jung, far more than Freud, whose conception of personality was dialectic, of a pressure-counter-check kind of equilibrium, conceived the human psyche to be incessantly striving for completeness, wholeness and congruity. Newcomb seemed to have echoed some basic tenets of Far Eastern philosophy of aesthetics when he introduced into social psychology the individual's "strain toward symmetry". Congruity and symmetry may presumably be regarded as special instances of a deeper harmony that is inherent in Unity. The consistency mechanism as expounded by Heider has initiated a vogue in social psychology,[11] notably Cartwright and

Harary's work on the Balance model, Osgood and Tannenbaum's congruity model and Festinger's Theory of Cognitive Dissonance.

As a proper epilogue for our present survey of the literature on congruity we may quote a citation from a paper on a "Sociological Model of Consensus", in an issue of *The American Sociological Review*:

> Consensus should have an importance in sociology comparable to that of energy in physics – namely, as a unifying concept, an abstraction that will include and relate more specific concepts and data. Light, heat, sound and electro-magnetism are forms of energy; so I think, culture, structure, norm-role, symbol and so on, should be treated as forms of consensus.[12]

This, no doubt, is a gross exaggeration and the epitome of sweeping generalizations. It shows, however, the importance imputed by some social scientists to the congruity principle and similar mechanisms. The scarcity of etiological, functional and other non-phenomenological analyses of congruity makes it even more astonishing. One possible reason is that the "whys" of the congruity principle are on the far borders, not even on the threshold of knowledge. We shall try to examine in the following pages some of the reasons and functions of congruity in a rather rudimentary form, thus risking a just censure from potential critics for dealing with "science fiction", or worse still for dabbling in metaphysics.

The Paralyzing Effect of Incongruity

One reason for the very existence of the congruity principle (suggested by Brown[13]) is that incongruous and contradictory normative mandates tend to paralyze action. This is incapacitation, passivity, or, if regarded with some pomposity, partial death. Therefore, the life force itself (without invoking Bergson's semantically similar, but discredited, concept of "vital impulse") is against normative dissonance. A partial verification of this premise may be found in the research carried out by Miller as to the resolution of the various types of conflict in goal-directed behavior.[14] An individual is dragged out by congruous decision making from the vacillations of an approach–avoidance conflict, the cringing of an avoidance–avoidance conflict and the starvation by an excess of riches of an approach–approach conflict.

However, this function of congruity would apply to a rather limited area of personality processes. Many theorists would be reluctant to impute any application to this inertia-through-conflict reason for congruity above and beyond some simple forms of decision-making involving relatively few variables.

On a deeper level of analysis, we recall some perfectly contradictory drives, pressures and normative mandates to which the human personality is exposed without their having necessarily a paralyzing effect on action. Lind and many others have collected some value contradictions inherent in our cultural mandates. For example, "this is a world in which it is every man for himself and the devil take the hindmost". But, "no man lives for himself alone; you should love your neighbor as yourself". "It is smart to have the newest model automobile, the most modern industrial processes, and the latest technical equipment". But, "anybody who proposes tampering with our fundamental institutions of government or industry is a dangerous radical and should be shipped back where he came from". "Hard work and thrift are signs of sound characters; they are dependable roads to success". But, "the smart boys know how to make money and go places without working".[15]

These conflicts are all around us. Many of them remain contradictory within the cognitions of individuals. They are not resolved and not glossed over by a dialectical synthesis. At most they are compartmentalized into different cognitive regions so that frontal clashes among the conflicting norms would be rare. Yet in most instances, except for occasional neuroses, we manage to carry on our overt and covert behavior without these conflicts paralyzing our actions. Moreover, if Freud was right, our whole existence is an arena of constant struggles between *Eros* and *Thanathos*. On a more abstract level, we may note a value judgment (inevitable in the sciences of Man), relating to the function of congruity as an antidote to inertia. The formal school of sociology regards the contradictory conflicts as holding both the social structure and the individuals within it in dynamic equilibrium. Conflicts here are "functional" and are described as bringing forth a strained equilibrium and not inertia, stability and not stultification. For lack of any better choice, the adoption of one of these two mutually exclusive value judgments becomes a matter of sheer taste.

Homeostasis

The tendency of the human body to maintain some steady states, which are apparently vital for its bio-physiological functions, may be related to a perceptual and behavioral balance and congruity. The human abhorrence of rupture, disjuncture or dislocation of some physiological processes are extended and transferred to cognitive phenomena and the perception of values and norms. Bio-physiological homeostasis thus serves as an etiological basis for the congruity principle in human behavior. Stagner builds a model of concentric circles leading from bio-physiological steady states to constancies in an individual's social environment. With some stretching of our theoretical imagination, we may find support for the present etiological function of homeostasis in the Freudian hypothesis of tension reduction through congruity and in Wynne-Edwards' theory of the function of social norms. The latter relies heavily in his homeostatic theory of society, both animal and human, on the congruity principle. He believes that natural selection has favored the evolution of man into a species that can feel the force of socially transmitted values. This capacity frees man from the necessity of evolving new innate releasing mechanisms to meet every change in the world around him. He can remain continuously adapted by changing acquired values from one generation to another.[16] This new phase of social Darwinism makes conformity to new normative mandates as necessary to the survival of Man as the ability of his ancestors to develop lungs in place of gills. The homeostatic basis of cognitive and normative congruity also imputes to the latter the functions of a defense mechanism against dissonance. If cognitive and normative homeostasis is as vital, or nearly as vital as the biological steady states, the congruity principle serves as a safety mechanism not unlike the sweating of the body and the widening of the arteries to regain temperature constancy. The immediate application to our theme is that if the congruity principle has been successful in rationalizing away any given cognitive dissonance and closing normative gaps, the involvement has been accomplished and no further value breakdown may be expected. Only those whose congruity defenses were weak or ineffective would be vulnerable to the subsequent value breakdowns.

As a supplement to the present premise, we note that the group also utilizes the congruity principle as a defense mechanism. Apparently, society is also geared towards preserving its homeostasis[17] by defending itself from the harbingers of disrupting innovations. The congruity principle would be linked here to some defenses against over-rapid social change. Cultural development, scientific discoveries (progress in the Spencerian sense) might be too quick, too sudden, or too revolutionary, if the pace of innovators were not curbed and slowed down. The innovating virtuosos had it perennially very tough; they had to encounter the resisting walls of previously accepted routine and mountains of sanctified tradition.

We may, however, perceive the individual innovator's plight as a corollary of the congruity-motivated self-defense of society. First of all, most self-styled innovators are more or less crackpots. For every Modigliani and Soutine there are thousands of brush and canvas dabblers who range between sheer fakes to sincere nonentities. An Alan Ginsberg or a Norman Mailer trails after him scores of bearded, dope-hazy imitators. For every Rickover, there are the numerous constructors of the latest model of a *perpetuum mobile* that "really works". Society has a built-in distrust and suspicion of *all* the innovators. This defense mechanism is reinforced by the sadly low statistical incidence of real genius. The latter, apparently, have to pay the price for their rarity; they too crash into society's bumpers against innovators, both real and phony. This is a quantitive defense mechanism. However, the congruity principle guards the homeostasis of society against innovators in a qualitative way as well. The perennial harsh treatment of innovators by society may be regarded as a filtering device against too revolutionary and therefore disruptive innovations. Over-rapid "progress", in any given area of culture, is disproportionate to the slower pace of development in other tangential areas, causing a cleavage of geological layers after an earthquake. Moreover, previous achievement and knowledge in the field might be too meager to support radical innovation and to absorb it in a process of organic growth. Ethically, society may not be mature enough to handle an innovation. Apparently, this defense mechanism had one of its lapses when it allowed the work of Einstein and Oppenheimer to culminate into the Manhattan Project.

Some of the implications of this qualitative congruity mechanism are: the slowing of the pace of innovations by the cult of mediocrity, the cherishing of the modes, means and medians, the standardization of consumption, production, and tastes, and the rounding off of protruding appendages in the bureaucratic structure. The impersonal *cum* streamlined *cum* adjusted *Homo Conveniens* brandishes the banner of "nothing in excess".

The present hypothesis has a science fiction bias, depicting society as stultifying, maiming, limiting, defacing, and clipping the wings of its creative innovators to serve its congruity-based homeostasis. A madman genius, who should know, enrolled even the psychiatrists to the cause of society's homeostasis. Antonin Artaud writes:

> A lunatic is a man who preferred to become what is socially understood as mad rather than forfeit a certain superior idea of human honor. A vicious society has invented psychiatry to defend itself from the investigations of certain superior lucid minds whose intuitive powers were disturbing to it.[18]

The congruity-based homeostasis of society operates, therefore, not unlike an electronic regulation device – passing on only a limited quantity and quality of innovations and innovators, decapitating the rest.

Congruity as Metaphysic

On the ontological and metaphysical levels, the congruity principle provides the most logical and relatively easily attained ever after. If the individual, the particle, becomes unified with the whole, which in turn is incorporated in the universal whole and the latter has seemingly no finality and temporality to its existence, the individual achieves immortality in his lifetime through participation in the universal whole.

Camus expounds this function of congruity as metaphysical rebellion, "a demand for clarity and unity . . . The metaphysical rebel . . . attacks a shattered world to make it whole . . . Metaphysical rebellion is the justified claim of a desire for unity against the suffering of life and death".[19] As in the traditional escatology, the quest for the hereafter is proportional to the pain and misery in the Here and Now. Plotinus, the third-century philosopher who was a most profound explorer of Unity, lived in an age of political disintegration, social decay and insecurity. He preached a *mystical union* with the divine, a negation of the parts by the whole, leading to the beholding of "a marvelous beauty; then more than ever, assured of community with the loftiest order; enacting the noblest life, acquiring identity with the divine".[20] This metaphysical function of congruity ties up with our previous exposition of the latter as an escape and defense mechanism. Indeed the words of Dean Inge, the modern disciple of Plotinus, may serve as a prime illustration for our premise. "In times of trouble like the present he (Plotinus) has much to teach us, lifting us up from the miseries of this world to the pure air and sunshine of eternal truth, beauty and goodness".[21] This brings us back to the main theme of our present work. The disregarding of temporal misery through unity with the transcendental (which is not dissimilar to the immersion of the individual in the immortal and infallible Party), and the escape from painful disintegration by regaining homeostatic stability, are but different phases of the same thing (i.e. overcoming normative disjunctures by means of the congruity principle).

Methods for Achieving Congruity

In the first part of the present chapter we surveyed some of the phenomena and functions of the congruity principle. In the following section, we shall proceed to analyze some of the actual processes of involvement to bridge over normative gaps.

Triadic Methods: Conflicts are "Good for You"

One of the most common modes of bridging normative disjunctures and conflicts is to postulate the functionality of these conflicts. It should be stressed that we are not concerned here with evaluating various theoretical attempts to picture the harmonization of normative contradictions (e.g. Simmel's conflict theory of society or, for that matter, Hegel's triadic compromises). Our concern is with the congruity-based involvements *by themselves*. Simmel utilizes the notions of equilibrium through conflict and Hegel explains almost everything through the dialectic harmonizing of opposites. But whether these theories are "false" or "true", empirically "sound" or "faulty", is irrelevant in the present context. Our interest is solely in the mechanisms that bind normative ruptures together so that the cognitive value-structure of individuals, who avail themselves of these mechanisms and methods, regains its internal consistency.

The "functionality-of-conflict" method of theorizing about congruity is one of the oldest. Heraclitus adopted it by advocating strife:

"Homer was wrong", he said, "when he prayed that strife might perish from among gods and men. He did not see that he was praying for the destruction of the universe; for, if his prayer was heard all things would pass away . . . Man does not know what is at variance agrees with itself. It is an attunement of opposite tensions, like that of the bow and the lyre."[22]

The main molders of Western thought, Kant, Hegel, Marx and Freud, have expounded this mode of conciliating among disjunctures later. The latter even summarized the whole of psychoanalysis as "a dynamic conception, which reduces mental life to the interplay of reciprocally urging and checking forces".[23]

Indeed, this triadic mode of congruity-motivated involvement is the easiest refuge for the perplexed. It is the least resistant avenue for regaining cognitive consonance, both in relation to a person's *Weltanschauung* (e.g. the contradictory forces of history), and the petty inconsistencies of everyday life (e.g. the female gossips of suburbia who are full of bile for one another but will stick together for better or for worse). Most of the phenomena involving inconsistent normative pressures, from emotional ambivalence to class conflicts, have been subject to this triadic theory of congruity.

The basic model of the latter is that two contradictory or inconsistent cognitive states are resolved into a congruous third state. The dynamic involvement in this triadic model takes the form of an obstacle course. Every new normative disjuncture is perceived as a novel task, an incentive for activity and creativity (e.g. an oyster encountering another limestone particle to cover with mother-of-pearl). Creativity becomes, thus, a process of catharsis accomplishment through the need to overcome a blockage. Normative disjunctures may, no doubt, be perceived by individuals as obstacles to be overcome by creative efforts. Freud stressed throughout his entire works that the libido soars to heights of expression only by the process of forcing itself through barriers (the stronger the latter the richer the ensuing creativity). He said, "It requires an obstacle to drive the libido up to a high point, and where the natural obstacles to satisfaction are not sufficient, men have at all times interposed conventional ones to be able to enjoy love".[24] Moreover, Freud imputes to the human sense of guilt, which is, by definition, on the cognitive level at least, a disjuncture between some normative mandates and the actual behavior of an individual, or in other words, the creation of culture. The pangs of Oedipal guilt through repressed parricidal-*cum*-incestuous wishes are responsible, according to Freud, not only for the genesis of law and order but also for the evolution of religion and art.[25]

One aspect of the process of involvement itself is that the harder it is the greater would be the value attached to the desired achievement of congruity. This is apparent in any task whose performance requires unusual hardships. The numerous obstacles, the harsh initiation rites, irrespective of the objective results, endear the end product to a person. The dissonance theorists try to explain this by a person's need to justify the great efforts he might have invested in a given task. Although the final outcome may not have been worth the trouble, he convinces himself of the higher intrinsic value of the projects to which he devoted so much energy or so many assets. The harder the initiation rites, the greater the prestige of the current "in" groups or castes is. Nobody can bear the thought that he wasted his life or part of it on trivialities or that his hardest and longest working hours were devoted to Sisyphian drudgery. This may lend another hue to Camus' revisiting of the Titan's plight, forever rolling the stone uphill. "The struggle itself toward the heights", he says, "is enough to fill a man's heart. One must imagine Sisyphus happy".[26] The pushing of the burden upwards by itself becomes finally a cherished routine. The expending of energy in the aimless task endears both hill and stone to Sisyphus. The efforts, the labor and the hardships involved build up the affective links between Sisyphus and his stone. The vested interests become ingrained in the climbing and pushing, *per se*, the end and goals are superfluous. Festinger's ingenuous investigations of the circle of believers in the prophetess of doom, whose proselytizing zeal increased after the doomsday predictions failed to materialize,[27] is another appropriate illustration of the triadic congruity technique. It would seem, however, that similar or even deeper insight into this congruity technique following a failure of expectations would be gained by studying the later phases of the seventeenth-century Kabbalistic Messianic movement initiated by Shabbetai Zvi. When the latter converted to Islam a shattering normative blow tore apart the cognitive structure of his followers. Shabbetai Zvi was undoubtedly the Messiah, how otherwise could he have raised their inner feelings of redemption to such heights of authenticity? However, the undeniable facts were that this Messiah became a formal apostate. Many of the followers regained their cognitive congruity by agreeing with the Rabbinical authorities, that the apostate Shabbetai Zvi proved himself to be a false Messiah and left the movement. Not so the inner core of believers led by Nathan of Gaza, who had recourse to the triadic technique of congruity by arguing as follows:

> After the original sin many sparks of saintliness have fallen and scattered among the secular powers and apostate religions, which were the realms of sin and pollution. The Messiah, the holy of holies himself, must therefore immerse himself in the filth of apostasy, so that he may gather these sparkles of saintliness from amongst the perfidious heretics and the secular powers. The latter's whole existence is balanced precariously on these holy sparks. If these are gathered and extracted by the Messiah, who had to pollute himself for this sacred task, the kingdom of evil shall crumble and true salvation shall reign supreme.[28]

The parallels with Christianity are of course striking. An apostate Messiah and a crucified Messiah have taken upon themselves the sins of humanity as a prerequisite for salvation.[29] Both Christianity and Shabbetaism have gained their initial impetus after the prophesied temporal triumphs failed to materialize.

The Kabbalistic terminology is also strikingly adapted to the triadic technique of congruity. "*Shevira*" is literally a rupture, a disjuncture brought about by the original sin and another flaw in creation, "the Breaking of Vessels", which gave birth to sin and evil. "*Tikkun*" is literally repairing, mending these ruptures so that a new cosmic harmony may be regained.

Dyadic Methods: Love = Death

The triadic congruity process described above involves the synthesizing of a third consonant state out of the incongruous ones. In the present section, we shall deal with a dyadic technique of congruity, which achieves consonance through excluding, defining and contrasting one part of the dissonant dichotomy with the other. Of the almost inexhaustible range of illustrations we may take four instances from four ascending levels of analysis:

(1) On the subjective level of affectation, the personalized perception of rupture and hurt as contrasted with homeostatic contentedness is pain. The congruity mechanism would operate here through the medium of sensitivity. The latter makes for a range of perception and emotions that are deeper, fuller and wider. These very same traits make a person more vulnerable to hurt than blunted sensitivity. Pain may thus be regarded as incidental to a fuller emotive and sensual life. The "romantic agony" may be invoked here not in the perverted love-is-pain of de Sade, but in the words of Musset, "*Les plus désespérés sont les chants les plus beaux*".[30]

(2) The widest application, however, of the dyadic congruity technique is in ethics and social interaction. Plotinus codified the principle, considered ancient even in his time, that otherness and sameness help to define and emphasize each other.[31] The definition of the socially conforming by contrast with the socially deviant, the law-abiding by exclusion of the criminal, and the socially "in", through excluding the non-deserving "out", is the societal application of this definition of otherness through contrast with sameness. "People like us" need the criminal to assert through him their image of righteousness. In psychoanalytic terminology, the quest for primitive justice, i.e. the allocation of evil to where it belongs (the criminal), reinforces the super-ego of righteousness. The "righteous" use the criminal as a contrasting medium to define themselves. Therefore the darker he is the brighter they shine. The criminals, the deviants and the pariahs serve also as a receptacle for the overflow of the aggressiveness of the legitimate citizens. The festive curiosity in the arena of the courtroom and the reports of crime in the news presumably stem from the same source. Genet voices a far deeper dyadic congruity technique. He claims that the sheer existence of social institutions such as justice and religion are functional corollaries of criminals and sinners. Judges owe their existence to their task of declaring guilt and making distinctions between criminals and non-criminals. The institution of justice stems, therefore, from crime and not vice versa. Likewise, the priest has the ability to declare guilt and absolve it, but the sinner has a trump

card up his sleeve; he may refuse to acknowledge guilt and worse still he may be reluctant to confess. What then would remain of the priest but a gesture, a form, and an empty shell covered by a robe and a miter.

(3) On the transcendental level, the dyadic technique of congruity is apparent mostly in second-century Gnosticism and the dualistic creeds, notably Zoroastrianism and the Manichean heresy. A clear conception of evil anchors one, by contrast, on the side of right. Righteousness has its borders honed and delineated through comparison with a viler sin. The perceptual gap between the two opposites becomes wider and one can safely assert one's virtue by separating oneself from any tangential proximity to sin. The dyadic technique of congruity, as applied to transcendental matters achieves a *reductio ad absurdum* lucidity in the words of Jacob Frank, the eighteenth-century Jewish apostate Messiah. He states:

> The subversion of the Torah can become its fulfillment . . . a man cannot ascend a mountain before descending beforehand the slopes of the valley leading to the mountain. We have first to degrade ourselves to the bottom of the vilest of pits, only then shall we ascend to eternal heights. This is the secret of Jacob's ladder of which I had a vision and he appeared to me very distinctly in the shape of V.[32]

(4) Most ethical expositions are dyadic in their essence: good and bad, evil and just, guilty and innocent. Some of the greatest minds of humanity – Spinoza, Kant, Nietzsche, Dostoevsky and Camus – have tried to find a significantly congruous basis for ethics. Some thought they actually found a measuring rod for the postulates of what *ought to be* as distinct from what *is*. One of the ingenious efforts to evade an ethical judgment seemed to be through Freudian psychoanalysis, which professed to operate on a totally distinct plane. However, as a therapeutic discipline it had no choice but to join the clamor of all the mental health advocates that maladjustment to the prevailing social and normative structure is *bad* and sanity as displayed by adjustment to society is intrinsically *good*.

The stultification through conflict might be a coveted state in some circumstances. The renunciation of temporal greed and eventually of all sensuous perception and cognition has been cherished by some Far Eastern creeds – consequently normative conflicts may be valued as the proper means to achieve this desired cognitive paralysis. The Taoist *Wu-Wei's* "action through inaction" may serve as a proper illustrative instance. Lao-Tzu postulated the avenues towards this cherished state of inaction as follows:

> To yield is to be preserved whole.
> To be bent is to become straight.
> To be hollow is to be filled.
> To be tattered is to be renewed.
> To be in want is to possess.
> To have plenty is to be confused.[33]

This is the way to suspended animation and to partial death. The crucial point is that the Taoists indeed regarded cognitive conflicts as a sure path to inaction, and this was meant to be avoided precisely by the operation of the congruity motive.

Monadic Methods

The monadic congruity technique has been mostly utilized in metaphysics. Leibniz used it for proving the eternity of the soul and the necessity and sufficiency of God as the prime mover.[34] Plotinus describes existence as the unifying process carried out by the soul through its ascension from plurality to unity. "It is through the soul's power that this world of plurality and variety is contained within the bonds of unity".[35] In Jewish mysticism, the ecstatic ascent of the soul through all the ordeals of the seven heavens is an obstacle course for the ever-diminishing number of the worthy souls striving to achieve ultimate bliss and fulfillment by unification with the Godhead, which holds court in the seventh heaven. This technique either blends the differences by integration or destroys them through choice. De Sade and Genet, who raised evil to the stature of sole reality and dismissed virtue as a tasteless illusion, whose only excuse was its non-existence have perfected destruction through choice. Monadic congruity operates through blending postulates – for instance, that suffering is not defined by contrast with love; pain *is* love. Christ on the cross, the hideous beauty of Medusa, the defiled sanctity of St. Jerome.

Conclusion

In this chapter we illustrated the importance of the congruity principle as it appears in literature in all periods. This provides the background to the theoretical analysis we must now pursue of accidia and the absurd. In Chapter 1, the absurd was defined as a value-disengagement generated, in the first instance, by gaps between a man's self and new norms, and in the second instance, by the failure of his attempts, motivated by the congruity principle, to bridge these gaps. Our background discussions in this and the preceding chapter have pointed in a particular direction. We began with an account of accidia and the absurd, which in fact is the end product of a process. Then, we discussed the congruity principle and congruity-motivated involvement, which is a contributory feature to the process. We must now go to where we are pointed, to the beginning. We shall present an analytical model that reconstructs and retraces the ground we have already opened up, but in the opposite direction and in a more systematic manner. We must begin therefore from an analysis of the self and its previous internalization of norms. We may then proceed to analyze new norm transmissions, their reception as disjunctive by the self, the self's efforts to make them congruous and the accidic disengagement or value breakdown produced in the case of failure.

The Broken Image and the Absurd

A Theoretical Analysis

We begin this chapter with an analysis of the self, which deals mainly with its cognitive and in particular its perceptual features. This will enable us to understand how normative disjunctions, incongruities and gaps are perceived between elements of the receiving–perceiving self, and elements of the newly transmitted norms.

To deepen our analysis of normative disjunctions, we then turn to study the efficiency and effectiveness of society's norm-sending processes. Having established the nature of the "broken image", normative disjunctions, by a further analysis of the self's knowledge and internalization of previous norms, we then turn to the self's reactions. A typology of the self's efforts to bridge the gaps and disjunctions, its "innovative involvements", is proposed and the potential creativity of this situation is noted. Finally a typology of the self's reactions to the failure of its efforts and its innovative involvements is put forward and illustrated.

The Perceiving Self: Elements and Processes

The self consists of internalized others, self-image and objects, all of which make up what we shall call the apperceptive configuration (AC). Our basic premise is that a normative disjuncture may occur between the AC and the subsequent normative transmissions directed towards him, which we shall call the transmission configuration (TC). This triadic division of the cognitive structure is, of course, not new; our only innovation is to apply such a division to the analysis of normative disjunctions. The difference between our triadic model for instance, and one of Freud's triads – id, ego, super-ego – is that he relates these three parts of the personality to the outside world taken as one whole, whereas we take the self as one unit and examine its interaction with a phenomenologically divided world.

Our basic model has also some Heideggerian elements in it, although these elements incorporate only his phenomenology, not his value judgments. He

38

conceives of three modes of cognition, "The world of things into which ego is 'thrown', the relationship with others that is totally negative, and the 'pure' subjective *Dasein* which is a self–self dialogue".[1]

But we can dispense with his conception of the self as a transcendental entity. For our present purposes, only components of the personality that can be traced to the impact of interaction and socialization on the bio-psychological potentials of the individual can be considered. Basically, we agree with Mead and other "symbolic interactionists", that the self is a "looking-glass" entity formed through interaction with others. We may, therefore, express our model as a disjuncture between a set of interactions as already absorbed and processed by the self and a new dissonant set of communications.

Before we proceed, two reservations must be made. First, the concept of self is notoriously elusive in epistemology and is full of contradictions and ambiguities in the field of social psychology (see for instance Wylie's *Survey of the Literature*).[2] Secondly, the Meadian interactionist hypotheses are difficult to operationalize and to test empirically. Our analysis of the main components of our model is not to be taken as another exercise in epistemology; hopefully we will be able to point to possible applications and tests. To those who see a rift between the phenomenological existentialist and the sociologistic conception of self, we may offer the rather frequent compromising distinction that these two operate on different levels of analysis. The first deals with ontology asking *what* the self is, whereas the latter is concerned with the "hows", i.e. the processes of the formation of the self.[3]

The phenomenological treatment of the contents of the self is manifested *in extremis* by Husserl's statement, "The transcendental ego exists absolutely in and for itself prior to all cosmic being".[4] This resonates with the central theme of existentialism that each one of us to *himself* is the center of creation. All reality flows through the particular cognition of ego. When I am awake, the world exists. When I am dreamlessly asleep or unconscious, there is no awareness, either of the self or of the world. Each ego, or its subjective cognizer, might wish to know why he has been chosen as the channel for the awareness of creation. This is the rarefied realm that transcends knowledge, the domain of questions without answers. However, ego's being the groove for the awareness of creation makes him unique, an existential prime source of being not only of himself but also of everything within his perception. This is not a revival of solipsism but an elucidation of the primary role of awareness in the structure of the self.

The sociologistic "hows" relating to the formulation of the self are indeed embodied in the postulates of the symbolic interactionists. In Mead's theory of the formation of the self through the continuous feedback of responses from others, in Cooley's description of the self as a molding of refractions from the relevant others, and in the quite common conception of the self in modern sociology as a complex of reflexive attitudes that arise in the process of socialization.[5]

One attribute of the self, which is equally stressed by both existentialists and behavioral scientists, is the centrality of self-esteem and dignity within the structure of the self-concept. With the existentialists, this would tie up with the uniqueness of the self as a source of awareness. As the self is the only authentic reality and the sole basis for transcendence, what could be more important than ego's self-esteem, which makes bearable "the futile passion that is man" and lends some dignity to his awkward striving to be a prime mover. Without dignity Sisyphus would be crushed under his rock. How could the myriads of rock-pushers bear their stultifying routines without a rebellious grinding of teeth, a straightening of the back and a defiant stare? This is not the megalomania of Le Roi Soleil or Le Grand Charles, but the realization of a Camus, a Mediterranean Pied-Noir, that life without dignity is worthless. Indeed, the Mediterranean conception of dignity is quite different from the European chivalrous honor. The latter is a pose, a conglomeration of forms, which may be reduced to a handbook of etiquette for debutantes as well as for officers and gentlemen. Dignity, however, for an Algerian colon, a Greek, or a Sicilian is the essence which keeps his spine straight. The near starvation, the scorching sun, the meager land are met with a snarl of perseverance. Dignity makes for the ability to stand and not slump in the gutters. For Sartre, man's striving to be God is a useless passion but for di Lampedusa's Don Fabrizio, a true Mediterranean, dignity is the panacea:

> The foreigners came to teach us good manners, but they won't succeed, because we think we are gods . . . the Sicilians never want to improve for the simple reason that they think themselves perfect; their vanity is stronger than their misery; every invasion by outsiders . . . upsets their illusion of achieved perfection, risks disturbing their satisfied waiting for nothing; having been trampled on by a dozen different people, they consider they have an imperial past which gives them the right to a grand funeral.[6]

This is the core of existential dignity common to the sisyphian brand of Camus' Rieux in *The Plague,* the hedonistic type of Kazantzakis' Zorba and di Lampedusa's tragic Don Fabrizio.

With the behavioral scientists, we find that self-esteem is considered by psychiatrists as crucial for sanity and by social psychologists as essential for congruity. Again, the existentialists provide the ontic "whys" for the prominence of self-esteem within the self-concept, whereas the behavioral scientists take it as a given datum that interacts with the other components of the personality. Roger Brown characterizes this stance when he says, "We have come upon one respect in which the self is unique among perceived persons. The organism is partial to itself and prefers to assign to it a positive value".[7]

Others

Although there are some arguments for the epistemological similarity between the perception of things and others[8], there is a clear basis for a distinction between the two in our present context: alters, through their constant feedback to ego of approvals and disapprovals, consensus and dissensus, are the major source of ego's own normative decision making, whereas inanimate objects, flora and fauna, are not. The latter may, no doubt, play the role of relevant others in the ego–alter dyad when they have been *personalized.* The pantheistic Ojibwa culture imparts symbolic life to "person–objects".[9] The Hindu reincarnation cult makes some animals the equivalent of human beings and for the Bedouin the desert hyena is the personification of evil. However, in these and many other similar instances the things, plants and animals concerned discard their non-human attributes and assume a role of *persons* who interact as such with ego. The uniqueness of the perception of alters, as distinct from the perception of non-persons, is described phenomenologically by Merleau-Ponty:

> Around the perceived body a whirl forms itself, which attracts and, as it were, sucks in my world. And in so far as that is the case, my world is not any more exclusively my own. It is not only present to me, it is also present to X . . . Already, the other body is not only a simple fragment of the world but the place of a certain elaboration and of a certain "view" of the world.[10]

Another generalized characteristic of the perceptual mutuality between ego and alter is the former's tendency to label the latter. The number of the pigeonholes used by ego for this purpose is surprisingly small when related to the almost unlimited logical possibilities. One reason for this lack of imagination can be related to the link between ego's categorization of others and the contrasting stereotypes which he applies to himself.[11] This rather limited number of tags and stereotypes proves, no doubt, an asset to the study of dyadic interaction between ego and alter.

One of the key issues here is that the norm and value consonance or dissonance between ego and alter is closely related to their mutual attraction or repulsion. If I like somebody, it would hurt me personally if he does not hold my views on some issues that I consider important. If I hate someone, it is almost impossible for him to be right on any issue. I shall probably have some logical argument to dismiss his reasoning as trivial, irrelevant or internally inconsistent. If worse comes to worse, I can always resort to an *ad hominem* refutation that a person that foolish must be wrong or that there must be a hitch to "that crook's" reasoning.

We really do not know very much about what makes persons attractive or repulsive to one another. Most social psychologists either grope in the dark when dealing with this issue or offer hypotheses on such a high level of abstraction that they hardly mean anything. Such hypotheses include, among others, the tendency for group members to change each other's opinions, the degree of conformity to group-induced standards of productivity, or the amount of defensive aggression that can be released against an attacker.[12]

Perceptual attraction or rejection is highly relevant for our purposes, but short of having any meaningful clues to the mechanism of this process we must content ourselves with two phenomenological observations, which are at best hypothetical.

The first relates to the partiality of ego to himself. Self-esteem, dignity, ego identity and other equivalent concepts denote the basic independent centrality of ego as an *ethically positive entity as defined by ego himself.* This ethical partiality must inevitably clash with the partiality of alter to himself which is, no doubt, conveyed to ego bluntly or subtly, depending on alter's temperament. In the dyadic relationship between ego and alter, the natural state would be continuous conflict and strife unless some harmonizing defense mechanisms gloss over these seemingly inevitable disjunctions. Indeed some of these mechanisms, e.g. the congruity principle, the pressure towards conformity, the subjective modifications of new dissonant perceptions, make possible and sustain the rather precarious *modus vivendi* between ego and alter.

The second premise is that ego's greater sensitivity in the perception of alter makes for his own greater vulnerability to cognitive dissonance and breakdowns of relationship with his relevant others. In our first premise, we postulated that the coexistence of the ego-centred ego and alter is made possible through a whole battery of defense mechanisms. These tend to blunt the edges, blur the fine demarcations of perception, bow to the consensus of the majority, and present to oneself gross contradictions as minor dissents. If ego is more sensitive, his perception more accurate and his insight deeper, his capacity for self-deception and make-believe would consequently decrease. He would be more liable to define his stance as diverging from the one held by alter. This would tie up later with our premise that the creative innovators, precisely because of their keener observation, would tend to suffer more from the conflicts and dissonant breakdowns because their overall sensitivity counteracts the streamlining effects of conformity and self-deception. Roger Brown, commenting on Bronfenbrenner's work on interpersonal perception says, "Knowledge, for the sensitive, can be bruising. The interests of others are often in conflict and having all the information may be paralyzing".[13] This, in essence, describes the interpersonal aspect of our model when ego realizes that no patching up can plaster the mutual feelings of estrangement between himself and alter.

Things

The main difference, for our purposes, between the perception of persons and things is that persons can direct and control ego's perception of themselves, whereas things cannot. Alter's behavior, or for that matter his sheer presence, imposes on ego a sharing of existence. Also the feedback of images, which ego receives from alter relating to his own existence and behavior, is beyond the power of things. Goffman's insightful work on the mechanism of social encounters[14] reveals the intricate subtleness that governs the face-to-face interaction and rituals, which are exclusive to *Homo sapiens*.

Rather than delving into epistemology and metaphysics for which we do not have either the training or the inclination, we shall adopt the pragmatist stance on object perception. This would imply that "outside realities" are the things we can perceive by our senses or deduce or induce logically. The proverbial stone smashing the window of Professor Fichte's study is an illustration of the former, whereas Freud's logical interpolation of the illogical subconscious is an instance of the latter.

Another test for the reality of the perception of objects is the teleological one. As stated by William James, the arch-pragmatist himself, "It means that ideas, (which themselves are but parts of our experience), become true just in so far as they help us to get into satisfactory relations with other parts of our experience . . . by realities or objects we mean either things of common sense, sensibly present or else commonsense relations such as dates, places, distances, activities or even mystical experiences if they have practical consequences".[15] The perception of things is real in so far as we can find consistencies and co-variations among different sets of phenomena, or if we can perceive them directly as concrete facts or abstract symbols.

Perceptual Stereotyping

There is ample evidence that ego tends to distort any incoming perception so that it does not diverge too much from any previously internalized one.[16] Ego's capacity for self-deception has been shown to be quite remarkable. For instance, a pen pusher in a clerical department was equipped with an adding machine to do his calculations and was paid for this easier task twice the wages of his colleagues who performed the *same task* by hand. They did not grudge him his better deal because they differentiated his mechanical adding and defined it as a "mathematical task".[17]

There are various manifestations to this twisting of ego's perceptual intake to fit his already internalized stance. One of the most common is the perceptual blinders which expose ego selectivity to contradictory stimuli. Goodman demonstrated that the moral of a story culminating in the admonition that "God will punish him" was very much remembered by children of a religious upbringing and almost totally ignored by atheists.

Another powerful technique of perceptual twisting is the reductionism through stereotypes and categorization. The tendency to pigeonhole our new perceptions and relate them to types already known to us is almost universal. To varying degrees this relational tagging involves a blunting of edges and a blurring of conspicuousness so that it fits within the preconceived category. Moreover, our ability to identify a novel perception and compartmentalize it into a familiar stereotype makes us happy. Indeed, the congruity principle, which we analyzed at length in chapter 2, is conceivably related to this stereotyping tendency. The comparison and reduction of the new unexplored and undigested perception to the rubric with known parameters makes one comfortable. When the new stimulus is not so easily reducible to a stereotype, efforts are made to squeeze it into a type to assure its contented internalization. As words are rather more flexible than the phenomena they describe, the manipulation of incoming perceptions is quite often verbal. Psychiatrists, for example, by tagging a patient with the name of a disease or sociologists, or by pigeonholing a given human interaction under the rubric of a paradigm, often feel that they have cornered and understood the behavior itself. This, no doubt, is another way of streamlining phenomena so that they fit the familiar stereotype. Buchanan and Cantril, indeed, showed that attitudes towards nations are dependent on some polarized stereotypes, which people tend to identify in the arena of international power politics.[18]

Related to our tendency to categorize is our desire to group together people whom we define as having identical or similar attributes. This tendency, which is, no doubt, linked to the consistency principle, reduces strain and inner conflict. We apparently feel happy and secure when we are able to classify people into groupings by some common denominators. Mostly, however, we classify groups of people (this is apart from the traditional social stratification of class, caste, etc.) in order to attach to them value-laden labels. Significantly, the "good guys" are "people like us", whereas the "bad guys" cannot possibly be like us. Here is the crucial point as far as we are concerned. Apparently we go to great lengths to attribute things that we like and ideas that we have to people that we like – to the "good guys". In a like manner we impute everything we detest to people we detest. In reality, people and their attributes and ideas are very seldom so clearly divided, but we ease our minds by *perceiving them* as such and a great deal of subjective twisting does indeed take place so that the "right ideas" are linked to the "right people".

Another hypothesis, that of "selective exposure", which also relates to the streamlining of incoming information, has almost the status of a truism, but it encounters considerable empirical difficulties, since, as in the following two examples, the link between selective exposure and specific attitudes has not been

44

empirically conclusive. A Mexican and American were fleetingly exposed to two pictures in binocular rivalry – the American perceived the baseball game and the Mexican the bullfight. Similarly, mostly the people who already were favorably predisposed to the United Nations noticed a series of campaigns promoting it.[19] The hypothesis here, which has not been empirically verified, is that the "blinder" effect of manipulating incoming information is related to the magnitude of the initial gap. The greater the disjuncture between the previously internalized information and the incoming one, the greater is the tendency to selective exposure. One thinks, for instance, of the very orthodox Jew never writing the addition sign as a cross, the Catholic priest piously averting his gaze from the bulging female curves on a movie ad and the businessman looking through the conspicuous evidence of a competitor's success as if it was so much hot air.

This leads us to the claims of the dissonance theorists – that the distortion of incoming information to fit the previously internalized one is a basic tenet of human nature. The greater the dissonance, the greater ego's tendency is to distort the incoming information. Moreover, this tendency would increase with greater uncertainty or inner doubts about formerly held convictions.[20]

A special case of distorting incoming information is by explaining away the apparent disjunction between the latter and the previous perception. This is rather similar to Osgood and Tannenbaum's "refutation treatment",[21] glossing over and smoothing verbally obvious contradictions that claim, "he really didn't mean it" or "he directed his remark to a fellow in his department and he did not mean us people". The variety of this kind of explanatory "distinction" is almost endless. It was perfected in the scholastic works of the church, where every new statement had to be ratified by previously held dogma and doctrine. The casuistry of the Talmud was built on the rigid ascending hierarchy of truths of the Mishna and the Torah. Jurists practice this kind of semantic juggling as a matter of course in systems that have a written constitution or a doctrine of binding legal precedents.

Finally, we have to relate ourselves to the subjective twists in our perception of other human beings and human groups, so that they are closer to the previous perception we had of them. One finding indicates that ego's self-concept is more closely related to his estimate of the generalized attitude toward him (i.e. to the generalized other) than to the perceived responses of a particular group (concrete others). The second relevant finding is that ego's perception of the response of others is more closely related to his self-concept than to the actual response of others. In other words, ego's subjectivistic bias twists, so to speak, his perception of others to be more in line with his previously internalized conception of them. The immediate application of these findings to our context are:

(1) We may disregard in our model the *actual objective* responses of others, partly because of their epistemological non-verifiability and mainly because value deviation is a state of mind. A breakdown of involvement is defined

subjectively by ego alone. (2) The perception by ego of the generalized other would be tainted by ego's subjectivity and anchored on his self-concept. The generalized other would necessarily vary from individual to individual. Moreover, this tendency would vary with every individual's subjective twist of his own private generalized other so that it fits his self-concept. (3) Our present premise is related to the congruity models in social psychology, e.g. dissonance–consonance, balance–imbalance and the problems of measuring this "subjective twist" would indeed be formidable. However, our operative conclusion is that the lower the tendency of ego to adjust the generalized other to his self-concept the higher the initial gap is between the transmission and apperceptive configurations. Only a relatively small number of individuals are exceptions to the proven tendency of human beings to twist incoming perceptions of others. Thus only these few would actually experience the initial disjuncture between the internalized image of others and the new diverging image to which they are subsequently exposed.

Perceptual Conformity

The subjective bias of ego's perception of the novel normative transmissions to which he is exposed, serves to adjust or bring, so to speak, the new norms of the group closer to his own stance, that is to reduce their "novelty". However, we do also have evidence of a norm rapprochement, which is initiated from the other direction: Mohammed's tendency to go over to the normative mountain if the latter fails to comply with the Prophet's perceptual wish that it moves over to him.

Ego's tendency to conform to the normative transmissions of the group have been recorded by Sherrif, Asch, Crutchfield and Stoner. Their studies reveal that individuals tend to renounce their own factually correct perception and to adjust to the incorrect perception of the group, which is a collusion in illusion. Bogdonoff and his associates even found a physiological correlate to conformity. They observed in an Asch-type perceptual conformity study that the non-conformist had a high level of fatty acids, indicating an anxiety-correlated arousal of the central nervous system, whereas the conformists had a low acid level indicating nervous system relaxation and well-being.[22] George Orwell, in 1984, appeared to have anticipated this finding when he described the main character, Winston, as feeling suddenly relaxed and happy after conforming to the postulate that two plus two equals five.

Of even more importance is the so-called Stoner Effect, according to which individual perceptions tend to conform to the mean judgment of perception of the whole group after the individual judgments have been openly compared by the group and discussed therein.[23]

Finally, this tendency to conform has been found by Crutchfield and others to be linked to other personality traits in measurable mutual predictability relationships.[24]

The motivation for conformity would seem quite apparent when the person who is imitated or the group conformed to have control over resources or gratification of needs. In the family, for instance, the young of the species are exposed to the normative transmissions of their parents and are bound to absorb them because an infant is utterly helpless. In a rather crude way we regard socialization as a give-and-take relationship. The child fulfills a vast array of emotional needs of his parents, so he therefore receives basic shelter and nourishment. However, the compliance with the normative mandates of parents is related to a subtle interplay of the child's need for acceptance, approval, affection and emotional security, which stems from a feeling of belonging and mutuality.

By the same token, the generals who first saw their king with trousers pressed accidentally lengthwise rather than sideways would hasten to imitate the new "fashion". A more complicated mechanism is the conformity to a new mandate because we happen to like the source of the new norm. Here cognition follows affective attachment.[25] Conformity to a group in a face-to-face public situation seems to be more forceful than compliance through vicarious and anonymous communication. Moreover, when a public commitment has been made the conforming choice becomes more and more attractive.[26] This is related to dissonance theory in that ego has a vested interest in the stance to which he has conformed, once he has made a commitment.

The crucial point, however, is that conformity is a measurable personality trait, i.e. if one person tends to conform in one situation he tends to do so in other situations, which may not necessarily be factually similar. Finally, levels of conformity may be related to cultural differences. We like to believe that the French, for instance, tend to conform less in any situation because they have been brought up that way.

The content of the norms to which an individual is expected to conform may be divided into two unequal parts: the larger one serves as a source of information, whereas a far smaller one contains behavioral mandates. The latter is the focus of our present study because a normative rift, which might be linked to a value breakdown, is invariably related to sanction-backed actions or omissions and not to neutral information. It is generally agreed that an individual will tend to conform to a group he feels he belongs to, or aspires to be a member of, or which he thinks is homogeneously composed of "people like us". As a logical corollary to this premise, we find that when an individual feels that his status within the group is threatened or shaky he tends to go out of his way to overconform to the group's norms.[27] Another type of person who tends to conform to the mandates of the group is one who seeks leadership or power within it. However, once he has achieved the high status he aspired for he would allow himself some indulgence because "what is permitted to Jupiter is forbidden to the Romans" and "what the Rabbi can do is not allowed to every simple Jew". In other words, "rank *must* have its privileges". We shall conclude this part of our analysis by pointing out that the individual's tendency to conform to the normative transmissions of the group is complementary to his tendency to subjectivize his novel perceptions so that they accord more with his previously internalized norms. Consequently, the initial disjunction between the internalized norms and the newly transmitted discordant ones *as perceived by ego* would be smaller than the material "objective" normative gap. (We are well aware that an "objective" normative gap is epistemologically ambiguous).

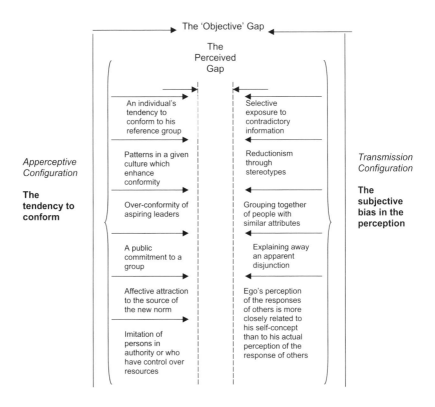

Figure 3.1   Ego's congruity-based tendency to narrow the perceived normative gap

The narrowing of the gap as perceived by ego depends, on one hand, on his subjectivistic bias in adjusting the new transmissions to the previously internalized ones and, on the other hand, to his tendency to conform to the judgment of others.

A wide initial gap would be related to a low subjectivistic bias of perception, and to a low conformity to group pressure and the judgment of others.

Consequently, individuals with keener perception and independent judgment – those who do not indulge in self-deception, or in the soothing opiate that the "voice of the people is the voice of God" – would be more prone to perceive this initial normative gap as being wide. Conversely, biased and conformist individuals tend to see the initial normative gap as narrow.

Later in this chapter we will discuss ego's congruity-based tendency to actively involve himself in order to minimize and bridge the normative gap. For the moment however, we are concerned with ego's perception itself, and not his subsequent action. But this, like the involvement-action, is governed by the congruity principle, first introduced in Chapter 2 and analyzed with specific reference to perception in this section. Schematically the congruity-based tendency of ego to narrow the width of the normative gap in his perception can be presented as shown in figure 3.1 (the arrows represent tendencies or forces).

Society's Norm-Sending: Its Efficiency and Effectiveness

For our present purposes we adopt Rommetveit's analysis of any group's "norm-sending" process. This requires, (1) a statement by the group about the desired behavior and the consequences to the individual if he does not comply, (2) group surveillance over the person in order to determine the extent (if any) of his compliance to the norm, and (3) group application of sanctions to non-complying individuals.[28] Defects in the process of norm-sending may be inherent in each of its three phases, thus reducing the efficiency and effectiveness of the normative transmission. Let us deal first with the statement phase.

Norm-Statement

This might be defective in so far as the rule or norm is unclear and ambiguous, or in so far as it contains patent or latent inner contradictions. Where norm-sending is performed by the primary socialization agencies, the statement of rules might be riddled with conflicting mandates stemming, among other things, from discord. Take for instance, parents and children, with the possible inconsistencies of parental discipline (and consequently the conflicts between verbally stated norms, and actual behavior of parents), as well as value and norm discord between the parents and other socializing agencies (e.g. school, church, youth club, etc.). The scaling of this variable should be based, of course, on theories of learning as to the possible effect of contradictory or inconsistent responses, reward, and withdrawal to the same (or similar) behavior of the child.

The efficacy of norm-sending may be enhanced by the high prestige of the norm source. In a similar vein, Allen reports, "traffic signal violations by a high-status person attired in a freshly pressed suit, shined shoes, white shirt and tie produced a higher pedestrian violation than the same transgression performed by the same model dressed in soiled, patched trousers, scuffed shoes, and a blue denim shirt!"[29] This means that pedestrians just about to cross a street would more readily follow the red light violation of a high-status pedestrian, as evident from his clothes, than of a low-status one. Conversely, it is clear that an injury to the prestige of the source of the norms would hamper the efficacy of the norm-sending. This may be apparent in communities that undergo a rapid or sudden social change, and especially immigrant families whose cultural tradition is markedly different from the culture of the absorbing community. These may undergo socio-economic injuries, which shatter the status of the head of the family. These types of conflicts stem basically from "external" sources (as viewed from the family's vantage point), namely, industrialization, urbanization, mass immigration, and social change in underdeveloped countries that recently gained their independence. However, the main effect of these types of social change is to blur the rules by creating conflict situations within the family between the immigrant parents and their native-born offspring (or children who were immigrants in infancy). The situations would raise the probability of injuring the prestige of the norm source and thus hampering the norm-sending process. In Israel, for instance, this type of conflict has proved to be a factor weakening the cohesion of the family unit, and loosening family control over the young.

The underlying feature of this process is that the family is a system in balance. Every disturbance of this balance, every "rocking of the family boat", is bound to be reflected in the way the child absorbs the conduct mandates of his parents. That is the child tends to absorb, within his personality, the whole family image as reflected to him by the elaborate and subtle inter-relationships among the family members.[30] The child's socialization is affected by whole networks of reciprocity between parent and child. Psychiatrists have studied extensively the so-called "symbiotic" relationships between parent and child. An aggressive mother, for instance, might make her child a receptacle for her aggression. Conversely, a guilt-ridden and self-blaming mother might unconsciously solicit aggression from her children.[31] Thus factors, which influence the strength or weakness of equilibrium of the family system, also affect the transmission of conduct norms to the young. The loosely-knit family would be a less effective organ of socialization than the tightly-knit and the internally cohesive family.[32] The mother's employment outside the house,[33] the nature of the father's occupation[34] and the quality of the family's housing,[35] are all further factors affecting the cohesion of the family, and therefore affecting children's socialization.

Defects of a more generalized nature in the statement of norms, legal and non-legal, may be related to a communication disjunction or breakdown between the norm-sender and the actual or potential norm-receiver. These communication gaps may be observed, very often, in technologically backward and mass-immigration countries. In these two examples, the norm-sending process is completely inefficient because the persons were never exposed to these processes and therefore were quite ignorant of the existence of the norms. Readers of the humane diary of Toufiq El-Haquim, a magistrate in a rural area in Egypt, realize how futile and tedious the administration of justice in villages is, where laws passed in Cairo never reached the Felahins' ears and eyes. Similar problems of external "culture conflict" are portrayed by the Yemenite Jew who cannot understand the Israeli laws which forbid bigamy, the Bedouin who dismisses the rumors that the "city laws" do not approve of avenging the blood of his murdered brother, and the mountain Jew from Morocco who does not know that Israeli laws prescribe life imprisonment for killing a daughter who becomes pregnant out of wedlock. These are extreme cases, but many laws are passed that do not reach the people. The norm-sending process here did not even begin to operate because the individuals were not exposed to the myriads of laws, by-laws, rules, and other prohibitions, which are enacted every day by the various authorities. Here the legislator can avail himself of the famous maxim that "ignorance of the law is no excuse"; otherwise the wheels of government and justice would be hopelessly clogged.

The trend towards state control of many fields from the economy to education, not only in totalitarian and welfare states but also under capitalism, results in a continuous flow of rules and regulations, which engulf the individual and restricts his area of "free movement". The sheer quantity of these prohibitions also subjects him quite often to inconsistent pressures. A Kafkaesque situation is produced where the web of bureaucracy leaves the individual in utter confusion as to what the rules are, who stated them, and when and where they are to be observed. Thibaut and Kelley refer to this danger of over-regulation of situations when they write:

> Under these conditions [of too many norms] said to characterize bureaucracies, the rules governing behavior can be so complex that people are unable to master them fully. The result is an unwillingness to act or make behavioral decisions. The individual may also become so engrossed with the internal structure and interpretations of the norms that he loses touch with the outside world.[36]

Norm-Surveillance and Norm-Enforcement

The surveillance of normative indoctrination in the family has very little reciprocity. Mostly, it is a unilateral flow of authority and power from the parents to their children. However, it has been noted that in families where the mother is the principal disciplinarian in the family, children tend to develop guilt (i.e. to internalize norms) more readily than when the father performs the main tasks of surveillance.[37] Also, there is evidence that middle-class children are more likely to adopt their parents' occupational and educational goals than children in working and low-class families.[38] But the most crucial phase of norm-transmission is conditioning by the application of sanctions, which are punishment for noncompliance and rewards for compliance. It might be said that we are trained like rats in a maze to refrain from actions that are associated with pain and resort to behavior, which is reinforced by rewarding experience. Where sanctions are sporadic, erratic and inconsistent, conditioning does not take place. Also too severe punitive sanctions are detrimental to the internalization of norms, as some findings have indicated.[39] Similarly, too intense punishment is ineffective in suppressing undesired behavior.[40] Another finding indicates that children who have experienced rejection or extreme punitiveness from their parents are likely to show weak internalization of a sense of duty and responsibility, and have bad control over their tendencies to behave aggressively.[41] A survey of delinquent group members revealed consistently that their parents were unusually punitive and rejecting.[42] Kohlberg summarizes this premise as follows:

> Parents of delinquents tend to be more punitive than parents of nondelinquents, although they do not differ in extent of "firmness" of socialization and home demands. They are less warm and affectionate and more inconsistent and neglectful than parents of nondelinquents. Delinquent boys tend to have overtly hostile relationships with their fathers.[43]

Conversely, the parents', and especially the mother's warm and affectionate treatment of the infant greatly enhance the effectiveness of socialization. Consequently, withdrawal of affection or the threat of it are the most durable and effective sanctions.[44] More important is the finding that the delay of reward as a sanction has been most effective in suppressing undesirable behavior.[45]

Middle-class families resort more to withdrawal of affection as a sanction in socializing their children, whereas the lower classes inflict more repressive punishment.[46] This might help explain the lower incidence of violence, delinquency and reported norm-violation in general among middle-class youth, whose socialization was presumably more effective in producing "law-abiding citizens".

As far as the normative system as a whole is concerned, Daniel Drew, a shady business associate of the "robber barons", once declared, "Law is like a cobweb: it's made for flies and the smaller kinds of insects, so to speak, but lets the big bumblebees break through".[47] Drew's assertion illustrates a prevailing view in many societies, and especially in the under-privileged classes, that the sacred maxim of equality before the law, which is solemnly engraved in many constitutions, is largely a myth. Here the differential surveillance of compliance to norms and the application of sanctions have a direct injurious and shattering effect on the norm-sending process, because this differential treatment of

lawbreakers is encountered in many business, political, economic and professional activities. One of the commonest types of offenses, where differential law
enforcement is presumably widely practiced, is "white-collar crime", or the
criminality of the upper socio-economic classes in the course of occupation in
business, politics, and the professions. Sutherland, who initiated this branch of
criminology,[48] demonstrated the colossal volume of offenses committed by
large corporations, especially in the defrauding of shareholders and the submitting of false financial reports. The food industry sells products that are quite
often against legal specifications and sometimes actually injurious to health.
Bribery is practiced by many as an inseparable part of routine business transactions. Politics are riddled with graft, millions are embezzled by employees, and
the advertisement colossi help extract money by false pretenses by attributing
to their clients' goods qualities which they do not possess. The point relevant to
the present context is that white-collar criminals, so it is argued, are treated
differently from the more conventional criminals by the law-enforcement agencies. If this hypothesis is correct, we have a clear case of conflict in surveillance
and in application of sanctions, which results (or have already resulted) in a
severe injury to the norm-sending agency. Let us suppose then that the rich
descendants of the "robber barons" are among the social elite of the United
States and that the chairman of railway companies who embezzled a quarter of
a million dollars is elected as president of the Chamber of Commerce. Let us
suppose that white-collar criminals have connections in the law-enforcement
agencies who see to it (for good consideration) that their friends are not pros-
ecuted. Furthermore, social class and social background similarities exist
between white-collar criminals and the higher echelons of government officials
and law-enforcement agencies, producing "softer" treatment for their offenses,
even to the extent of turning a blind eye to them. In this hypothetical situation
the norms, which prescribe these "white-collar" offenses, are not transmitted
effectively. A direct outcome of this differential treatment is that the public gets
accustomed to the idea that businessmen must commit offenses in the course
of their occupation in order to be able to survive cut-throat competition.
Businessmen, therefore, become "sons of bitches", as the late President John F.
Kennedy candidly described them, but this should be followed by the old Jewish
saying, that "money cleanses, purifies, and makes these 'sons of bitches'
respectable".

Many criminologists point out the tremendous sums of money involved in
white-collar crime, which makes ordinary criminals look like peanut pilferers,
but our concern is centered on the effect of this type of crime, and especially of
the relative immunity of its perpetrators from detection and prosecution, on
the norm-sending process. Ordinary crimes, burglary, theft, and violence are
committed by persons who are in many ways outside law-abiding society. These
persons are clearly stigmatized as criminals and sooner or later will be forced,
by social ostracism among other things, to cross the barrier to the criminal

subculture. However, white-collar criminals belong as a rule to the respectable circles in a community and to its social elite, but if this elite not only commits grave offenses against the state, the economy, and the public at large, but also gets away with it; the public (lower-classes and middle-classes alike) tends to revoke the legitimacy with which they invested the political and legal system, and perhaps even the normative system in general. We observe therefore that white-collar offenses, more than any other type of offense, enhance cynical attitudes towards the law and law-enforcement agencies, and promote distrust, suspicion and bitterness towards agencies of government and authority as a whole.

A similar derogatory effect on the efficacy of norm-sending is caused by the "fix", which is, presumably, closely associated with the symbiosis between organized crime and law-enforcement agencies, especially when the latter are staffed with elected chiefs of police, district attorneys and judges. Here a whole class of persons, who have the appropriate connections with the political machine and are able to get their cases fixed, gains a relative immunity from prosecution.[49] A similar injurious effect on the norm-sending process is caused by legislation that is passed by the pressure of a powerful minority against the interests of the population at large or a considerable part of it, e.g. big business and industry lobbying against the interests of the consumers, employers against the interests of employees, landlords against the interests of tenants, etc. Finally, we must not overlook the situation where an increasing rate of certain behavior contrary to social norms leads to the realization (which is used also as a rationalization after the act) that "everybody does it". The law comes into disrepute here through its inability to be enforced and further law breaking is encouraged by the fact that people can "get away with it". Communication research has pointed to further factors in which the machinery of norm-sending may be clogged because the sources of norms are over-committed and saturated (e.g. a harassed and bemuddled traffic coordinator during a traffic light breakdown). In an over-centralized system of norm-sending, some peripheral norm-sources may become ineffective. Finally, when the source of norms is united unanimously against a threat of disaster, a dissenter would be towed back into conformity far more effectively than in cases where his dissenting stance is supported by individuals within the norm-sending group itself.[50] From the *norm-sending* process we turn to *norm-receiving* and to the factors which are linked to the depth or strength of norm-internalization.

Self's Norm Reception: Knowledge and Internalization

Degrees of Norm-Internalization

We have already discussed ego's perception of new norms and of the possible disjunctions, incongruities and gaps he may see between these new norms and the old ones he feels committed to. But we have not yet discussed the nature and degree of these previous commitments. How receptive is ego to new and different norms, given that he has perceived them as such? We hypothesize three degrees of internalization of, or commitment to, previously held norms: (a) sanction–orientation, (b) reward–orientation and (c) moral–orientation.

Norms are least internalized when ego has a sanction–orientation to them, when he complies with rules and regulations merely out of fear of the possible consequences of not doing so. Reward–orientation implies more of a commitment to, and internalization of norms; it is a utilitarian and perhaps pragmatic kind of attitude. Moral–orientation is the greatest possible commitment to and internalization of norms. Here ego will "follow the rules", "do what is right", or "do what he is told", not out of desire for reward or fear of punishment, but because it makes him feel joyful, righteous, or whatever, to do so.

Clearly, ego's degree of internalization of old norms affects his receptivity to new and different ones, and this is interwoven with the type of knowledge he has of the norms he holds. We will turn to this in a moment, but first we must look further at some of the factors enhancing ego's receptivity to normative transmissions of both familiar and unfamiliar norms, which he is constantly monitoring in daily social life.

(1) *Mode of exposure*: Ego's knowledge can be direct or indirect – he can either monitor normative transmissions in actual interactive situations, or scan various forms of mass media. It has generally been assumed that the former is more potent and effective – the "school of life", "experience" and so on. In criminology, Sutherland postulated[51] that criminal behavior is learned this way, by ego's direct association with criminals. But the other, indirect modes of exposure, particularly mass media channels such as television, can apparently be just as effective. Bandura and Walters demonstrated the effectiveness of the mass media in producing imitative aggressive behavior.[52]

(2) *Weaving of a single norm or group of norms into a comprehensive system*: This technique, addressed to ego's deepest moral orientations, is a potent feature of all scholastic ideological systems, from Roman Catholicism to Maoist Communism.

(3) *The personalistic effect*: The norm is structured so that the perceiver feels that the norm's transmission is directed towards him personally. "God loves

you and wants you to do good". "Big Brother is watching you!" "Your Country Needs You!"

(4) *Self-esteem and self-assurance*: These are effective barriers against persuasion and attitude change. Conversely, the shattering of self-esteem, the leveling effects of some degrading institutional routines or prolonged social isolation may weaken the previously-held normative orientation and thereby facilitate the onslaught of contradictory norms.

(5) *Inoculation*: This process has been recognized as a potent barrier against normative receptivity and change. In immunology weakened microorganisms are not able to spread a disease, but they are active enough to induce the body to create antibodies. Similarly, training-exposure to contradictory norms and ideas may serve as an inoculation against persuasion and brainwashing. A person is unpracticed in defending his beliefs if he is never called upon to defend them and the motivation to defend a normative stance is lacking if one believes it to be invulnerable. Hence the Talmudic maxim that a scholar should be conversant with the doctrines of heresy so that he may refute the blasphemies of an apostate.

Context and Emotion in the Knowledge of Norms

All knowledge can be placed on a continuum running from sensory stimulation to full moral and emotional involvement by the subject with the object of knowledge. We assume that this continuum can, in addition, be understood as one of an increasing context in terms of which to know the object. Context here refers both to the "internal" context of the knower's whole personality, and to the "external" context of the known object's physical and (but more particularly) its social situation. Thus, mere perception or sensory stimulation is barely knowledge at all in that no context is provided for what is sensed and there is no emotional commitment to it.

The vessel recorded as a shape on the retinas of Man Friday's eyes did not relay the information or the concept of an "artifact" to his understanding. What he saw he could not fit into his previously absorbed information, his existing "stock of knowledge". What stimulated him, what he saw in this sense, he did not know. Knowledge involves the provision of a context for what is seen. The voiceless politician in Tony Richardson's screen version of *The Loneliness of the Long Distance Runner* was out of context. A politician without a voice (and very often with it) is a succession of meaningless facial gestures. Sartre's Roquentin in *La Nausée* sees the glass of beer on the table as devoid of relational significance to himself or to the other objects in the room. Camus' Meursault perceives the taking of a life as a mechanical act, because for him the normative mandates of doing and not doing have lost their substance and power for justifying or negating.

Thus the meaningful scope of cognition is seen to be ethical. It is the norms of information or mandates of behavior, which provide contextual meaning for perception. Chisholm bears out our interpretation, and defines knowledge in ethical terms as distinct from descriptive ones. "To know that h is true will be not only to have true opinion with respect to h, but also to have a certain right or duty with respect to h".[53] This conception of knowledge could be illustrated also through a scholastic side-glance. The implications of knowledge for rights and duties were quite harshly inflicted on the first knowers after they had eaten from the Tree of Knowledge. Ecclesiastes was more forthright in proclaiming his creed, "he that increaseth knowledge increaseth sorrow".[54] But even sorrow of duties and the burden of obligations do not exhaust the wider scope of cognition that we are proposing here, and which must involve an emotion.

The wider scope of cognition, which we shall call, according to our assumptions, the greatest degree of knowledge, consists of full affective normativeness, when one is attached *emotionally* to a norm. And of course this is intrinsically connected to the degree of internalization of norms. Thus, any attempt to change ego's norms would be met with much stronger resistance where he is emotionally committed to them than where he simply has a neutral kind of cognitive awareness of them.

Schematically these two continua (which we depict triadically for the purposes of demonstration) can be represented as parallel and complementary, as follows:

Normative-Knowledge Continuum		Norm-internalization Continuum
Perception — — — — (least)	— — — — — —	sanction–orientation
Cognition — — — — ↓	— — — — — — —	reward–orientation (and identification)
Emotion — — — — (greatest)	— — — — —	moral–orientation

The Self's Reaction to Norm-Gaps: Innovative Involvements

A Typology of Innovative Involvements

At any given time there could be, as we have already mentioned, various combinations of dissonance between ego's AC and the relevant altars' subsequent norm-sending, the TC. These initial disjunctions or gaps are normative conflicts, but they would not, by themselves, constitute the final breakdown of involvement. At this stage ego is still involved – he still desires and hopes to bridge the gap between the various components of the AC and TC. He is urged and pressed to accomplish it by the congruity principle (as analyzed in

Chapter 2). Ego's efforts are related, among other things, to the following four variables:

(1) The degree to which the AC has been previously internalized
(2) The degree of ego's affective knowledge of the AC
(3) The potency of the new TC
(4) The width of the gap between the AC and TC

The last variable relates to the *contents* of the norms. A wide range of normative discrepancies/clashes can be relevant, as the content of new rules may be contrary to previously internalized norms. These clashes of rules have been studied in relation to social change, and especially to industrialization/urbanization,[55] and to political subjugation of nations or to their newly gained independence, as a by-product of internal/external migration or of group conflicts among ethnic minorities, political rebels and labor unions. Besides their content, many disjunctions of norms in relation to their form may also be relevant – conflicts between newly transmitted universalistic norms and particularistic norms which might have been previously internalized by the individual.

Transmission Configuration

	E W	E Na	NE W	NE Na
d A	Involvement + Rejection	Acceptance	Rejection	Rejection
d c	Involvement + Acceptance		Rejection	Inertive rejection
Sh A	Involvement + Acceptance		Rejection	Inertive
Sh...C	Acceptance		Rejection	Inertive

Where:
E = Effective norm-transmission
NE = Non-effective transmission
W = Wide initial gap (between the components of the TC and the AC)
Na = Narrow initial gap (between the components of the TC and the AC)
D = Deep internalization (of the components of the AC)
A = Affective knowledge (of the components of the AC)
C = Mere Cognitive knowledge (of the components of the AC)

Figure 3.2 A typology of innovative-involvements as reactions to norm gaps

Moreover, regarding content, the newly transmitted norms should be defined subjectively by ego as relevant. They should be important enough to him to cause the predicted dissonance and strain in relation to his *weltan-schauung*. This subjective definition of relevance would vary, no doubt, from individual to individual and through different periods of their lives. The hypothesis here is that a wider gap in content is less susceptible to changes, but the empirical evidence in this respect is far from being conclusive.[56] Figure 3.2 presents the interrelationship of the four dichotomized variables, which we have now examined and their link to ego's involvement to bridge the normative gap.

"Involvement + rejection" signifies a high probability (alternative, of course) of both involvement to bridge the gap and rejection of the new normative transmission. "Involvement + acceptance" signifies a high probability of involvement and alternatively acceptance of the normative transmission, i.e. attitude change.

Inertive stability is an outcome of a complete (or almost complete) lack of any tangential proximity between the TC and AC. We are only concerned here with a primary and, to be sure, quite crude hypothetical relationship. A relatively small proportion of relationships (3) in figure 3.2 are very highly predisposed to involvement and a small proportion would be inertive (3). The modal relationships are of low involvement probabilities with a high probability of either attitude change (5 relationships) or rejection of the normative transmission (5 relationships).

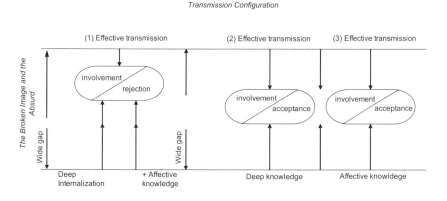

Figure 3.3   Three relationships with the highest probability of involvement

At one extreme we have the highest probability profile for innovative involvement (i.e. effective normative transmission, a wide normative gap between the transmitting configuration and the recipient one, a previously deep internalization of the recipient configuration and its affective cognition). At the other extreme we place the lowest probability of involvement profile. It is related to non-effective normative transmission, a narrow gap between the transmission and recipient configurations, and shallow previous internalization of norms and their cognitive knowledge.

For our theoretical purposes, the most relevant relationships in figure 3.2 are those displaying the highest probability profiles of involvement. This is because we are theoretically analyzing a dynamic process in which a value-breakdown is linked and follows the innovative involvement to bridge the initial normative disjuncture. The three involvement relationships may be displayed schematically, as shown in figure 3.3 (page 59).

Both involvement and the subsequent breakdown would require, as preceding conditions, the deeper internalization and full affective attachment to the previously held norms (as indicated in 1, figure 3.3). One must first feel for and care for something in order to be subsequently disenchanted. The highest probability profile for involvement is also characterized by an initial pressure for stability and against change. There is the tendency to reject any novel normative mandates, which are very markedly contrary to the previously deeply internalized and affectively meaningful normative system. This is the very common fear of new mandates. Man feels secure with his old customs, mores and values. He cherishes his homeostasis and his initial tendency, backed by the principle of consistency, is to reject the new normative transmission, which threatens to "rock the boat". The second high-involvement probability relationship displays effective normative transmission and deep previous normative internalization (2, figure 3.3), or its affective knowledge 3. Here, the initial polar discrepancies between the transmission and recipient configurations are considerable. And the chances are very high for an active involvement on ego's part to explore, differentiate and try to reconcile the discrepancies or to try to change the normative transmission. However, one element in the AC is lacking in each of the relationships: i.e. cognitive knowledge in 2, and shallow previous internalization in 3. Thus the alternative possibility, that of attitude change (as opposed to rejection), is also very high. Schematically the combinations of disjunctions in our basic model may be presented as shown in figure 3.4.

These combinations apparently display all the possible disjunctions. However, figure 3.4 presents a problem, for are we not omitting from our analysis the interrelationship between the self as such, and each of the three pairs of components? Before stating our views on this question we have to point out that our model makes a dynamic process static for expositional purposes only. Ego's absorption, rejection or conflict with the continuous flow of his own social image as transmitted by his surrounding alters is, *inter alia,* one of the many processes which crystallize ego's self-concept. However, at any given "frozen" instant, the discrepancy between ego's self-concept and the relevant images of himself as transmitted back to him generates ego's involvement to bridge the gap and lead ultimately to a value breakdown. If we turn now to our problem, we have to rely on some of our previous assumptions. Both theoretical and empirical knowledge of this premise, as in other epistemological problems is, alas, sadly meager.

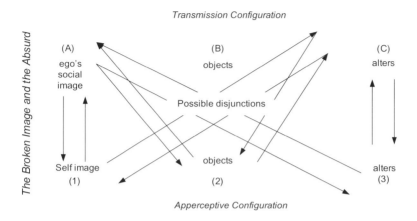

Figure 3.4 Possible disjunctions between the transmission and apperceptive configura-

What, however, of the possibility of a further separation between ego and himself, besides the gap between self-concept and social image? Barring the metaphysical conception of a human soul or the distinct animistic psyche, this possibility is, to say the least, unwarranted. Ego's self-perception – seen organically, as performed by "inner" and "outer" sensory and nervous systems – does not reveal or make possible any such *a priori* essence. There are, however, some pathological states, notably paraphrenia, in which a person might hallucinate himself outside of his organism, or construct a delusive entity distinct or partly separate from his person. Yet these are outside the scope of the present work. The sheer complex psychopathology of these cases makes untenable the assumption of a psychic entity separate from the self-image and social image, particularly in more straightforward non-psychotic cases. Even Sartre's objectification of oneself (*en soi*) cannot be for oneself but for others. A self separate from inanimate objects, fauna and flora, is *prima facie* possible. Through deeper analysis we shall conclude that it is already included in our differentiation between previously internalized objects and the normatively transmitted ones. We adopted the ethical conception of knowledge, which means that perception of objects outside their normative context would be like the eye physically "seeing", but cut off from the associative center in the brain, which relates the perceived image to past experience. The self-concept is formed by and interrelated with the internalized perception of objects, and, therefore, incorporates all the previously perceived objects which are confronted with the newly transmitted ones. As for a possible additional relationship between ego and alter, we have Brown's assertions based on empirical research findings. "The self-conception is created by a process of impression formation much like the process by which conceptions of others are created . . . The organism's conception of the self and of the other persons are highly interdependent entities".[57] We do not have to resort to Mead's other-orientated self-concept, according to which ego can build his self-image only through the eyes of the relevant alters[58] (this is what we denote as ego's social image). This might be too farfetched. We conclude that, fortunately, there is no immediate need to encumber our paradigm with three additional variables; this may well be at the price of sacrificing some epistemological finesse, but at least we have weighed and calculated this risk.

The Creative Potential of Innovative Involvement

Congruity-motivated involvement consists of a tension generated by a disjunction between two entities: *the appreciative self and the transmitted self.* These two concepts are a direct corollary from our basic epistemological model in this work, related to the initial gap between the previously internalized norms and newly transmitted ones as components of ego's self-concept. These two entities have, of course, tangential and overlapping similarities with Meadian and other symbolic–interactionist conceptualizations, as well as the Sartrian dichotomy of *être pour soi* and *être en soi*. However, most of the contents of our concepts, and especially their outer boundaries, are novel and are primarily molded for our present purpose.

The apperceptive self is ego as a channel, as a receptacle of consciousness and therefore as a center of creation. Without ego introspecting, perceiving his surrounding as well as inanimate objects, other human beings, flora and fauna, all these might as well not have existed. Our present conceptualization of the "apperceptive self" is nearest in meaning to the "Soul" component of "Being" as expounded by Plotinus:

> Each soul should first remember that it was she who by an infusion of the spirit of life produced all the animals on earth, in the air, and in the sea as well as the divine stars, the sun, and the immense heaven. She does all that, while yet remaining distinct from the things to whom she communicates form, movement and life . . . they are born or die in the measure that she imparts to them or withdraws from them their life.[59]

Ego has, so to speak, been singled out to perceive all of creation through his cognition. Every individual human being must inevitably be aware of his uniqueness in being singled out for the privilege and burden of serving as a life-giving agent to his surroundings. Many of us play at "shutting off the world" by "shutting off" some of our perception. This may remind one of Kazantzakis urging his Greek rooster not to heed the lies that his crowing does not make the sun rise – it does indeed. This epistemological nonsense is existentially sound. We know only by interpolation that alter also perceives the world through *his* cognition as the channel through which all essence flows into Being. Should my consciousness wane or fade, so would all creation. The *apperceptive self per se* is essentially unique and congruous, but dissonances are bound to occur when it is confronted with the *transmitted self*. The latter consists of the internalized normative transmissions of alters and is crystallized by a "looking glass" process, as expounded by the symbolic interactionists. The crucial distinction is that ego anchors himself on the relevant alters in order to construct his transmitted self. It draws its existence from his surrounding alters. It defines its individuality *vis-à-vis* the collectivity of others. Others essentially mold the transmitted self, whereas the apperceptive self may have and indeed does have an essence by itself. The present premise supplements our previous exposition in Chapter 2, according to which the self is formed by a continuous absorption of new normative transmissions, which are being incorporated through integration or conflict into the previously internalized normative apperceptions. Our present premise distinguishes between the self as the source of cognition and the self as built by ego through his internalization of the normative transmissions of others. These two have been confronted and made to conflict with each other in the conformity studies of Asch, Crutchfield and others.[60] The apperceptive self of the bona fide research subject has been contrasted with and made to contradict the collusionary consensus of the others. The stress and strain generated by the disjunctures between the apperceptive and transmitted selves on the one hand and the pressures of congruity on the other hand are the essence of the dynamic process of involvement. They may manifest themselves in many ways; some of the most conspicuous are creativity, achievement and the quest for knowledge, which may or may not overlap.

(1) *Creativity*: Strain is not only of the essence of *Creativity*, but the best creations have been realized through the most potent strains and stresses to be experienced by creative minds. It is an acknowledged premise that the latter produce best under pressure, for "Damocles never danced better than beneath the Sword".[61] The release of energy entailed by the act of creation is triggered, presumably, by the strain of involvement. The Nietzschian command to "create . . . or else" singles out creativity as the sole means to the survival of meanings; creativity through stress, through agony, the surging out of a new life through a suffering womb. For Nietzsche, the alternative to creativity is non-being. God is dead, and the man-God dies too if he cannot assert his being through creativity. The alternative to involvement through creativity is also a partial death, the finalization of the normative dissonances and value breakdowns. Arthur Koestler, in his voluminous treatise *The Act of Creation*, does not seem to adhere to the strain process of creativity. He even claims that conflicting inner identifications might lead one to immaculate passive bliss. "To be both Caesar and Brutus", he says, "in one's imagination has a profound

cathartic effect, and is one way of approaching Nirvana".[62] Koestler himself, however, may serve as a prime refutation of his thesis. His masterpiece *Darkness at Noon* rings with the profound and searing strains between Roubashov, the Utopian revolutionary, and Gletkin, the brutal brainwasher. The strains are generated by the disjuncture between Koestler's apperceptive self as an idealistic Marxist (who is gladly sacrificing his life to fight misery, exploitation and starvation) and his transmitted self as the creature of historical necessity. This strain between Koestler-Roubashov and Koestler-Gletkin gave birth to *Darkness at Noon*. Its greatness lies in the authenticity of character, feasibility of stance and credulity of argument of both Roubashov and Gletkin. They are not a "bad guy" and a "good guy"; they are the tortuous stresses generated by the two divergent components of a self. This strain, if not released through the ringing dialogues of *Darkness at Noon,* could have played havoc with Koestler's sanity rather than cushion him onto the suspended animation of Nirvana.

(2) *The achievement motive*: The achievement motive may be described by our conceptual framework as a strain between the apperceptive self as a solitary existential egocentrism and the flow of assailing normative patterns introduced through the transmitted self.

The strain of involvement in this case is the apperceptive self's striving to overpower and/or to manipulate the incongruous cognitive elements sent over to him through the transmitted self. Weber's classic thesis on the achievement motive may be quite fruitfully linked to our present conceptualization. He stresses the self-reliance element in the Protestant Ethic as a corollary of its rejection of the ecclesia and sacraments as the sole avenue to salvation. Self-reliance, individuality, puritanism, asceticism, hard work and thrift make the accumulation of worldly goods and wealth (without enjoying them sensuously) an almost natural outcome. Moreover, the achievement of the latter becomes the wages of virtue, and striving to achieve them is the symbol of virtue. Gothic architecture has marked elements of a stratification of the achievement motive. A soaring precursor of the Protestant Ethic, it "struggles with outstretched arms to grasp some glory above". The individual standing alone *vis-à-vis* the world without the comforts of an intermediary church and the coddling of an ecclesia is actually the cold solitude of the apperceptive self as conceptualized by us. It tries to cope with the incongruous transmitted self by the outer-involvement mode of achievement.

The Weberian hypothesis, as reformulated by McClelland, starts with a need to reach a certain goal and proceeds with the efforts to overcome external or internal obstacles to the attainment of the goal.[63] McClelland does not, however, agree with the genesis of this need for achievement. Our present conceptualization may supplement McClelland's model in so far as it explains the strains inherent in the need to achieve itself. This model will be presented later, together with an analysis of the paradigm and the resultant typology of involvement.

(3) *The search for knowledge*: The third instance illustrating the strain of involvement is man's striving for ontological comprehension. Kaufmann recruits original sin to explain love and creativity. Precisely the striving to overcome the cardinal proscription brought out in man his creative and effective potential.[64] This may be so, but we might as well interpret the scriptural episode of the Fall as depicting man's prime passion to know. The mouthful of the apple was evidently quite small. Far from being "as God", we had only a meager glimpse, and a blurred one, of the mechanics of matter, and a limited insight into logic, itself a limited tool, before being chased away. Our ontological knowledge remains as poor as it was then. It is enclosed in a minute space of existence flanked by two walls of darkness: the obscure prime movers and unknown ultimate goals. The passion to know is, therefore, a basic strain – the striving of the disconnected "apperceptive self" to comprehend his relationship with all the incongruous patterns reaching him via the "transmitted self". This passion for knowledge, clarity and meaning dwarfs the social goals of wealth, status and power and turns wine, women and song into an insignificant drudgery. The passion to know, this striving to be God, served Camus as a basis for his philosophy of revolt. We go further and give this ontological interest the stature of a prime mover. Whoever propels us installed both an ontic blackout about our origins and aims and a passion for clarity. This makes man the foundling of no origin and no destination, forever roaming the solar system and aiming at Alpha Centauri, probing into the subatomic Omega Minus and the workings of the synapses in his own cerebral cortex. The foundling is installed with a need, a strain for a seemingly impossible search for his ancestry and heritage. This seems desirable to Morris Cohen, who says, "All that is absolutely worthwhile has something of the unattainable about it".[65] To others, however, it may seem like a sinister and a not very funny experiment with us as guinea pigs. We nevertheless have to retain our sense of humor as our only means of protest, and humor is indeed a prime and choice mode of involvement.

The Self's Reaction to the Failure of Involvement: Breakdown

We may proceed now to analyze some types of value breakdown. The following figure presents a three-dimensional "property space". The basic variables are the three pairs of discrepancies among the six components of our two configurations. The components of the AC are: previously internalized objects, others and self-concept, and the hypothetical gap among these and the respective components of the subsequent normative images of objects and alters. L signifies a low gap between two corresponding components and H stands for a wide gap.

65

The Broken Image and the Absurd

NORMATIVE GAPS			INVOLVEMENT TO BRIDGE GAP		FAILURE AND BREAKDOWN	
Disjunction btw. Self and social image	Disjunction btw. Internalized objects and the normatively transmitted ones	Disjunction btw. Internalized alters and the normatively transmitted ones	Direction of involvement	Type of involvement	Type of breakdown	Non-involvement breakdown types.
L	L	L	---	---	---	Ideal type alterist
H	L	L	Inner involvement	'Exploration of inner space'	'Iyun': the defacement of self	
			Outer involvement	'Social climber'	Resentiment	
L	H	L	Inner involvement	Perceptual innovation	'a knife through the canvas'	
			Outer involvement	Invention	'the universe is out of control'	

Figure 3.5 A typology of value-breakdowns

L	L	H	Inner involvement	dialogue	objectification	
			Outer involvement	moralist	'Hell is other people'	
H		L	Inner involvement	transcendental subjectivity	existence is not essence	
			Outer involvement	logical metaphysics	*credo quia absurdum*	
H	H	L	Inner involvement	solidarist	'The lonely crowd'	
			Outer involvement	ideational innovator	'The end of ideology'	
L	H	H	Inner involvement	Hedonism	'The moment after'	
			Outer involvement	achievement motive	ritualism	
H	H	H	---	---	---	alienation

Figure 3.6 Failure of involvement

(1) *The first and the last types* (L-L-L and H-H-H) are the noninvolvement-non-breakdown. In the extreme is the ideal type alterist who is "other-directed", to use Reisman's phrase, or who is in the ultimate state of *alteration* as conceived by Ortega y Gasset. He is a conformist swayed by every normative change, the follower of every new craze, fad and fashion. At the other extreme, we have the one who is completely divorced in his recipient cognitive configuration from the components of the transmitting one. He is alienated, and his knowledge of self, objects and others is weird and endogenous, unshared by others. He is the person diagnosed as mentally ill. The concept of conformity both semantically and materially is far from being clear. If we regard it statistically (which is in the last analysis the only possible way), conformity would be in compliance with the modal values and behavior of a given group at a given time. It would, no doubt, vary with the shifting of the modes, means and medians. Moreover, there can be no *a priori* exposition or typology of conformity because one type of behavior, which is denoted as deviant, might become modal and vice versa. Merton's typology of adaptations, for instance, specifies "ritualism" as an individual's anchorage on routine,[66] the raising of means to the stature of ends in themselves. In case it appears (which we suspect it will) that the modal types in our industrialized bureaucratized societies are the assembly line technician and form-filling clerk, the ritualist would be the conformist. The industrial psychologist in Western societies and the "thought reform" councils of Communist China would see to it that the workers sanctify their routine drudgery. The cultural goals are thus merged into the means to achieve them. Conformity is also not synonymous with solidarity and cohesion. We visualize societies that advocate individualism or preach passivity and retreatism. We can, therefore, define conformity only structurally, but never by its contents.

Social psychologists dismiss as nonsense the presumably coercive nature of the normative system of society,[67] which is supposedly imposed from above to ensnare the free souls of individuals, first, because norms are created through the interaction of individuals. The symbolic interactionist sees the self-image as being molded through the constant reflection of ego's image in the "looking glass" self as presented to him by the generalized other. This excludes any transcendental set of standards implanted in the "soul" of the individual, the "will of the people" hovering in the ether and demanding conformity. Second, the conformity studies according to which *Homo Conveniens* tends to defer to the consensus of the group if it is in conflict with the perception of his own senses.

Third, conformity in the formative years is induced through the utter dependence of the child on goodwill and acceptance by the relevant adults. The present work, however, is concerned with the later phase. After a person has already achieved his post adolescent ego identity, he can be confronted by normative transmissions emanating from any given social institution, which are liable to be inconsistent with his previously internalized norms. These are the initial normative gaps that may lead eventually to value deviation. We propose to deal rather extensively with the insane and compare them in Chapter 4 with other formal deviants: the criminals. Our claim here is that there is a marked similarity in the pressures towards insanity and morbidity.

(2) *The remaining six typologies* have been dichotomized by inner and outer involvement. The latter are based on a person's presumed reaction to frustration as conceptualized by Rosenzweig.[68] The passive "impunitive" type of reaction, which expresses itself in condonement of others and self, is not relevant in the present context. On the other hand, the active reactions – "intropunitiveness", i.e. the condemnation of self, and the "extrapunitive reaction", i.e. condemnation of the outer world, for failure – are relevant indeed. The initial normative gap between the transmission configuration and the apperceptive configuration, which is our key epistemological model, could be taken as a dissonance, an obstacle and therefore, in a sense, a frustration that ego has to respond to. If he tends to "intropunitiveness", there is a higher chance that his involvement to bridge the gap would be more towards his own self and person. If he tends to explain his failures by factors and processes outside of himself in the outer world, he would tend to bridge the initial normative gap by involving himself with the external novel transmissions, i.e. with the components of the transmission configuration. The present comparison is quite fruitful, because we thereby relate some given personality traits with our conceptualization of inner and outer involvement. Moreover, these personality traits are measurable as demonstrated by Rosenzweig's own studies. In other words, a person's "intropunitiveness" or his "extrapunitiveness" are adequate predictors for his inner or outer involvement, as we conceptualized.

One assumption underlying the typology in Paradigm B is in line with the dissonance theories. The likelihood of involvement is greater in relation to components between which the relevant gap will be wider. The need for consistency, as well as the efforts to bridge the discrepancies will be greater, and the resultant innovative involvement would also be of a greater magnitude.

We have thus arrived at twelve basic types of initial disjunction between the components of the transmitting and recipient configurations followed by involvement and its breakdown.

Lazarsfeld has described the typology presented in Paradigm B as "pragmatic", in the sense that it "consists in matching a given system of types with that attributed space and that reduction from which it could have originated logically".[69] As a matter of fact, we have looked for a concretization to fit the cells of the paradigm. We searched a composite of attributes personified by an illustrative type. Unlike the type analyses of inductive casuistics from the Talmud to Jung, the ontological validity of our typology is sadly meager. In technique we have followed Merton's typology in *Social Structure and Anomie*.[70] Putting it crudely, the variables coordinated in a given property space of the paradigm are likely to be associated with the attributes converging on a type of person. The following presentation of the types is rudimentary; it is more of an initial description than an exhaustive analysis.

The Defacement of the Self

When the initial normative disjunction between the self-image and social image of ego occurs, the congruity motivated involvement concentrates presumably in these components and not in the other pairs of relationships in the paradigm. The latter, displaying a low initial gap, are in a relative state of homeostasis. They do not require ego's focused attention and they do not call for his involvement. Strictly speaking they do not bother him. One is aware of the existence of a tooth or a nail when they hurt. The inner involvement in this case tends to hold ego's social image as given, probing into his self-concept to understand the rifts, blemishes or even collapse of his "life theory", *weltanschauung*, dignity and self-esteem caused by the onslaught of his social image.

Examples are furnished by the marginalities following internal or external migration or ethnic admixture – Europeans grafted into Africa or Asia, for example, who are trying to integrate themselves into the indigenous culture. Their social image as transmitted to them by the natives is that of a European with all its implications. Their own self-image is that of one who is trying to internalize his adopted culture so that it harmonizes with his European back-ground; they abhor leventinization by shallow absorption of the native culture. The predicted involvement in this case is towards self-searching. Ego feels unable or is unwilling to attack his European social image with the natives. Rather, he strives by introspection to find the clue to effective presentation of his "true self" to his adopted cultural peers so that the gap between his self-image and social image narrows. Moreover, all his dignity and self-esteem is based upon his self-appointed carriage of the "white man's burden", his role as harbinger of "progress" and "enlightenment" to his culture.

When a rift occurs between the self-image and the social image because the mother culture disowns a person's right to power supremacy and threatens to sever the umbilical cord, he might bridge the gap by rejecting it in turn, claiming that the mother culture has been adulterated and that he is the sole true survivor, the authentic torch-bearer. Whether such a venture is politically successful is irrelevant.

The breakdown occurs when ego's inner involvement leads to a debasement of his self-concept. For example, the Algerian Pied-Noirs coming over to France after carrying for generations the banner of French culture in the Maghreb and shedding their blood for an Algérie Française. Their own self-concept was staunchly French, honed and sharpened by years of combat and struggles. Their social image, however, as broadcast to them from the mainland and the metrop-olis, was of Pied-Noirs – crude Levantines of obscure origin, not far removed from the Moslem Algerians and other Moghrabites also living in Algeria. For the Pied-Noirs, who sought the key to this dilemma by probing into their self-concept, and who chose not to question the integrity of the mother culture, the verdict of the metropolitan French was hardly assailable. After all, the others were, by definition, the "true" and authentic French. Apparently their own self-image of Frenchness was all wrong (how could it be otherwise) and a process of self-doubt, self-debasement, self-hatred and self-degradation set in.[71]

In Jewish mysticism, this process is denoted as "*Iyun*", the defacement of the "*Ani*", the self.[72] A relevant episode witnessed by the author took place as a sequel to an argument by a bus-driver and a commuter (both Moroccan Jews) who emigrated to Israel. The commuter asked the driver aggrievedly, "Where is your traditional Moghrabite-Jewish dignity?" "Everything is lost here", answered the driver in a philosophical mood, "in this confused melting pot, you don't know whether you are an Israeli, a Moroccan, a Jew, a Frenchman. Over there we were Jews, over here we are Moroccans. In truth we cannot claim to be either this or that". Such instances illustrate the failure of inner involvement, the loss of identity following the probing inside the self, and its debasement in face of an overpowering social image.

Resentment

In the case of outer involvement, ego strives to close the gap between his self and social image by trying to change the latter. The "social climber" who will "show them" is a slum kid, a typical grammar school boy, a Jew-boy, a dago, a pint-size Ajaccien. Many means can be used to assail the social image so that it approaches the "true" self-image. Money, knowledge, reputation, another hit, another play, another pair of antelope horns, another notch on a sniper's gun, a shark's tail or a woman's body. The end is social status. One keeps chasing it all one's life. The breakdown comes when the contestant realizes that he is chasing a will-o'-the-wisp; the distance remains constant whatever the efforts to shorten it. This is the case of the snob in Maugham's *The Razor's Edge*, whose breakdown after a lifetime of status-chasing is pure "sour grapes". A more profound breakdown of outer-involvement is the case of the Camusian Judge-penitent, who finally realizes that by devoting his life to striving for wealth, fame and social status, he has devoted himself to ends which are, in the last analysis, meaningless, absurd and boring. This might be another case of disenchantment through achievement. When the triumph of changing the social image to fit the self-image has been finally reached, the victory tastes stale. On the other hand, this kind of breakdown might follow ego's realization of the inherent incompatibility between his self and social image, and his sole refuge to coherence is to be able to see himself apart from the misleading setting of the group.

Failure of Involvement

Innovation

In one of the most articulate passages of *The Myth of Sisyphus*, Camus describes, as if for our present purposes, the disjuncture between previously internalized objects and their novel normative perception:

> Strangeness creeps in; perceiving that the world is "dense", sensing to what a degree a stone is foreign and irreducible to us, with what intensity nature or a landscape can negate us. At the heart of all beauty lies something inhuman, and these hills, the softness of the sky, the outline of these trees at this very minute lose the illusory meaning with which we had clothed them, henceforth more remote than a lost paradise. The primitive hostility of the world raises up to face us across millennia. For a second we cease to understand it because for centuries we have understood in it solely the images and designs that we had attributed to it beforehand.[73]

This rupture between the habitual image of things and their new perceptual impact, when followed by inner involvement, might lead to novel aesthetic insight of inanimate objects, flora and fauna, in the plastic arts, poetry and literature. This, of course, is only one illustrative instance of the direction in which the inner involvement in this case might lead. The aesthetic innovation of a Van Gogh is a proper example. In his letters to his brother Theo, he writes:

> It is not the language of painters but the language of nature to which one ought to listen . . . The feeling for the things themselves, for reality, is more important than the feeling for pictures, at least it is more fertile and more vital . . . I see that nature has told me something, has spoken to me, and that I have put it down in shorthand. In my shorthand there may be words that cannot be deciphered, there may be mistakes or gaps, but there is something in it of what wood or shore or figure has told me.[74]

This is the involvement, the proposed solution to the artist's perceptual, emotional normative dilemma, caused by a discrepancy between the conventional perception of objects by other artists and his own new perceptual insight. He expresses this dilemma:

> A peasant woman by a Parisian who has learned drawing at the academy will always indicate the limbs and the structure of the body in one selfsame way . . . I should be desperate if my figures were correct . . . I do not want them to be academically correct . . . my great longing is to learn to make those very incorrectnesses, those deviations, remodellings; changes of reality, so that they may become, yes, untruth if you like – but more true than the literal truth.[75]

However, the breakdowns in these cases are quite violent and mostly symbolic. In Van Gogh's case he wrote very shortly before committing suicide, "Well, my own work, I am risking my life for it and my reason has half-foundered owing to it".[76] Others drive a knife in impotent rage through the unyielding canvas, while others stare gloomily at the failed efforts of expression on a flat canvas with nothing in it or behind it.

The Universe is Out of Context

The corresponding outer involvement in this case might take the form of technical invention or the probing to various depths into the intricacies of nature and matter. The lines of progress here could superficially be traced through the triumphs of Leeowenhoek, Pasteur, Ehrlich and Sal, or by the as of yet unfinished escalation from Newtonian physics through Rutherford's model of the atom and quantum physics to the Manhattan project and thermo-nuclear reaction. The Spencerian idea of "progress" hardly distinguishes between triumph and disaster. However, an outer involvement in the present case could lead to value breakdown in the form of Promethean remorse, the chained Titan striking his chest in atonement for the fatal tool he gave man to manipulate his physical environment. This is reminiscent of the agonies of an Oppenheimer for his part in the development of the Manhattan project. The realization of impending total disaster as a direct corollary of outer involvement is but one possible instance of value breakdown. A more common one, depicted by Ionesco, could be labeled "the universe is out of control". Technology, assembly lines, and gadgeteering turn boomerang-like on their initiators. The Sorcerer's Apprentice is smothered by tides of his own making. Better than any other playwright, Ionesco has captured the ludicrous panic that invades modern man in an age of rapidly changing technology. Ionesco produces tragic farce by using the proliferation and acceleration of physical objects. In *The New Tenant,* furniture inexorably chokes up every inch of space until the hero is entombed amid his belongings like a petty, bourgeois Pharaoh. But as the props become more animated, the people become more desiccated. The insides of Ionesco's characters are like the outsides of computers. The most acute breakdown, however, is one's realization that he makes no headway in his outer involvement. For all his "progress" he seems to understand (which is the ultimate in successful involvement) less and less his natural and physical environment:

> Matter, substance, time, space, causality, precision of measurement and the belief in the predictability of behavior of the measured, have run like sand through the physicists' fingers . . . Nineteenth-century physics describes a sharply defined world with a blurred initial stage; contemporary physics describes an evenly blurred world, like a film with coarse granulation; whether we describe this world as "Pantheistic", "Free", "Undetermined", "Statistical", "Spiritual", or "Voluntaristic" is more or less a matter of taste. What really matters is that the physicist's instruments of measurement indicate the presence of physically immeasurable factors".[77]

Objectification

The initial disjunction between the others is already incorporated in ego's self-image and Camus portrays the subsequent impact of their newly perceived image:

> Men, too, secrete the inhuman. At certain moments of lucidity, the mechanical aspect of their gestures, their meaningless pantomime makes silly everything that surrounds them. This discomfort in the face of man's own inhumanity, this incalculable tumble before the image of what we are, this "nausea" as a writer of today calls it, is also the absurd.[78]

The inner involvement to bridge the gap would be presumably in the *Dialogica* tradition. We hold the new alter, the *thou,* as constant, as given, and try to find a place for him in our subjective consciousness composed, among other things, of previously internalized alters. For Buber, this dialogical involvement is the supreme medium of "real" existence. "The I is real in virtue of its sharing in reality (with Thou). The more direct the contact with Thou the fuller is the sharing (of reality) . . . The Thou meets me, but I step into direct relation with it. Hence the relation means being chosen and choosing . . . "[79] However, this subjective grasp of alter is, even according to Buber, a moment of grace bordering on the miraculous. Moreover, it is of short duration and inevitably deteriorates into an objectification. The *I–Thou* relationship breaks down into an *I–It* relationship. "This is the exalted melancholy of our fate that every *Thou* in our world must become an *It.* It does not matter how exclusively present the *Thou* was in the direct relation. As soon as the relation has been worked out or has been permeated with a means, the *Thou* becomes an object among objects".[80] If the mystic and optimistic Buber dooms any successful dialogical involvement to eventual breakdown by the objectification of alter, Sartre foredooms the involvement at the outset. Ego is continuously stifled by alter. Alter is by definition an objectified entity (*être en soi*) for ego. An inner involvement by ego to bring alter to a subjective relationship with him is an ontological impossibility. In a Sartrian world populated by objectified alters, whose sheer existence limits ego's freedom and makes his life hell on earth, a dialogical involvement is a spurious delusion. One should accept the breakdown as an inevitable sequel to an attempt at involvement that has failed before it has even begun.

Hell is Other People

The corresponding outer involvement is that of the moralist. He tries if possible to impose, or at any rate promulgate, his own internalized image as an active assault on the diverging normative image of alters. This includes a vast array of normative doctrinaires from the law-giver, through the preacher, to the Hyde

Park orator. This type seems to be too wide to be of operative value in a taxonomy. Whether this is so or not becomes apparent after the whole paradigm is subjected to empirical testing. The status of ego and the amount of power that backs his moralizing is not really important in the present context. We are concerned with value deviation and the social position of the indoctrinator; whether he is a Hammurabi, a Savonarola or a skid row sage is hardly relevant. The breakdown here occurs as a corollary to a lack of meaningful communication between ego and his audience if rapport is lacking or impossible. If an exchange of meanings is not feasible, violence becomes the ultimate sequel to the outer involvement of the moralist – violence *by him*, if he has power, or violence *to him* if he is powerless. The intolerance bred out of ego's powerlessness to convey to alters his proposed normative mandates is by itself violence, of the type portrayed by Sartre in *No Exit*. If the comprehensive transmission of norms is blocked, relations deteriorate to a stigmatic repartee between ego and alters, an interchange of derogatory tags and labels. Modern literature and drama is rife with this engulfing violence and the Kafkaesque victims and the brutes of Pinter both epitomize the tyranny of imposing norms. If not based on a meaningful meeting of minds between ego and alter, these are nothing but a mindless force.

Existence is not Essence

In case of a disjuncture between self and social image, the previously internalized objects and the newly transmitted ones, the involvement would, presumably, take a transcendental form. This double disjuncture of self and nature has perennially driven man to transcendence. Augustine posed his basic enigma, "*quid ergo sum, Deus ineus? qua natura mea?*" Buber interprets this as being a double query about Man's relationship with himself and his relationship with his surrounding nature.[81] This actually resembles our present double normative disjuncture. To risk a wild generalization, we hypothesize that most religious premises stem from an initial stance of normative disjuncture, of a sense of meaninglessness and relative futility of the temporal world. The ingenious constructs of the ever-after – the Jewish "*Olam-Habba*", where the just dine with golden cutlery at a golden table, the Moslem "*Genna*", where the faithful live it up with voluptuous hours – these and many other similar *post mortem* promises of inheritance to the meek serve as an expedient panacea for meaninglessness, misery and normative contradictions in the here-and-now. The involvement here is by trying to bridge the initial normative gap with transcendental artifacts or belief systems which need no empirical verification and are invulnerable to refutation.

Our contention that a transcendental involvement is more feasible in case of a self–object disjuncture with a relatively low discrepancy in the social variable needs, of course, further elaboration, which has to remain outside the scope of the present work. Many anthropologists and sociologists of religion from Weber and Frazer to Malinowsky and Radcliffe-Brown stress the functionality of religion in reconciling man's struggles and ordeals with his physical surroundings and self. Man's dependence on the hazards of nature, his symbiosis with the world, and the dangers in his daily encounters with his physical environment have bred most of the deities and rituals of religion and magic. Man's insoluble queries about his own being, essence and existence, have also been directed towards transcendental solutions. These belief-systems are conveniently anchored on non-logical premises. O'Dea states, "Rites in both religion and magic display two characteristics: reinstatement of an earlier situation with the arousal and catharsis of appropriate feelings and the displacement of attention from some aspects of the situation and the focusing of it upon others".[82] These are precisely the patterns of transcendental involvement hypothesized in the present context. We are well aware that the Durkheimian conception of religion as a transcendentalization of social relations is diametrically opposed to our hypothesis, but a further elaboration of this controversy is, again, outside the present description of a mere typology. The inner transcendental involvement strives to bridge the normative gap of self and universe by probing into oneself and seeking mystical union of the normatively ruptured cognitive elements. This achieved union of self with the ultimate is the mystical fusion of whatever cognitive disjunctures ego may experience between his self and its diverging images transmitted over to him. The mystic and, therefore, non-logical or cognitively consequential links of the discrepancies are achieved by a union with the transcendental invisible. This *Unio Mystica* with the Divine Presence is the essence of mysticism. The Kabbalists cherished it as "The Redemption",[83] as the final solution to inner disharmonies. This is also apparent from the interpretation of Deuteronomy 5:5, "I stood between the Lord and you", by the Kabbalist Rabbi Michael from Solotov. His belief was that I–ego, as a separate cognitive entity, is the partition, the wall that separates one from his God.[84] This separateness is supposed to be overcome by the mystic union between the whole self (not only the cognitive part thereof) with God.

St. Maximus of Turin forces this mystical union into a pseudo-naturalistic fusion. "In the Savior we are all risen, we have all been restored to life, we have all ascended into heaven. For a portion of the flesh and blood of each of us is in the man Christ".[85] To risk an unwarranted concretization, we visualize the mystical union as an endless progression of Rutherfordian models of the atom. The solar system structure of electrons, protons and neutrons is incorporated in the human person, in the way that the solar system is an atom of a universal transcendental entity, which again might exist in a solar system or its equivalent on another dimension and so on *ad infinitum*. Nicholas of Cusa sets the bridging of cognitive disjunctions of ego's material surroundings through mysticism:

> The place wherein Thou art found unveiled is girt round with the coincidence of contradictions, and this is the wall of Paradise wherein Thou dost abide. The door whereof is guarded by the most proud spirit of Reason, and unless he be vanquished the way will not lie open. Therefore, I observe how needful it is for me to enter into the darkness, and to admit the coincidence of opposites beyond all the grasp of reason, and there to seek the truth where impossibility meeteth me.[86]

This is very much like the Kabbalistic *Tikkun*, the mystic striving for the harmonizing[87] of the conflicts, contradictions and imperfections of the world. The breakdown of mystic involvement may occur in many alternative directions, one of them being Satanism, the salvation-through-the-gutters phase of the religious nihilists, notably the followers of Shabtai Zvi and Jacob Frank who had to account for the apostasy of the Messiah by the doctrine of redemption-through-sin and the purifying nature of evil. This Genet-style form of sanctity is found in the Frankist maxim, "The subversion of the Torah can become its true fulfillment".[88] This is paradoxical, and the breakdown is precisely the destruction of the belief system, the involvement of which is intended to be a harmonizing act. It is as Scholem says, "as if an anarchist rebellion had taken place within the world of Law".[89] An opposite direction of breakdown is a Kierkegaardian theme of self-destruction through a "fear and trembling" relationship with the divine. However, the most common breakdown of a *Unio Mystica* attempt at transcendental involvement is the subsequent lack of ability or desire to bridge over paradoxes by non-rational means. The breakdown here is a regression to reason, back from *Tikkun*, The Way of Perfection, Yoga and Nirvana to cognitive logic.

I Believe in the Absurd

The transcendental outer involvement is the cushioned orderliness of institutionalized religion; the *Ecclesia* and the *Kerygma* of the Apostles, the security of the tightly knit infallible dogmas of the heir to Jesus Christ. The pulsating bosom of the Torah has all the tranquilizing answers for the perplexed. Contradictions are only delusions and death is a mirage.[90] The Moslem *Ulamma* have scholastically synchronized every violence of nature with every human deficiency. Logic is superfluous and normative gaps are bridged over by decrees supported by a metaphysical hierarchy.

Freud has described this outer transcendental involvement and has also stressed incidentally the dual nature-and-self disharmonies, which are presumably glossed over by institutionalized religion:

> For the individual, as for mankind in general, life is hard to endure. Man's seriously menaced self-esteem craves for consolation, life and the universe must be rid of their terrors and incidentally man's curiosity . . . we are perhaps still defenseless, but no longer helplessly paralyzed; we can at least react; perhaps indeed we are not

even defenseless, we can have recourse to the same methods against these violent supermen of the beyond that we make use of in our community; we can try to exorcise them, to appease them, to bribe them, and to rob them of part of their power by thus influencing them.[91]

The breakdown of outer transcendental involvement is evidently quite widespread, judging by the continuous secularization of modern society. This process has been accelerated by a self-destroying movement within the Ecciesia in the form of the Death of God theologians. Institutionalized religion may hardly survive a prescription of the sad truth that prime movers are logical absurdities. Indeed, inference in this matter is impossible, but Kyries cannot be sung if no vestige of hope remains for the appearance of Godot. We are concerned, of course, with value breakdowns. It is of secondary concern, therefore, if the rituals of institutionalized religion following the value breakdowns are perpetuated through the cynicism of the Borgias or the stoic resignation of Dostoevsky's Grand Inquisitor.

The Lonely Crowd

The solidarist tries to bridge the normative gaps of self-social-image and normative-others by adhering as closely as possible to the normative system of the group. This type of inner involvement is the "adjustment" process of the individual to the normative system of society, so highly cherished by advocates of mental health and social welfare. This entails the honing of edges and odd protruding corners in ego's self-image and internalized alters so that it fits better the new normative images transmitted to him. His inwardly directed involvement takes the novel normative transmissions as constant, as casts into which ego has to mold himself. These new transmissions are bound to be focused toward the central values, the mean, mode and median. There is almost a consensus of opinion that the more a society becomes urbanized, industrialized and specialized the greater the trend towards centrally focused and standardized norms. This is evident in the industrialist who has to gear his production to satisfy the demands of potential consumers as revealed by the curve of his latest market research (not wider than two standard deviations from the mean). The pop star will groan *ad nauseam* at the top tunes on the hit parade, all of which are geared towards a standardized taste. This leveling process creates a normative system, the edges of which have been blurred and its focal points unduly accentuated. This is the normative system to which the divergent ego (as defined by the inner involving ego) has to adjust himself to become a solidarist. The breakdown of the present involvement is a rejection of the mass culture and a "streamlined" normative system as a debilitating cult of mediocrity. The solitary group and its *esprit de corps* of the herd are both rejected as meaningless. Kierkegaard calls the group (the public) "an all-embracing something which is nothing consisting of unreal individuals who never can be united in an actual situation".[92] The new normative transmissions may have only a leveling, defacing and dehumanizing effect on ego.

Heidegger regards the normative system of society as representing the generalized other, *Das Man*, the embodiment of impersonality and indirectedness, and therefore tyrannizing.[93] Jaspers sees in modern mass society an entity devoid of existence and therefore unauthentic. It is a "phantom . . . supposed to exist in a vast number of persons who have no effective interrelationship".[94] The breakdown here negates, therefore, the attempt towards solidarity with the group and its norms because mass culture (including its norm) is by definition instrumental to the defacing and the debasing of ego. Moreover, the group itself is not solidaristic or cohesive, and might transmit centrally focused norms for mass consumption; but the crowd as such is atomized, anomic and lonely.

The End of Ideology

The corresponding outward involvement would strive to impose ego's previously internalized images and ideas on alters. In its extreme phase, this would take the form of ideational rebellion. The rebel with an ideology wishes to overthrow governments, change social, economic and religious institutions. His self-image and previously internalized alters assure him that the normative gap can be bridged by the alters accepting his version as to what is the desired state of affairs. He believes, and his faith is coupled with chiliastic charisma, that when his ideology governs the fate of the group, the road leads directly towards communal wealth and peace. Ideational rebellion might have been preceded, therefore, by a deep and effective internalization of some relevant systems of beliefs and norms in their absolute and authoritarian form. It would be interesting to investigate the link between ideational rebellion and a rigid early socialization by the agencies of sacred or secular religions. The etiology of a behavioral process is outside the scope of a mere typology. However, we may assume that the potential rebel has internalized at a relatively early age a defined and stable normative system from his primary socialization agencies. He expects the groups to which he is most closely associated to carry out or at least to adhere to a clear non-ambiguous normative system. The ideational rebel projects his inner images of the absolutes which he has internalized on society at large, or at least on his reference or membership groups. If the sacred religionist projects his abstracted subjective image of perfection on transcendence, the secular religionist projects his subjecting abstraction of monolithic absolutes on the group or the relevant alters. Despite arguments to the contrary, the ideologist is an intellectual who proceeds from himself outwards from his own inner convictions. He has scar tissues resulting from "the painful clash of these convictions with the insensibilities and insensitivity of alters". Bell says:

> The ideologist – Communist, existentialist, religionist – wants to live at some extreme, and criticizes the ordinary man for failing to live at this level of grandeur. One can try to do so if there is the genuine possibility that the next could be actually, a "transforming moment" when salvation or revolution or genuine passion could be achieved. But such chiliastic moments are illusions. And what is left is the unheroic, day-to-day routine of living.[95]

This is one mode of the breakdown of the ideological involvement. However, the most common form of breakdown stems from the sad realization that Utopia is not only semantically, but also by operational definition, a *fata Morgana*. On the long road towards the mirage the majority of rebels, social reformers, political innovators, labor leaders and founders of religions succumb intentionally, or by an inevitable occupational hazard of ideational innovators, to a pursuance of absolute power. To state that the pursuers of absolute *isms* end up as absolute tyrants is to voice a well-known truism which is, however, preferable to the argument that power does not corrupt but that corrupt people seek power. The latter has, to our mind, more value as a quip than a description of reality. The analysis of the breakdown of ideologies is the favorite pastime of political theorists. Right and Left have been equally vulnerable. Schumpeter delineated the self-destructive mechanism built into capitalism and the God-that-Failed iconoclasts eulogize their hangovers from dialectical materialism and the morning after spending the night with "historical necessity". Without the *élan*, an ideology becomes verbalism, a conglomeration of empty words and symbols hovering from paper or vocal chords through hot air.

Hedonism and Ritualism

When objects and others trouble ego, his inner involvement seems to be an easy way out. He makes objects of alters. He is the hedonist. He is Don Juan, whose present is concerned with the blotting out of the past, and with the ignoring of the future, a Dionysian releasing the reins of the Satyr's goat-half. The corresponding outer involvement is achievement motivated towards the imposition of ego's image of things and others on upper vertical mobility and higher status.

The etiology of the achievement motive has received a new vogue since the pioneering work of Weber on the Protestant Ethic as the prime mover of the "from-here-to-the-stars" drive inherent in capitalism. Atkinson and McClelland have initiated a veritable avalanche of modifications and empirical verifications of the Weberian thesis.[96] Other studies trace the achievement motive to diverse, often incompatible, sources, e.g. Winterbottom's claim that achievement is ingrained into the child by an early parental concern with independence-training coupled with hugging, kissing and patting by mother.[97] On the other hand, Dines, Clarke and Dinitz trace the achievement motive, in the psychoanalytic tradition, to infantile deprivations and the non-fulfillment of a child's basic needs.[98] We cannot at this stage of our analysis take sides. We are constructing a mere taxonomy and disregarding at present the causal processes leading presumably to a given type of involvement. The breakdown, however, deals with etiology because we have defined it as a dynamic causal chain. Avenues to the present breakdown are quite numerous. The sociological expositions start with Durkheim's description of the anomie casualties, "rolling down the slopes of the achievement pyramid".[99] Merton analyzed the retreatist rejection of both "unattainable goals and the institutionalized means to achieve them".[100] Cloward and Clilin stressed the role of the various ethnic and class barriers to upper-vertical mobility in the "breakdown of values and the breaking-away from the achievement motive".[101] Max Scheller delineated the "sour grapes" breakdown "The pre-achievement rationalization of impending failure through *ressentiment*".[102] Camus's Judge-penitent personifies the existentialist description of our present breakdown. His post-achievement waiving of status and wealth is an ultimate gesture of evaluation, or rather the lack of it, by a person in free-fall. This negation by Camus is the path for new meanings through the dialectics of opposite directions;[103] but for us, as far as the achievement involvement is concerned, Jean-Baptiste Clement went to his breakdown through a suicidal fall from the achievement pyramid.

We wish to point out two additional pressures towards the present breakdown that are indeed anchored in both the sociological and existentialist expositions previously mentioned. The first is related to the built-in self-defeating mechanism in the achievement motive. The sociological expositions seem to neglect the goals–means relationship in this motive, which stress the predominance of goals over means. Means are regarded as tools the expediency of which is *ad hoc*, instrumental to the realization of a certain goal. The latter, however, is flexible *by definition* as far as the achievement motive is concerned. It retreats like a mirage from the achievement-motivated pursuer. Intermediate goals are immediately discarded when achieved; the only reality lies therefore in the processes inherent in the activation of the means. But these are relatively deprecated. This preference for illusion over the dynamic reality of means predisposes the achievement-orientated climber to a value breakdown. Another premise, more linked to the existentialist attitude towards achievement, is the wider perspective one achieves by reaching the higher echelons of the upper-nobility pyramid and staring down. While one is kicking and clawing one's way up, one is too occupied to assess the value of the climbing itself. But from the "room at the top", the struggle down there in the arena might seem rather pointless. This is the value breakdown of the participant-turned-spectator.

In the construction of our present typology we have not used the concept of accidie, coined in the preamble to this work. Our omission is a deliberate deference towards the reader, to allow him to judge for himself the tentative adequacy of the proposal to portray value deviation as a breakdown of involvement.

The Absurd Revisited

> I accumulate the past, constantly making out of it and casting into it the present, without giving it a chance to exhaust its own duration. To live is to suffer the sorcery of the possible; but when I see in the possible itself the past that is to come, then everything turns into potential bygones, and there is no longer any present, any future.
> E. M. Cioran: *The Fall into Time*

In the previous chapters, we transplanted the concept of accidia from Christian theology into the socio-psychological analysis of human alienation, and then equated accidia with the Camusian Absurd, which we interpreted as the confrontation of the irrational world and "the wild longing for clarity hose call echoes in the human heart".[1] Finally, we defined the Absurd rather loosely and quite descriptively, as a state of mind, really a breakdown of value involvement. An individual is prompted by the congruity motive to bridge whatever normative disjuncture may arise between his previously internalized norms and new normative transmissions. But, if and when he fails in his efforts he is faced with the Absurd. The congruity motive, the human search for harmony and Man's striving for unity, which was our base line for the analysis of the Absurd value-breakdown, has been taken for granted in philosophy, theology and the behavioral sciences from times immemorial. We have also taken man's quest for congruity as an axiom, beyond which one cannot go further without delving into metaphysics. However, in a recent exposition of our ontological personality theory we tried to provide a bio-psychological explanation for the congruity motive.[2] Consequently, we shall revisit the Absurd in the present volume armed with new insights and new ideas.

The gist of our new personality theory relates first to the two opposing vectors, which constitute the scaffolding of the personality core. These are "participation" and "separation". Participation indicates the identification of ego with a person (persons), an object, or a symbolic construct outside himself, and his efforts to lose his separate identity by fusion with this other object or symbol. Separation is the opposite vector. These opposing vectors of unification–fusion and separation–isolation are used as the main axis of our personality theory in conjunction with three major developmental phases. The first phase of separation is the process of birth, the second is the crystallization of an individual ego by the molding of the "ego boundary", and the third phase of separation is a corollary of socialization when one reaches one's "ego identity".[3]

The strain to overcome the separating and dividing pressures never leaves the human individual. The striving to partake in a pantheistic whole is ever present and takes many forms. If one avenue towards its realization is blocked, it surges out from another channel, although actual participation is unattainable by definition. The objective impossibility of participation is augmented by the countering separating vectors, both instinctual and interactive. At any given moment of our lives there is a disjuncture, a gap between our desires for participation and our subjectively defined distance from our participatory aims. In *The Myth of Tantalus*, we denoted this gap the "Tantalus Ratio",[4] which is the relationship between the longed for participatory goal and the distance from it as perceived by ego. Sometimes this quest for congruity is directed against the limiting and dividing presence of the body itself. This necessitates coming to grips with various homeostatic and defense mechanisms of the organism.

The intensity of the participation vectors may be graded in the following decreasing order: first, the reversal of birth, which is the most radical and is linked, therefore, to the various techniques of *unio mystica* by the annihilation of the separate self; second, the dissolution of the ego boundary, which might result in extreme cases in insanity and autistic schizophrenia; third, the neutralization of the socionormative separation, which might display itself in crime and social deviance. Although our first examples of participation happen to be deviant, most attempts at participation are legitimate and institutionalized. For instance, the quest for the expression of creativity in any field is an institutionalized outlet for participation in the ontological sphere. The deviant counterparts to these institutionalized attempts at ontological participation are retreatism, autism, suicide and other modes of self-destruction. In some forms of schizophrenia the patient "lets go", for he does not wish any more to hold on to his ego boundary, which was crystallized for him by his relevant alters.

The institutionalized avenues for religious participation in modern western culture are sadly scarce. Consequently, many contemporary modes of participation are basically alternatives to mysticism. Love is the institutionalized melting down of partitions between individuals. This participation through affect has been considered by Sartre as an ontological impossibility, while Buber considered this fusion of souls as possible for some time, through a meaningful dialogue between ego and alter. The "love-ins" are intense attempts at affective participation, whether they succeed or fail is beside the point.

This quest for participation, for the reversal to an earlier developmental stage, is the explanation of the congruity motive. The earlier the developmental stage we wish to revert to, the closer we aim to partake in the pantheistic togetherness of early orality and the unity of omnipresence *in utero*. The congruity motive and the longing for the wholeness of unity are just two concurrent manifestations of our participation vector. It is necessary, therefore, to reexamine the processes leading to normative disjuncture and human alienation, since our quest for congruity in our interaction with our physical and social surroundings is not axiomatic or sanctioned by God, but determined by our bio-psychological longing to partake in Unity.

Another basic premise, which relates to our personality theory and has a direct bearing on ego's object relationship as expounded in the present volume, is the fixation of the separant and participant personality types. These are related in our theory to the crystallization at later orality of a separate self out of the pantheistic mass of totality and early orality. This is the ontological base line by which the self is defined by the non-self (the object). The coagulation of the self marks the cutting-off point for the most basic developmental dichotomy: from birth and early orality, to the phase where the ego boundary is formed around the emerging individual separatum and from later orality onwards. In the first phase, any fixation that might occur, and thereby imprint some character traits on the developing personality, is not registered by a separate self capable of discerning between the objects, which are the source of the fixation-causing trauma and himself as its recipient. (The experiencing entity is a non-differentiated pantheistic totality). Conversely, if the traumatizing fixation occurs at the later oral phase after the objects have expelled the self from their togetherness by a depriving interaction with it, the self may well be in a position to attribute the cause of pain and deprivation to its proper source, that is to the objects that are the source of the fixation causing trauma. We propose a personality typology, anchored on this developmental dichotomy of pre and post-differentiation of the self, and we rely on this typology in the present work.[5]

The molding process is the nature and severity of the fixation, which determines, in turn, the placement of a given individual on the personality type continuum. However, the types themselves are fixated by developmental chronology. The participant at pre-differentiated early orality and the separant after the formation of the separate self. The participant core personality vector operates with varying degrees of potency on both these personality types, but the quest for congruity manifests itself differently with each polar personality type. The participant type aims to achieve congruity by effacing and annihilating himself, by melting back (so to speak) into the object and achieving thereby the pantheistic togetherness and non-differentiation of early orality. The separant type aims to achieve congruity by overpowering or "swallowing" the object. The congruity aims of the self-effacing participant are denoted as exclusion, whereas the object devouring separant wishes to achieve congruity by inclusion, that is, by incorporating the object in his out-reaching self. We might intuitively sense that the Absurd breakdowns and alienation of human beings must differ with a person's inner involvement within himself or his outer involvement with things or other people. However, we have a more solid justification for the differences in the dynamics of alienation, depending on whether the tendency of a person is towards self-effacing exclusion or object swallowing inclusion.

Apart from revisiting, re-examining and re-evaluating our previous exposition of Absurd alienation, we shall be concerned with the wider context of the gaps between man's ontological aims and his actual relationships with his surrounding objects and other people. We shall, therefore, have to state some initial premises and make some primary assumptions before launching the exposition itself. First, we hold that the bio-physiology of man is not the basis of his interaction with his environment but constitutes its potential. The biological potential of behavior and interaction is activated by learning, which starts very early on by the fetus *in utero* and continues throughout life. Clearly, the biological programming of the potential of human behavior sets some obvious limits to the range of human action and fixes boundaries to the possibilities of interaction. The biological potential of man thus reduces the probability range of behavior and structures it into sets of finitudes.

Second, we observe and study ego's interaction with his surroundings from the only base we have, and this is ego's psyche itself, for the simple reason that there is no other point of vantage. Ego's psyche is the only seat of his awareness of himself as well as the source of his cognition of his surroundings. Our present exposition is ontological in the sense that it focuses on ego's flow of awareness and cognition as the sources of direct or inferred observations. We exclude from our analysis prime moves, ultimates and the "things out there", which by their very nature can only be the subjects of metaphysical conjecture. An ontological study of relationships is, perforce, a lopsided task because it stems solely from the awareness and senses of ego. The outside world is deaf and blind to the intricate nuances of ego's subjective feelings and perceptions. Ego cannot have any clue as to the reasons for his being the sole channel for his subjective perceptions, cognitions and sense of awareness. This ontological sense of uniqueness and choice triggers a positive feedback cycle of anxieties, which is reinforced by the relative meaninglessness of stimuli as perceived by the congruity spurred ego. Heidegger has rightly depicted man's being in the world without known origin or discernible end as "thrownness" (*Geworfenheit*). Camus has described with awesome force the everlasting sense of exile of man who is condemned to roam in a world with which he cannot reach any dialogue. Our task, however, is to explain why ego fails in his dialogue with his surroundings and not just to describe or elegize his failures of communication. The *hubris* of our aim may be compared to the Zen masters who set out to study not the sound of two hands when they are clapped together, but the sound of one hand only. Because ego is ontologically incapable of perceiving through the senses of alter the way he perceives through his cognition and senses, the study of ego's interaction with things and others can only be done through ego's own cognition. We shall study, *faute de mieux*, the sound of the clapping by one hand only.

Third, our exposition is synthetic, holistic and not analytic. Reasons given for the need for analytical specialization are that every few years the amount of new information in any given field is at least doubled. Although we see the value of applying text x to population y, counting the number of times the letter alpha appears in the *Septuaginta* or feeding a computer with all the adjectives in James Joyce's *Ulysses*, we feel there should also be some unifying ex-positions trying to link the various specialized findings and premises into a meaningful *gestalt*. Our hope is that the holistic scaffolding presented here will lend depth and perspective to a whole area of human behavior within the context of the whole personality of man, and not just a single trait of it. The synthetic holistic approach to human interaction seems to us rather appropriate because we have some solid evidence that man's cognition of his environment operates within *gestalts*, and not through distinct and disconnected percepts.

Fourth, our present work aims to be truly interdisciplinary in the sense that it tries to integrate the most varied areas of knowledge and sources into an organic whole. We do not mean just to collate and gather eclectically the separate disciplines into a multidisciplinary mixture, but integrate and fuse the sources and items of observation into a unified alloy. To this end we will utilize just one part of a measurement or a fragment of a source, which fits our overall design. For instance, dialectics may be utilized not as a universal panacea *á la* Hegel or Marx, but only as an apt dynamic describing some modes of interaction. Whereas a drama director regards a play first and foremost as an aesthetic display of form and action, for us the plays of Camus, Sartre and Genet are ideational texts, which are as salient to our synthetic structure as much as the insights of Freud and the research findings of behavioral scientists.

Being and Perceiving

The present work is essentially focused on ego's relationship with his surroundings, both animate and inanimate. Although we place the present volume into the general realm of social psychology, its ontological base sets it apart from other sociopsychological expositions. Our basic assumption is that ego senses himself ontologically unique. He sees himself as the seat of being, which is not shared by his surrounding objects. The relationships of ego with his surroundings are inevitably that of being with not-being. This has been voiced and philosophically elaborated by some existentialists but has not been, to the best of our knowledge, systematically presented as a sociopsychological exposition.

The unique position the self holds in any ontological conception of being lumps together everything that is not the self into a residual category of not-being. This makes our basic relationship dualistic, with ego on one side and everything else on the other side of the dyad. Yet, our ontological dualism is egocentric because there cannot be any communication between ego and his surrounding objects. In the last analysis we dealt with the relationship between two sets of ego's cognitions, the ones he has of himself and those that he has of his surroundings. However, both these sets of perceptions are still ego's because four thousand years of labyrinthine, yet fruitless, epistemology have not succeeded even remotely in introducing into the *dramatis personae* of ego's perception, the "things in themselves out there". Descartes recruited God to support his argument that there must be corporeal objects, which generate our ideas (sense impressions). Otherwise, says Descartes, God would be deceitful by definition. We are not privileged to have Divinity support our arguments, consequently we know nothing about the things "out there". The utmost concession we can make to "the outside" is to agree with Bishop Berkeley, that our wakeful perceptions, which do not stem from our bodies, fantasies or dreams are triggered by something other than ourselves. There is no way, however, for us to know the shape, contents, dynamics, origin and purpose of this "something other than ourselves".

The epistemological barriers between ourselves and the "outside" are sealed tight. The space–time structuring of our perceptions have rightly been conceived by Kant as moldings and dynamisms of and within our minds.[6] This gives a philosophical vindication to our two basic vectors, which are deemed to cast, process and structure experience into cognitive patterns and stereotypes, which in turn influence our sense impressions. If time, space and causality are structures of our personality, then developmental fixations and cultural imprints determine or influence our space–time perceptions. Consequently, our core personality structure and its dual polarities should be related to a corre- sponding polarity in the perception of time, space and causality. This makes for a subjective basis of cognition and a vulnerability of the spatiotemporal struc- ture to even minute changes in the dynamics and moods of our psyche. It also supports our conceptualization of vectors that are subjectively more or less involved with space, time and causality, which are themselves constructs of the human psyche. Moreover, spatiotemporality ceases, thus, to be a metaphysical or epistemological concern, and becomes a correlate of man's biopsychological development. The subjectivity of the spatiotemporal structuring of cognition is not really far from the phenomenological approach of Merleau-Ponty, who posits the source of cognition in the subjective psyche. He says:

> I am the absolute source, my existence does not stem from my antecedents, from my physical and social environment; instead it moves out towards them and sustains them, for I alone bring into being for myself (and therefore into being in the only sense that the word can have for me) the tradition which I elect to carry on, or the horizon whose distance from me would be abolished if I were not there to scan it with my gaze.[7]

This would lead directly to a contemporary exposition of mind, the essence of which is its "privacy" or rather its exclusiveness as far as ego's epistemic perception is concerned.[8]

All this leads to and supports our conception of an ego who not only regards himself as the source of cognition, but also as chosen to serve as the channel for the awareness of all creation. This sense of ontological uniqueness provides the self with a touch of built-in megalomania. The self expects too much from his surroundings, yet these expectations cannot be fulfilled by definition. The self is therefore plagued by longings and quests, which can never be quenched. These inevitable gaps between the self's expectations, as determined by his sense of ontological uniqueness and the incoming stimuli from his perceived surroundings, constitute the base line of our present exposition.

The Fallibility of Perception

We are not concerned with optical or visual illusions, such as the sticks in the Muller–Lyer illusion, which show the line with arrowheads pointing outwards to be shorter than the line with its arrowheads pointing inwards, though the two lines are exactly the same length.[9] We are not concerned with the twisting of perception by motivation, needs, values and personality difference. We are, however, interested by the fact that the sticks in the Muller-Lyer illusion appear to be of different lengths to different people, and to the same person at different times and places. In this issue we side with the motivational approach to perception, according to which we are very likely to misperceive because of a projection of needs and wishes on the stimuli. Consequently, we cannot adhere to the psychophysical approach of Gibson and his disciples, which stress "the correspondence between certain mathematical properties of the retinal image and certain phenomenal variables of the visual world".[10] The psychophysicist anchors on the stimulus with a scientistic zeal for measurements, whereas we joint the motivationist in trying to relate the individual's perceptual response to his needs and motives. Moreover, we hold that because ego's motives and wishes as determined by the dialectics of his personality core vectors, largely determined his percepts and perceptual responses, they also play a crucial role in his interaction with his surroundings. To be more precise, our interest in ego's value involvement with things, nature and people makes us more concerned with the relationship between his motives and his perceptual responses than with the epistemic nature of the stimuli, which impinge on his senses.

There are, of course, some links between stimuli and their percepts, which are not based on motivational pressures and their projections. These have been studied and supposedly measured by an impressive number of experimental psychologists, from G. Fechner to the modern psychophysicians.[11] We do not believe, however, that the non-motivational components of the percept can be effectively isolated from the motivated and projective ones, and then related separately to the stimuli. The Science of Man has not yet reached the level of sophistication to conduct the controlled experiments that are necessary for these kinds of measurements. Yet, we carry on our reasoning and theorizing by assuming a given constancy of relationship between the stimuli and their non-motivated percepts (which serve as a raw material for the final product of perception). This, in turn, is influenced and molded by the vast array of motivational and wish-based personality traits and cultural pressures. Some scientist psychologists may question this assumption. Our defense is in reference to one of their own cherished assumptions: the behaviorist black box analogy of intrapsychic dynamisms, which is very much like our present assumption about the constancies of relationships between stimuli and their sensory percepts.

Even if there are some psychophysical constancies in the relationship between stimulus and percept, they are bound to be twisted and remolded by the dynamics of the organism and the psyche. The intensity of the needs of the body, and some endocrinal secretions, diseases and drugs on the biological level, developmental fixations and core personality characteristics on the psychological level, and cultural imprints and social character traits on the social level, all influence the form and quality of the percept. The complexity and variability of the configurations of these variables are so vast that the chances of one person having even a closely similar percept to the one perceived by another person of the same stimulus are very remote. Yet perceptual theory links "meaning" and "reason" to similarity.[12] Consequently, the inevitable dissimilarity of perceptions makes the possibility of meaningful communication of percepts from one person to another sadly remote. Meaningfulness in the present context relates to the intersubjective domain and not to the mere mechanical transmission of symbols and signs.

Worse still, even the meaningfulness of ego's own percept is related, according to perception theory, to the resemblance of a given percept to a previous one. There is evidence that time differences may be related to different motivations, body chemistry and moods, and these are also bound to influence the form and contents of the percept.[13] Thus the meaningfulness of a percept varies not only with the motivations, fixations and cultural imprints on ego's personality, but also on the time of perception by ego himself. We may conclude, therefore, that the meaningfulness of ego's perception is not only non-communicable from the ontological point of view, but in all probability also statistically unique. This premise that perception is essentially a "private language" will have wide implications for our subsequent examination of ego's ability to reach a meaningful dialogue with his surroundings.

Time and Timelessness

Time, space, causality and logic are some of the scaffolding on which our separant cognition of the world is sustained. These, as Kant has rightly observed, are the mind's modes of interpretation of ego's percepts.[14] They have nothing to do with the *Ding-an-Sich*, because we can never have any knowledge of it, neither are they related to the stimuli, which impinge on our senses. It is the congruity-motivated structures within our minds that order the percepts into schemes of *gestalts*. We differ here from Kant's conception of time and space as psychic binoculars through which stimuli are structured into spatiotemporality. This structuring is related to the congruity motive that stems from our striving to unify and regain wholeness, which is inherent in our personality core vectors.

Time is the most volatile, and therefore the most vulnerable component of our cognition of spatiotemporality. This is why participation-oriented philosophers and mystics who wish to reach "authentic existence" or mystical union find it more expedient to assault time. They hope that when time is "extinguished" or "dissolved", the whole edifice of the illusion of spatiotemporality would crumble down. There are two basic premises relevant to our present context of understanding ego's cognitive interaction with his surroundings. First, because time is a manifestation of our congruity motivated perception of the world it is related to the personality core vectors and the cultural imprints on it. It is therefore bound to vary with personality structure and cultural factors. Second, and more crucial, time is subject to the dynamic interplay between our polar personality core vectors. Heidegger and Merleau-Ponty have noted, each in his own style, some problems in time perception which are relevant for the present work.[15] Heidegger, in his almost non-intelligible obscurantism, seems to convey the ingenious observation that we have expectations of the future and experience of the past, but no authentic present.[16] The present, which is a swift *augenblick* (eye-blink), has no temporal dimension because it jerks immediately from future to past the moment we focus our attention on it. Jonas recalls that when he tried to arrange Heidegger's "existentials" into the categories of "authentic being" the column for the present remained empty.[17] There is no authentic present in Man's galloping "*Geworfenheit* unto death".

Meleau-Ponty is puzzled by the fact that time is inherent in ego's relationship with the object, and yet cannot be grasped by its consciousness. Merleau-Ponty's dilemma may be related first to our congruity-based vector of separation. We recall that separant manipulation of reality is by the process of inclusion, that is, by trying to manipulate the object that is subjectively meaningful to us into a scheme, and thereby incorporate it into our psyche. This is the separant's quest for dominion over the object through meaningful cognition. For example, if I say that yesterday I saw the eruption of a volcano, I have projected my separant object manipulation onto two totally unrelated stimuli, the revolution of the earth on its axis and a geological eruption. These events become, through the ontological mediation of myself as observer, an integrated spatiotemporal cognition. Heidegger's exposition of temporality may also be fruitfully related to our personality core vectors. The separant component of our personality core perceives the object in concrete sequences. As a result, its focus on a given eye-blink of time turns it immediately into past. It also projects by logical inference its past experience onto the future, but then the same process of discrete sequences makes the moment of the future become instantaneously the past the very moment our sequential act of attention focuses on it. Consequently, the separant component of our personality knows no present, only future and past. On the other hand, our participant vector and personality component strives for holistic unity and a non-sequential flow of cognition. It looks for the permanent present of timelessness. This, like Bergson's "*Durée Reel*", is perceived not by discrete sequence and logical inference, but by intuitive and boundless immersion into the object.[18] Our daydreaming, our short spells of meditative reaching out to the object, the mystics' quest for union with the ultimate unity, and the Middle Eastern coffeehouse patron who "loses himself" (i.e. loses the discreteness of time and finds the continuous present with the help of a waterpipe full of hashish and the undulation of torch singing), are all manifestations of the participant quest for the everlasting present, which is anchored in the timelessness of the pantheistic unity of non-differentiated early orality.

We pointed out in *The Myth of Tantalus* that the three time sequences of future, present and past, are the dialectical combination of the two core vectors.[19] The separant vector supplies the future and the past, whereas the cognition of the present, or the quest of it, is supplemented by the participant personality core vector. This explains the more fragile and vulnerable structure of the temporal dimension of objective reality. All the other dimensions (e.g. space, causality, logic) are totally separant and object bound, whereas the sequences of time are a dialectical combination of both separation and participation. The chain is as strong as its weakest link, and time seems to be the weak link in the cognition of objective spatiotemporality. Mystics, Zen Buddhists and Kabbalists, to mention only a few seekers of participant salvation, have tried to concentrate their attack on reality mostly on time and its manifestations. The "collapse" of time, they believed, would bring about the inevitable annihilation of spatiotemporal reality.

The existentialist conception of time may be clarified by reference to our developmental model of the personality core. We have shown that our perception of time is dependent on a dialectical dynamic of our personality core vectors. Our cognition of time is therefore largely determined by the peculiarities and subjective structure of our personality. As time is of the essence of spatiotemporal reality, our whole cognition of our surroundings is dependent on our intrapsychic structure. This again indicates the statistical uniqueness of our cognition, and the impossibility of its meaningful communication to other people, a premise to which we shall return in chapter 5.

The Troubled Encounters

In *The Myth of Tantalus* we specified that ego's interaction with his environment is essentially deprivational.[20] This is because he conceives himself as statistically unique, and ontologically chosen to be the channel for the cognitive awareness of spatiotemporality. Ego's congruity-based quest for omnipresence and exclusiveness, determined by his early developmental phases, makes all other people and objects his ontological rivals. The ontological dyad between ego and the object is constantly under attack by ego's own motivational structure. If he is a participant he strives to annul the dyad by "excluding" himself, that is, by effacing his separate self and melting into the object. If ego is a separant he aims to "include" the object into his personal domain by gaining dominion over it. This may be related to Simmel's insight that ego's conception of his freedom involves his self-proclaimed right to dominate and exploit other people.[21]

The underlying, ever-present motive of ego is to achieve union with the object, but the separant vectors of growth and development constantly oppose this participatory aim. We discussed in *The Myth of Tantalus* that ego's active involvement with the object with participatory aims is a self-defeating venture.[22] First, because the deprivational interaction with the object at the oral phase of development thickens the scar tissue of the separate self, and thereby creates a more insulating ego boundary. Second, the deprivational interaction and the rites of passage of later socialization enmesh the individual in more and sturdier layers of social norms, thus making for further separation. Third, the Least Interest Principle specifies that the keener the interest we display in a certain objective in dyadic/social relationships, the less likely we are to attain it.

The vicissitudes of our efforts to fulfill our craving for participation with the object begin at the outset with the process of our quest for a meaningful communication with the object. In order to seek participatory congruence with the object we have to perceive him meaningfully. That is, we have to perceive him in keeping with our own cognitive system, and this is where severe trouble begins. In order for any participatory process with the object to be initiated, a pattern of meaningful communications with it has to be reached. The question is whether or not this is viable. We have already specified that our perception of the object is largely determined by our own personality core characteristics: cultural imprints, needs, motives, and our vast array of subconscious and cognitive defenses. Consequently, our perception of the object and other people is less dependent on them than on our own intrapsychic structure and dynamics. This is without taking into account the various possible epistemic disjunctures between the stimuli and the percepts impinged on our senses.

We hypothesize that a decisive part of ego's perceptual and cognitive biases are related to his personality core vectors. The separant vector (which is related to the differentiation and distinction in the perception of space, the discrete sequences of time, and causality) underlies the bias of the analyzer who looks for contrasts and sharply defined boundaries between objects. The need to differentiate tunes our senses to more sharply defined distinctions among objects and people. This separant bias makes for an initial exaggerated disparity between self and object. A separant culture socializes its young to pay the utmost attention even to minute detail. Persons who can point out in conspicuous relief the differences of certain parts from others in a given context are considered to be a prized asset. The participant biases of perception and cognition are rather more elaborate. They vary with the level of cognition whether it is affected by the core personality type or by the whole coordinating ego, which we denote as the *Ity*.[23] These biases vary with the process of exclusion (i.e. the self's self-effacing deference towards the object), or inclusion (i.e. the self's egocentric and separant wish to incorporate the object within its dominion). The following is a paradigm that may guide our discussion:

Modes of Participant Cognitive Biases

	Inclusion	Exclusion
Core personality type	Sisyphean leveling down of object	Tantalic self-deprecation
Coordinating ego function (Ity)	Adjusting incoming cognitions	Tendency to conform

Figure 4.1   The process of exclusion and inclusion

1. The Tantalic participant tends to tone down his conspicuousness *vis-à-vis* the object and other people. His quietest *Weltanschauung* would make him ignore stimuli, which pushes him to a more active deprivational interaction with his environment. He has a cognitive screen against too many and powerful stimuli and this aversion to stimuli makes our Tantalic type reduce both the volume and range of his cognitive input.[24]

2. The Sisyphean, on the other hand, tends to "adjust" his perception of the object to his preconceived plans of its manipulation. If ego expects the object to fit into a given scheme, he tends to perceive more clearly the attributes of the object that are relevant to the scheme, and disregard the attributes that are defined by him as irrelevant for his purposes.

3. On the coordinating ego level (*Ity*) the participant exclusionary dynamics tend to induce the self-effacing ego to conform to the incoming norms. When his own normative convictions are in conflict with the mandates stemming from his environment and relevant others, ego's internalized norms tend to give way to the external group norms. Consequently, he tends to impute greater potency to the incoming norms than to his own. Furthermore, the source of the norms are favorably colored by the value judgment inherent in the perception of the norms themselves.

4. A separant activist, however, tends to twist the incoming normative information so that it fits his own internalized normative configuration. The whole subject of cognitive dissonance and its biasing effects on incoming information is relevant to the present premise.[25]

The essence of our argument is that our participant core vector makes us seek closer communication with the object and other people, and brings cognition to twist its perception to enhance this participatory goal. The separant core vector, on the other hand, interferes with and blocks our longed-for communication with the object and others, and biases our cognition accordingly. Thus, in any encounter with objects or with people, we wish to attain a deeper and fuller communication than the level of communication we have actually reached. If, for instance, we encounter people on a routine level of interaction, we aim to have a deeper meeting of minds on the level of a dialogue. If we think that we have reached a dialogue with a certain person, we still aim at a more complete "fusion of souls" when the partition between ego and alter, hopefully, melts down and an intersubjective communication is attained.

The separant core personality vector is, we presume, not only responsible for augmenting the disparities between the self and the object, but also for the initial disjunctures between the stimuli and percepts. The more distinct differences between the self and its environment make for a sharper definition by contrast to the dichotomy that is the initial event of separation. Also, the more pronounced disparities between objects and sequences enhance the perception of spatial relationships and temporal discreteness, which is the basis of the separant cognition. This indeed is a far-fetched hypothesis, but without it we shall have to resort to metaphysics, the occult, or the devil to explain the seemingly senseless confounding of our senses in their perception and cognition of objects and other people. By hypothesizing a separant function to this perceptual and cognitive distortion, we provide a bio-psychological explanation, without resorting to axioms or beliefs in the away and beyond.

The dialectical conflicts between the separant and participant core components of our personality express themselves on two levels. First, the participant component which longs for meaningful (as defined subjectively) communication with the object and other people is opposed by the separant component, which interferes with the process of communication by twisting perceptions and distorting cognitions. Second, whenever the participant component wishes to deepen communication between ego and the object and other people, in order to attain a more fulfilling (from ego's point of view) participant encounter, the separant component tries to hold both communication and encounter on as shallow a level as possible.

We first argue that for any meaningful communication between ego and alter to be effective, ego has to convey to alter the level of communication he aims at. This may range from a formal encounter in the street to the fusion of souls in eternal love. Alter must then absorb the message, be willing to communicate with ego on the same level of encounter, and be able to convey his intentions to ego in a manner which is both meaningful to ego and acceptable by him. We shall devote a considerable part of our efforts in chapter 5 to showing that this is impossible for two reasons. First, for ego's intentions to be meaningfully conveyed to alter and vice versa, there must be a way for inter-subjective communication, and there is no such way. Second, ego's developmental fixations, personality traits and cultural imprints may predispose him to aim for a specific level of communication, which is hardly likely to be shared by alter.

We argue secondly that ego's aim towards a certain level of encounter with alter is determined by the participant component of his self. This aim is countered by the separant component of ego's self, which twists perception and biases cognitions in order to impede a meaningful communication with alter. Ego's own internalized separant social norms would serve as a barrier against the desired level of encounter. At any given moment, ego wishes to reach a deeper level of encounter with alter than he is actually able to reach. There is always an inevitable gap between the desired depth of encounter and the level that has been reached. Even in routine daily encounters we wish that others would understand us, that there be a meeting of our minds as to our expectations from them, and that a large measure of grace would be awarded to our routine mistakes. This unrealistic quest of our participant personality component is rarely present in the impersonal and rather alienated routine encounters between human beings. A deeper level of encounter is the dialogue. Ego strives here for meaningful, two-way communications with alter. The participant component of the self aims, so to speak, to "punch holes" in his own boundaries and alter's ego boundaries, so that a direct Buber *I–Thou* communication is effected. The level of encounter aimed at here is inter-subjective dialogue. But intersubjective communication is impossible, due to the separant barriers and deprivational interaction between ego and his surroundings, including other people. Finally, the deepest level of encounter is the totality of love, and the fusion of ego and alter into an ecstatic unity. This ultimate participation through love longed-for, sung to and worshipped, is unattainable. More often than not, alter is not even as keen as ego to be swept into the absorbing totality of love. This may account for the usual short duration of affective infatuation, especially if ego's expectations for the totality of the relationship are greater and deeper than alter's. Generally, the keener ego is for a total relationship, the less interested alter is; also, the deeper the totality of affective relationship expected by one party to the dyad, the shorter the duration of the encounter. Finally, the duration of the encounter also varies directly with the width of the gaps between the mutual affective expectations between ego and alter. These initial generalizations are some of the vicissitudes of the separant forces, which make the totality of love a cherished ideal projected onto poetry, fiction, art and confession magazines, but never attained in the separant reality of dyadic encounters.

We propose now to schematize the various gaps between participant expectations and their fulfillment on the various levels of dyadic encounters. It would be useful to relate our scheme to the three personality components, which we have defined and described in *The Myth of Tantalus*.[26] The *Ity* is the overall coordinating ego function of the whole personality, and represents the daily encounters of the self with his surroundings. Ego's dyadic encounter with alter on the *Ity* level is the most shallow one of routine formal and impersonal interactions. The deeper level of encounter is related to the *Atzmi*, the separant interactive component of the self. The *Atzmi*, motivated by the separant core personality vector to be deeply involved with the object, represents the dialogica level of encounter. Finally, the *Ani*, the participant core component of the self, represents the deepest level of encounter where ego aims to fuse with the object. These are just three illustrative signposts on a continuum, which ranges from the most shallow to the deepest level of encounter. The major hypothesis, which will guide our exposition throughout our present work, is that on each point on the continuum, ego wishes to attain a deeper level than the level he actually perceives the encounter to be at. At a later stage, ego may wish to terminate the dyadic relationship with alter, or even avoid an additional encounter at all costs, but the initial wish of ego is to have a deeper rapport with alter than he thinks he has.

At the *Ity* coordinating level (chance meetings with drinking mates in a bar or a random encounter with a lady on the street) ego aims to have a varying measure of a meeting of minds with alter. He wants to know if the lady would agree to go with him to the theatre if he suggests it to her. To put it more precisely, ego wishes to attain a dialogue with alter and not just a mere shallow encounter even in routine transactions. If ego thinks that he has achieved a certain level of dialogue with alter, that is, when he thinks that his *Atzmi* (his interactive self component) has attained a rapport with the *Atzmi* of alter, he wishes for an even deeper encounter. For instance, in a relationship between teacher and disciple, the latter is continually unsatisfied with whatever dialogue he thinks he has reached, but aims for a deeper participation. On a deeper dyadic level, as in love, ego aims at the totality of participation – to melt into the beloved alter in a spaceless union and a timeless forever. What makes these encounters frustrating for ego is that his quests for a deeper level of encounter with alter is ontologically impossible. We shall elaborate at greater length in the following chapters the manner in which ego's desire for deeper dyadic levels of encounter with alter is incessantly frustrated. If he tends to be a separant type, his inclusionary efforts to dominate ego will be aggravated in a Sisyphean manner of ever trying to manipulate a stubborn and treacherous rock. If ego is more of a participant type, he will try to woo alter into an exclusionary timeless union choosing thus an ever-receding Tantalic mirage. Schematically this may be presented as follows:

Ego's perception of actual level of initial encounter	Ego's desired level of encounter
Ity-Ity Ego-alter routine coordination	
Ego-alter dialogue	*Atzmi-Atzmi* Ego-alter 'meeting of minds' dialogue
Ani-Ani inner-core contact	*Ani-Ani* direct contact between inner cores or selves
	Grace of complete union

Figure 4.2   Levels of encounter

The initial disparity between ego's perception of the actual level of encounter and his desired depth of encounter makes for a predisposition for the breakdown of the encounter and any dyadic communication. The initial gap between the perceived level of encounter and the desired one is, of course, the primary disposition for the breakdown of communication. The intensity and nature of ego's motivation for the encounter are also crucial factors. We envisage the extreme case of someone who discovers the "queen of his dreams" in a crowd and starts chasing her with fiery orations of eternal devotion. Chances are that he will soon find himself cooling of his amorous passions in a police station, nourishing a swollen cheek because of a slap on his face. The first phase of dyadic encounters starts, therefore, with ego's definition for himself of the desired level of communication with alter, and the actual level which he perceives it to be at. The second phase is ego's inclusionary efforts to bring alter to reach his own desired depth of communication, or to effect an exclusionary rapprochement by accommodating himself to what he perceives to be alter's desired level of communication.

These efforts, both on the *Ity* coordinating level, and on a deeper core-personality level, to close the gap between perceived and desired levels of encounter, result in most cases in a dialectical *modus vivendi*. In many cases, the precarious equilibrium between the perceived and desired levels of communication is disrupted and a breakdown of communication ensues. We hypothesized a three stage process leading to alienation, but did not at that time have the insights into the core personality dynamics, which we have gained through the formulation of our personality theory set out in *The Myth of Tantalus*. Our first insight is the enormity of contrast between the separant forces of growth and the participant quest of non-being. The galloping progression (or regression of time, depending on the points of vantage and value

	ITY		ATZMI		ANI	
Level of encounter	*Routine coordination of interaction*		*Dialogue*		*Merger of selves*	
Direction of participant effort	Inclusion	Exclusion	Inclusion	Exclusion	Inclusion	Exclusion
Aim of encounter	Soliciting	Accepting	Dominion	Initiation	Possession	Sacrifice
Breakdown of communication	Misunderstanding	Rejection	Betrayal	Deceit	Subjugation	Self-annihilation

Figure 4.3   The scheme of encounters and their disruptions

judgment) consists of a non-existent future, an equally non-existent past and an eye-blink transition between the future and the past, which is mistaken for the present. The participant "awakening" from this temporal *fata Morgana* is embodied in our "pure-self" core vector, which aims at nothing less than the annihilation of spatiotemporality and merging, thereby, with pre-differentiated unity. Our second insight is that our perceptual and cognitive biases should be traced to our participant and separant core personality vectors and the dialectics between them, and not to the vicissitudes of epistemology or to the rarified borders of knowledge touching on metaphysics, as proposed. Our third insight relates to the precipitating process of the breakdown of the dyadic encounter. The predisposition to this breakdown, as we have already discussed, is inherent in the size and nature of the cognitive gap between ego's perceived and the desired level of encounter. This gap, which is bridged dialectically, may be ripped open again through an internal or external catalyzer that upsets the precarious dialectics of the separant and participant dialectics within the personality core. Figure 4.3 (page 98) shows the scheme of encounters and their disruptions, which shall guide our study throughout the present volume.

On the *Ity* level of routine coordination, the separant ego tries to manipulate alter into his personal sphere of influence. This may range from the salesman who tries to convince a customer to buy a vacuum cleaner he doesn't really need, to the dandy who walks in the boulevard flashing out his attire and demeanor in order to attract the admiring attention of the onlookers. The exclusionary efforts of the participant would be to seek the approval of alter. He would do his utmost not to be conspicuous, in order not to risk any sanction or disapproval for his extravagant manner. He would strive in a self-effacing manner to be "approved" by his relevant others. His troubles begin when he tries to please as many alters as possible for the wishes of these alters are inevitably discordant.

The breakdown of communication between ego and his surroundings on the *Ity* coordinating level result in tragi-comic misunderstandings, in the classic tradition of a comedy of errors. The meek exclusionary efforts of ego to be accepted by alter may be rude or gentle, but firmly rejected by the latter, especially if ego's efforts to be accepted are too obvious and strenuous. In extreme cases, the breakdown of coordinatory communication between ego and his surroundings result in psychosis. This is in line with the social interactionist approach to mental illness. We shall present in this volume an empirical follow-up of our conception of psychosis and crime as forms of communication disjunctures. Crime may be conceived as a rift with the normative system of society, whereas psychosis may be envisaged as a complete disconnection and retreat from the object in the case of autism, and a delusive hallucinatory rupture with the object in the case of paranoia.

The dyadic dialogue, the *Verstehen* meeting of the *Logos*, and the inner meaning between separata has been dealt with by such *dialogica* philosophers as

Kierkegaard and Buber.[27] Ego's separant inclusionary efforts at the dialogue level is to reach through to the *Atzmi*, the interactive component of alter's self, in order to gain influence over it. There are many examples: the teacher's efforts to make disciples out of pupils, the leader's aim to make people his ideological initiates, the psychiatrist's seemingly therapeutic goal of achieving transference with his patient, and many domestic dyads where relationships are a means of conducting the household. In all these cases, one party to the dyad may try to dominate the other in order to have a decisive role in conducting the affairs of the relationship. The self-effacing participant party to the dyad tends to accept the submissive role. The interactive dyad may be envisaged as a system in balance where there is a complementarity of roles between the separant charismatic domineering partner and the willingly submissive dominated partner.

The breakdown of the efforts to achieve dialogue, or the rupture of the dyadic communication, is usually accompanied by a traumatic cognitive shock. The doctrinaire proselytizing Freud felt betrayed by what he defined as a heretical desertion of the Freudian psychoanalytic doctrine by Jung and Adler. The disciple, on the other hand, may experience a "God that failed" disenchantment with the master. In extreme cases, the sense of deception is so acute that a Tausk commits suicide in a Japanese-like feat of *resentiment* against what he defined as an unbearable betrayal by Freud. There may also be the external deference of a disciple towards a master, as well as a formal submission but without the internal conviction. The ex-disciple may go through the motions of submission to the master because of expediency or power politics, but his quest of a participant dialogue with the master has ended in failure. The dyad remains formally intact but materially disrupted.

The quest of the merger of selves (the *Ani* level of encounter) is attributed by the romantics to love. Indeed, the great lovers who were depicted as courting their beloved to gain their hearts were mostly separants who aimed to possess their beloved and incorporate him/her into their psyche by the process of inclusion. The affective participation of ego would correspondingly take the form of a self-obliterating sacrifice. In extreme cases, it would express itself as a *mourir d'amour* romantic agony, or a literal willing sacrifice of a Pere Goriot to his carnivorous daughters. The breakdown here seems inevitable because of the enormous gap between the affective goals of ego and the possible level of his participatory achievement. Sartre, for instance, assures us that any affective liaison between ego and alter ends in the servile submission of one party of the dyad to the egotistical subjugation by the other.[28]

A Dramatic Interlude

It is a measure of the viability of our major hypotheses that language, our main medium of symbolic communication, is poor, limited and ineffective. And yet novelists and playwrights have been able to depict the misery and dilemmas of the human condition with keener sensitivity than behavioral and social scientists. We shall try to illustrate our three levels of dyadic encounters and their breakdowns through three plays. They portray, in an exaggerated polarity, the striving for communication and the frustrating failures to attain it. The plays were chosen not for their dramatic virtuosity, but for their ideational relevance.

The first level of encounter will be illustrated by Camus' play *The Misunderstanding*.[29] The macabre plot was adopted by Camus from an episode that actually occurred in a small resort town in Czechoslovakia. A son who left home for many years overseas has made a small fortune and returns home with his new wife to his innkeeper mother and sister. He wants the meeting to be a surprise, so he does not reveal his true identity when he takes a room in his mother's inn. At night the mother and sister murder him for his money. All four characters in the play long for deep level of communication with one another, but the circumstances and their own lack of any means for insight into the expectations of the others keep the communication at a shallow and formal level with disastrous results.

The second play, Sartre's *No Exit*, depicts three people, two women and a man, in one room. Each tries to reach an authentic dialogue with the other but the conflicts, different expectations, diametrically polar desires, and above all a lack of communication, petrifies the triad and makes the male character announce that "Hell is other people".[30]

On the deepest level of encounter, we have as an illustration Genet's play *Deathwatch*.[31] The cast here also consists of a triad, where three homosexual convicts are immersed in consecutive throes of violence and love. The structure of the play and the repartee in some of the dialogue brings to mind an ever-growing similarity between Genet's *Deathwatch* and Sartre's *No Exit*. It occurred to the author in a fit of wild imagination that one could produce the two plays together, simultaneously, on one stage divided by a partition in the middle. The dilemma of *No Exit* is extenuated by the violent jealousies of *Deathwatch*, and one character's effort to regain the love of the other by murdering the third. The lack of dyadic communication seems to be solved in *Deathwatch* through the finality of murder. This is the black passion solution to Sartre's dilemma in *No Exit*. One may disentangle oneself from the misery of human relationship by the ultimate participant act of murder that involves one's own execution, and constitutes, therefore, a merger into unison through annihilation. This is the rather macabre, yet philosophically simplistic answer to Man's plight rejected by Camus, contemplated with ambivalence by Sartre, and glorified by Genet.

The Cognitions of Dialogue

Each man contemplates in his own personal way the stream of events
upon which he finds himself swiftly borne.
                George A Kelly: *A Cognitively Oriented Theory of Behavior*

In the previous chapters, we were mainly concerned with the theoretical-philosophical expositions of the feasibility of dialogue. In the present chapter, we shall try to survey some of the research findings related to the possibilities of dialogue as an empirical anchor to our largely theoretical presentation of ideas, hypotheses and models. Our approach is holistic, observing the behavior of the whole human being rather than just some isolated aspects or traits. Having discarded the scientistic orthodoxy prevalent in the behavioral and social sciences, we accept a wide range of observable phenomena as empirical anchors. Our present work, being a holistic phenomenological synthesis, is more concerned with overall trends, perspectives and vectors, and less with the depth analysis of details.

Our focus is on the interplay of ideas concerning human dialogue and its rupture. Our central thesis is that effective interpersonal communication is so unlikely that it borders on the impossible. This is because ego's cognition is related, first of all, to his biological potential, to his core personality fixations, to his peripheral personality parameters, and to the cultural imprints on his personality affected by socialization. The permutation of all these factors makes the cognition of ego unique to himself and not shared by any other human, being almost like his fingerprints. Consequently, there is no cognitive common denominator between ego and alter, and even if there was, there are no adequate means of transmitting ego's cognitions to others. We assume that there are no effective direct means for intersubjective communication. Telepathy, even if it exists, is not developed and widespread enough to serve as an effective and universal means of interpersonal communication. Language, as discussed in the previous chapter, operates on a very shallow level of encounter and is subject to the same twists and biases as other modes of cognition. To begin our argument we present the following model of dyadic interpersonal perception:

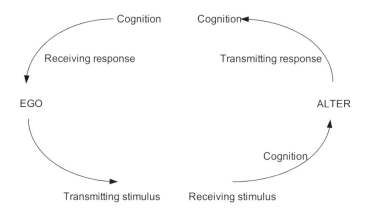

Figure 5.1 Dyadic interpersonal perceptions

Each stage of perception and response is subject to the biases and twists of both ego and alter's cognitions. The specific and virtually unique combination of ego and alter's cognitive processes intervene and stand between the reception and transmission of both stimuli and responses. As the accumulation and permutation of bio-psychogenic and sociogenic factors make the twists and biases within the cognitive process unique for each person, the effective transmission of stimuli and responses on a common denominator of meanings between ego and alter is practically impossible. As for the value-laden attitudes and affects inherent in the cognitive processes of an individual, they are even less transmittable. The personality and culture-bound attitudes color each percept and cognition of ego in hues and nuances peculiar to himself. They cannot be shared with alter or communicated to him.

The essence of our argument is first of all statistical, namely that the vast permutations of the cognitive twists and biases, together with the combinations of affects and value judgments, make the cognitions of ego peculiar to himself, and the possibility that they are shared by alter is so remote that it is virtually non-existent. Second, all kinds of symbolic and non-verbal means of human communication are blunt, coarse and inadequate tools for effecting an inter-subjective rapport of meanings. Finally, ego's psychological defenses and his congruity-based longing for dialogue create an illusion of communication. This illusion constitutes a further barrier against interpersonal communication, because the illusion itself and its projection on alter is peculiar to ego and cannot be transmitted to alter. Moreover, when this illusion of communication is projected onto the group the collective or society at large, it creates expectations by the individual from the group, which are again peculiar to a given individual and are not shared by others. This makes for the vast heterogeneity of views as to the social and political functions of society, and the inevitable rift, with which we shall deal later on, between ego's expectations from his membership and reference groups, and the latter's ability to fulfill them. The guideline for our analysis of the disjunctures in the process of dyadic communication is presented schematically as follows:

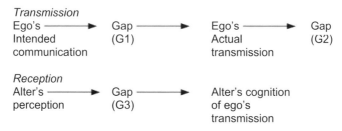

Figure 5.2   Disjunctures in the process of dyadic communication

The first gap, denoted as G1, is between the communications that ego meant to transmit and the actual product he presents. This gap may be the result of a wide range of reasons. Some instances are that ego lacks the necessary proficiency in verbal or non-verbal means of communication in order to convey his intentions. Many times language, or any other means of communication available to ego, cannot depict and hence convey the depth of his emotions, the range of his ideas, or the subtlety and nuances of his meanings. In art, and especially in the performing arts, the artist may feel that "he did not come through" or that "the music in his heart was not translated by his fingers into the music that actually emitted from the piano". Because of twisted perception and defense mechanisms of projection, displacement, pretence, illusion and elusion (double illusions boomeranging back at ego), one may present a communication in a form and content quite different from the manner in which ego intended to transmit it.[1]

The second gap, G2, relates to ego's communication as stimulus, and alter's twisted perception of it due to biological, personality and culture factors. The third gap, G3, is the transformation of alter's percept by his cognitive processes and the biasing effects of his defense mechanisms, personality peculiarities and cultural imprints. The cumulative disrupting effects of these gaps on ego's endeavors to communicate with alter are brought home to ego by alter's dissonant reaction to his communication. Ego is then likely to experience a frustration because of this initial breakdown of communication. Man is motivated by his early developmental phases to be a congruity driven animal. Consequently, ego is bound to try and overcome these gaps of communication (depending on his personality type) through either a separant inclusionary effort to reach alter by conveying his communication to him in an overpowering manner, or through a participant exclusionary effort of trying to achieve congruity by accepting alter's version of the communication as processed by him and fed back to ego. When these congruity-based efforts to close the gaps in the process of dyadic communication fail, the breakdowns in the communication process are final, and are recorded as such by ego's psyche.

The failure of dyadic communication is, of course, relative and varies in degree for every communication. Totally detached autistic psychotics are a very small minority in any human society. On the other hand, a mutually meaningful and successful dialogue borders on the miraculous. The middle range consists of near failure, semi-failures and partial dissonances. The main impediment to any measure of dialogue is that ego is motivated by his core personality vectors to achieve a deeper level of encounter with alter and his contextual object than the level he deems himself to have achieved. This is the fate of man's Sisyphean and Tantalic illusions, that he is forever chasing a stone he cannot control or communication he cannot achieve.

The Cognitions

We need now to examine whether our cognitions can in any way serve as a basis for human dialogue.

Homo Conveniens is the harmony seeker, the one who strives for unity and congruity implying that the quest for congruity is the basic human motive. In *The Myth of Tantalus* we provided, in a new personality theory, a developmental bio-psychological basis for the congruity motive.[2] We were able to see this quest for congruity at the base of the achievement–motivated personality in a separant culture, aiming to bridge the rift between himself and the object by overpowering it, and the self-effacing type in a participant culture trying to obliterate his separate self and melting into an engulfing Unity. We hypothesized that the quest for congruity is Man's basic motivation, precisely because it is unattainable. The Sisyphean activist can never dominate the rock and the Tantalic union while the Perfect Origin is always receding. The energy that kindles our cognition is a quest, a search, a craving for congruity, which is never fulfilled yet never relinquished throughout Man's life. The first corollary of this basic premise is noted by social psychologists, but not related to a wider theory, that Man's cognition tends to relate parts to wholes (including himself as a separatum), to the totality of his cognitions. Man also tends to arrange his cognition into systems and relate one cognition to the other within these systems.[3] The implications of this basic premise to the sciences of Man are universal. We shall try and trace it in the realm of perception, in the human efforts to overcome cognitive dissonance, and in ego's search for dialogue with alter by either overpowering him in an inclusionary manner, or by submitting to alter in order to effect an exclusionary participation.

On the social level, we described in *The Mark of Cain* how Man's attachment to congruity, consistence and stability is related to his tendency to stigmatize any form of deviance.[4] While in *The Myth of Tantalus*, we demonstrated how the congruity principle operates through the social character of the individual in politics, art and architecture.[5] In Israel, for instance, the Jewish activist social character assails the terrain with structures that tend to overpower and subjugate the landscape, whereas the participant Arab architecture tries to mold its buildings so that they integrate within the topography and are absorbed in it. However, the core of our argument in the present context is that the congruity principle operates through the psyche, as well as personality and cultural imprints of each individual, and affects a cognitive system that is peculiar to a given individual and not shared by others. We propose, therefore, to examine the implications of this argument on the cognitive process as related to the possibilities of human dialogue.

We claim that Man arranges the incoming information and his percepts into cognitive systems, which comply with his congruity needs as related to his core personality vectors and cultural imprints. These systems involve the molding of the percepts, so that the cognitive systems fit the congruity needs of a given individual at a given time. Consequently, the configuration of an individual's cognitive system is bound to be statistically unique. The implication of this process is that no two cognitive systems can be alike, or even similar, although the individuals may be exposed to the same source of stimuli. Therefore there can be no sharing of cognitive systems between ego and alter, and even if ego wishes to convey to alter the form and contents of his cognitive system, he does not have adequate means to do so.

The biased organization of incoming information to fit ego's specific congruity needs operate throughout the cognitive process from "perception" to "system construction" to "storage".[6] These congruity-based twists of the cognitive process are both conscious and subconscious. According to psychoanalysts the defense mechanisms twist perception and cognitive processes are largely subconscious. Even according to the more traditional psychologists, learning and conditioning (and hence cognitive biases) may occur subconsciously.[7] This means that the functioning of the human psyche both on the conscious and the subconscious levels, and in its psychogenic and sociogenic aspects is subject to congruity based twists and biases. This has led some social psychologists to declare that "no two persons live in the same cognitive world" and that "every perceiver is, as it were, a nonrepresentational artist, painting a picture of the world that expresses his individual view of reality".[8] George Kelly, in his Theory of Personal Constructs, states that persons differ from each other in their construction of events. Kelly cites with approval the neophenomenologists Snyog and Combs, whose basic postulate is that "All behavior without exception is completely determined by and pertinent to the phenomenal field of the behaving organism".[9] We therefore regard our cognitive system as an elaborate mold, as a system of scaffolding, which is not shared and is unshareable with others, into which our psychic experience is cast, processed and stored. There are, of course, some common features to human cognition, but these are blurred, distorted and screened by the congruity based arrangement and configuration of each individual cognitive system.

The dynamics of the cognitive processes make ego expect certain occurrences in conjunction with the state of his cognitive system at a given time and place.[10] However, these expectations vary and change with each new experience. Ego's cognitive system is not only unique to himself but also changes in different points of time. The statistical possibility of dialogue thus becomes more remote because ego's unique and ever changing cognition moves in a temporal orbit. The differences in cognitive points of vantage are compounded by missed temporal opportunities like the heart-broken old spinster who rejected in her youth many a suitor, or the sad lament, "*si la jeunesse savait, et si la veilleuse pouvait*".

The statistical uniqueness and hence unshareability of each individual's cognitive system is effected by the interrelationship among an almost infinite number of factors. For instance, bio-physiological factors, which may be inherited, acquired by injury or induced by chemicals, have been shown to have a distinct effect on cognition.[11] The bio-functional state of the central nervous system also affects cognition. Eyesenck has demonstrated that an "excited" cerebral cortex exerts a restraining and inhibiting hold on cognition, whereas an inhibited cortex loosens the reins over the individual with a resultant increase in cognitive excitation.[12]

The form and contents of cognitive processes are related to the core personality structure and its position on a separant–participation personality type continuum. The activist separant type anchoring on the object perceives and processes his cognitions differently than the inner directed, self-effacing and contemplative participant. The peripheral personality characteristics and some measurable personality traits affect cognition in varying degrees and manners. Rosenzweig's typology of reactions to frustrations is an example of measurable personality traits.[13] The extrapunitive reaction is characterized by aggression directed outwardly towards the object and others, accompanied by a tendency to projection, whereas the intropunitive reaction is characterized by inner-directed aggression accompanied by displacement and isolation. These polar reactions entail selective cognitions and differential orders of priorities that make for different cognitive systems. Jung's celebrated personality typology has the introvert's libido turn inwards so that "a negative relation of subject to object is expressed. Interest does not move towards the object but recedes towards the subject", whereas the extrovert turns his libido outwards so that his cognition focuses on the object.[14] Eyesenck operationalized Jung's types and defined the measurable traits of the extrovert by sociability impulsiveness activity, liveliness and excitability, whereas the introvert was characterized by diametrically opposite traits.[15] These polar personality traits, no doubt, affect the cognitive processes and the arrangement of the cognitive configurations in a diametrically polar manner.

The ingenious experiments of Petrie demonstrated that the "augmenter" increases the size of stimuli subjectively. Being averse to stimuli, the "augmenter" is more tolerant of sensory deprivation and is less tolerant of pain. The "reducers" tended to decrease the size of stimuli, and being tolerant of sensory deprivation demonstrated a hunger for stimuli.[16] Again, Petrie's polarity of stimuli, hunger and aversion is bound to be related to the form and contents of the cognitive processes and systems.

Witkin and his associates studied psychological differentiation as related to the object, setting and environmental perception while performing a task. The "field dependent" individual displays a low psychological differentiation, because he is dependent in his performance on cues stemming from the overall *gestalt* and the background set of the situation. The "field independent" displays higher psychological differentiation and greater reliance on his own cognitive cues than on the outward *gestalt* of the objects.[17] Needless to say, the individual's cognitive configuration vary with his field dependence or independence.

The experiments carried out by Klein and his associates also found significant links between cognitive processes and personality parameters. Klein identified the "sharpeners" as making accurate size judgments and perceiving better contrasts. In their personality they were more active, energetic, competitive and aggressive. The "levelers", on the other hand, made inaccurate size estimates, were less aware of contrast and were generally more passive, dependent and tended to retreat inwards into themselves. Klein also identified the "form-bounded" personality showing more objective accuracy and less imaginative interpretation, whereas the "form-labile" personality gave free, imaginative and sometimes bizarre interpretations of reality.[18] Klein's personality parameters are obviously related to the style and manner of the individual's cognitions.

The personality parameters mentioned above are by no means an exhaustive list, but merely an illustration of measurable personality traits that are strongly related to inevitable variations in the individual's form and contents of perception and cognition. The overall effect of personality parameters on the style and nature of cognition has been aptly summarized as follows. Personal factors limit the number of objects that can be perceived at any moment, they selectively sensitize the perceptual mechanism of the individual, and lower his threshold for recognizing and attending to relevant stimulus objects and aspects of objects. Personal factors may distort cognitions of relevant objects so that they "fit" the requirements of the individual.[19] These individual differences, as well as the strength of individual drives, goals, motivations and emotions augment the statistical uniqueness of an individual's cognition and lower the chances of its shareability.

The cultural factors of cognition are related first to the socialization of the individual. The sum total of our experience and cultural imprints not only shape our personality, but effect the structure and processes of our cognition. The selectivity of memory and the storing of experience are largely bound by culture. It has been demonstrated that what a person remembers and how he remembers it is largely related to his definition of social relevancies and interests.[20] Binocular rivalry studies revealed selected perception and cognition related to different cultural backgrounds. The Latin American student saw bullfights, whereas the American student saw baseball games. Cultural backgrounds are related to the manner of grouping, classifying and the choice of categories. The crucial point is that people, who are socialized by their culture to categorize items in one way, find it hard to communicate with people whose manner of categorizing is different. The cultural imprints on the individual add a vast layer of cognitive differentials, which interact with the personality and psychobiological peculiarities of Man to form a unique, unshareable and non-communicable cognitive process and system for every individual human being.

Our cognition is anchored on spatiotemporality. Yet, even this seemingly solid anchor is subject to the psycho-cultural differentials of perception and cognition. Time being the more volatile component of spatiotemporality, is also more vulnerable to the subjective twists and biases of Man's perception and hence cognition. We intend to substantiate our argument that Man's cognition of time (and hence space and causality) is totally subjective, statistically unique, and therefore essentially non-communicable to others.

The diametrically opposed temporal cognitions inherent in human cultures can be arranged on a continuum between two extreme poles.[21] The separant social character is time and particularly future oriented. The Protestant Ethic regards the fruitful and industrious use of time as a sign of predestined worth. The participant social character, on the other hand, seeks constancy in unity, which is infinite and therefore timeless. The Hinayana Buddhist state of *Jhana* is both a unified one pointed awareness (without substance), and focused in one moment (*ekok-sana*) of the present without a past or future. It is timeless.[22] The participant Sufi aims to free himself from the slavery of spatiotemporality by creating his own subjective time, which is the eternal present of "no-time".[23]

The separant social character is future-oriented because one has to have a life plan to prove one's worth in the here and now as a proof of worth before God, the Party, or historical necessity. "Remember", says Benjamin Franklin, "that time is money".[24] And money is a sign of grace, power and wisdom in the successful manipulation of objects. Consequently, the separant is ruled by schedules, dates and deadlines. He has to "fill the unforgiving minute with sixty seconds of distance run". The shape of the day as determined by orderly routines encased by fixed time sequences gives the separant a sense of security. It reassures him that by ordering his time he can control the space around him and determine his destiny. The participant social character, *per contra*, has a constant sense of temporal failure. He longs for infinity. For him history and time are just whirls and ripples of the Mayan curtain, the veil of illusions that the Upanishadic *Moksha* (liberation) disperses. The Mayan illusion is that both time and form (*Rupa*) are inseparably bound together. Consequently, the participant's vision of the "eternal now" involves the dispersion of the obscuring fog of time sequence, and revealing behind it the constancy of unity.

In our comparison between the social characters of Arabs and Jews in Israel, we contrasted the separant Zionist who has both past and future-oriented, with the participant Arab fellah who was present or no-time oriented.[25] The Arab is not just indifferent to temporal sequences; he outright rejects them. "*Ala-jala min a shaitan*" ("To hurry is to be under the devil's influence"), is a religiously sanctioned Arab saying signifying contempt and disdain of action structured and paced by time. When asking an Arab the time of arrival to a destination the answer is likely to be "*camen shewoy*" meaning "in a little while". This very same answer is given with relaxed constancy if the distance is ten or a hundred miles, and the travel time an hour or ten hours. Even today Bedouins measure distances by cigarettes (i.e. the time unit is the distance covered by a camel rider when smoking one cigarette). Time for the *Fellah* was vile because it harassed him out of his convenient fatalism and participant lethargy. He resented the temporal boundaries of finitude that curbed his participant longing for infinity.

In essence, the separant social character regards time as a linear sequence or a dialectical progression, which is bound to take him somewhere, whereas the participant social character regards time as an illusion, which gets him nowhere because it moves him around in circles. This polar perception and conception of time imprinted on an individual by the prevailing culture provides a basic polarity of time cognition that moves along a continuum from one extreme to the other.

On the personality level, the separant type aiming to manipulate his objective environment and other people is attuned to the past and future, whereas the participant striving for Unity and non-sequential flow of cognition longs for a permanent present. This makes for a subjective conception of time that varies with the position of the personality type on the separant–participant continuum. The separant's acute attention on temporal sequences might make him a slave of time. This type of subjugation is apparent in the total attention given by passengers in an airport to the electronic clock on the flight schedule board. The participant type, because of his sheer craving to escape the bonds of time, might be less subject to the dominance of temporal sequences.

The subjective cognition of time is apparent throughout the widest range of experience. A bereaved mother, for instance, feels the loss of her child as an ever-present pain hardly dulled by the passage of years. Yet her friends and acquaintances, some of them meaning well, ask themselves and others, "So many years have passed and she is still grieving as if her son died yesterday".

What they do not understand is that the passage of time for them is totally different than the passage of time for the bereaved mother.

Empirical findings have established that the cognition of time varies with a vast number of bio-psychological factors ranging from mood to body temperature.[26] Although the concept of a biological clock envisaging some objective time awareness by the human organism enjoyed a considerable vogue recently, the empirical evidence for inbuilt time cognition was far from conclusive, and a recent survey of the relevant research does not uphold the existence of an inbuilt human time pacer.[27]

A theory of time that seems to have received solid empirical support is the Storage Size hypothesis. M. Guyau, at the end of the last century, laid the basis for this hypothesis by postulating that time is a purely mental construction agreeing thus with Kant that temporality is an intrapsychic construct.[28] The experience of time was held by Guyau to depend on the intensity of the stimuli, the attention paid to the stimuli, the associations of the stimuli and the expectations called up by the stimuli.[29] According to the Storage Size theory of time, the more sequences experienced the longer the cognition of the duration is. Consequently, the cognition of time is totally subjective. Frankenhauser, a contemporary exponent of the Storage Size hypothesis, says:

> In respect of subjective time, succession is in itself an inherent characteristic of the experience. Thus the discrepancy between the immediate perception and retention of time is not an error caused by methodological inadequacies, which we want to eliminate, but rather a typical expression of the phenomenon we want to study.[30]

The cognition of time, according to the Storage Size model, depends first on the amount of occurrences in a given interval, which reach awareness, and on the efficiency of the coding and the storing of these occurrences. This is why pleasant or interesting experiences are bound to be regarded as "long" in retrospect, whereas monotonous yet quite long periods (e.g. prison terms) are likely to be remembered as "short" in retrospect.[31] This Storage Size mechanism of temporal cognition, with its subjective relativity dependent on both the personality core and the peripheral traits of the self, combine with the cultural differentials to affect a uniquely individual and unshareable cognition of time.

As for the cultural variant in the cognition of space as embodied in the object, we recognize that separant tool orientation reaches outward to things and structured relationships between objects in a manner described by Ortega y Gasset as *Alteracion*. He contrasts this outward reaching activity with a contemplative journey into one-self (*Ensimissmarre*).[32] Indeed, the symbol-orientated, quietist-intuitive manipulation of ideas has no common grounds with the activist goal-oriented manipulation of objects. A discourse between the two is bound to be very much like Maxim Gorky's fable on the dialogue between a hawk and a snake on the pleasures of flying.

Extreme separants, living in tool-oriented cultures, are primarily rational manipulators of their surroundings, because instrumental activities sustain their cultural goals of successfully coping with material needs and controlling their physical environment. However, symbol oriented participants advocate the non-rational, contemplative, intuitive preoccupation with the individual self in order to remove the confining boundaries between subject and object.[33] Consequently, the socialization of a given individual in a culture, which is skewed towards separant tool or symbol orientation, is bound to be related to the individual's cognition of the form and contents of space. This cultural component of spatial cognition is related in a multivariate manner to the personality dimensions, which we have enumerated earlier, and which are also bound to contribute to the diversity and ultimately to the uniqueness of the cognition of space of every individual. The "stimulus hungry", "reducer", "sharpener" and "field dependent" separant individual would regard space as the "world is my apple" object, to be manipulated and overpowered by him. *Per contra*, the "stimulus evasive", "augmenter", "leveler", "field independent" participant would tend to cringe away from the object with a corresponding effect on his cognition of space.

The interrelationship between space and time increases, in a multiplicity of permutations, the individual peculiarities of cognition, compounded by the subjective variations of the cognition of causality.

The imputation of meanings to one's environment, as well as the cognition of causal relationship, has been dealt with by attribution theory in social psychology. In our daily routine of interaction with our surroundings and other people, we tend to impute causal nexus to actions and processes in a rather naïve commonsense manner.[34] The attribution of causality in this manner is not a rigorous scientific or philosophic inquiry, but a one-sided definition by ego of the meaning of the relationships that he observes. Ego's attributions as defined by him become, to use W. I. Thomas's theorem, real in their consequences. The cognition of causality thus becomes a largely subjective affair linked to all the cognitive twists, biases and projections of ego. The crucial point is that whatever ego's reasons for attributing causality the way he does, it becomes a cognitive fact, which others cannot refute or share. Each individual thus has his own sets of causal attributions, which may only partly be communicated symbolically. Most of it is a conglomerate of inferences and linkages peculiar to ego's cognition because he has no criteria by which to describe or communicate them, rather like the spirochete trying to explain to its fellow bacteria what it thinks it does in the human brain. This rather extreme illustration enlarges in relief what the attribution theorists themselves feel, namely that the cognition of causality is dependent on ego's perceptual context and personality traits. "The information conveyed by the order of events", says Jones, "is contingent on the context in which these events unfold and on the nature of the entity being considered as an attributed target".[35]

As for ego attributing causality to himself and to his behavior, Nisbett says rather bluntly, "We do not have direct, fixed knowledge of our behavior".[36] Kanouse, one of the leading exponents of attribution theory, points out that the process of attributing meanings to one's surroundings either by naïve causality or plain description are value-laden.[37] Value judgments are, to be sure, a mesh of cultural biases imprinted on a specific psyche and projected outwards in a manner peculiar to a given individual. Attribution theory is not concerned with the accuracy of ego's attribution, but with the process by which he makes naïve, commonsense, causal inferences on his surroundings. Further, attribution theory does not seem to question the assumption that the cognition of causality is a subjective process unique for each individual. Because of a lack of common criteria for the cognition of causality, it is not likely to be effectively communicated by one person to another.

George A. Kelly's Theory of Personal Constructs is another attempt to explain how Man tries to imbue his surroundings with meanings, order, causal nexus and interrelationships. Personal constructs for Kelly are "transparent patterns", which Man creates and then tries to project and fit over the realities that he perceives the world to be composed of.[38] In this rather neo-Kantian conception of the dynamics of the human psyche, Man seems to project on the same events different meanings, expectations and predictions. These differ with time, place, and, what is crucial to our present context, the personal constructs differ from person to person. "Persons differ from each other", says Kelly, "in their construction of events . . . it seems unlikely that any two persons ever happen to concoct identical systems and even particular constructions are never identical events".[39]

Ego's personal constructs are therefore peculiar to himself, and insofar as these constructs are also projections of order and causality on ego's surroundings, they are not likely to be shared by the corresponding constructs within the cognitive system of any other individual.

Our statement as to the unique and unshareable cognition of causality within the framework of spatiotemporality is related both to personality differentials and cultural variables. The separant occidental and scientistic conception of causality (inference, correlation and the statistically significant, difference between measurements) projects its inclusionary designs on the object. By imbuing its surroundings with a systematic set of relationships, the separant culture attempts to dominate its environment. On the other extreme of the cultural continuum, the participant cultures reject the mechanisms of causality and dismiss it as just another illusory Mayan veil of spatiotemporality. Some Far Eastern cultures, for instance, accept what has been denoted by Jung as causal synchronicity – coincidences of events outside time and chance, and links between subjects and objects without the mediation of space.[40] Through synchronicity, fact and fiction intermingle within a timeless unity. A *déjà vu* is as valid (or invalid) a proof as a correlation matrix, and stars are eclipsed the moment they are extinguished within the mind of a Tibetan lama.

On the personality level, it has been shown that some people more than others tend to arrange their environment in cause and effect systems. Such organization is influenced by our value judgments and emotional states.[41] The pioneering experiments of Michotte demonstrated that we readily tend to impute causality to totally unrelated phenomena.[42] This enables a whole range of halo effects and projections, originating within the psyche of the individual and related to his needs, to impute causal relationships to chance or random phenomena. Gossip builds a cover story of romance and honeymoons on a chance nod of greeting exchanged between celebrities, and the political mudslinger links a routine handshake between a political candidate and Frank Sinatra as a proof of the former's direct links with the local Mafia. Yet the specific attribution of causality by a given individual is dependent on his own subjective needs and defense mechanisms, so that the nature and form of causal cognitions would vary from individual to individual. The context of the observed relationship is also important in the cognition of causality. When one is being persuaded by an individual of higher status, one's compliance is being attributed to inner direction and independence, whereas a lower status persuader would seem to have achieved compliance by undue pressure.[43] The cumulative combination of culture, personality traits and context would affect a cognition of causal nexus as unique and specific for each individual as his finger prints. Moreover, this uniqueness is compounded by the specific configuration of space, time and causality within the cognition of each individual psyche.

The "Unshareable" Perceptions

A percept is a mental image processed by the bio-psychosocial configurations of our personality, and is therefore very precariously related to the stimuli impinging on our senses. The mental image of a percept is an end product covered by layers of our personality biases and defenses, value judgments, cultural pressures, affects, motives and drives. It is virtually impossible to peel layer after layer of the bio-psychogenic and sociogenic components of our percepts in order to reach the pure epistemological core of the original stimuli. Moreover, it is not necessary for our present work because we are not concerned with the technical mechanisms of perception, but with the possibility that our perception in its final processed form awards us a viable basis for communication and dialogue. To this end we shall try and see how and if our percepts provide our cognition with the necessary means for interpersonal communication.

It is common knowledge that the synchronized perception through a number of senses of, for instance, a well prepared meal is not just partial and inchoate, but totally different when perceived by one sense only (i.e. when the food is only tasted, only smelled or, alas, only seen). Less known is that a combination of percepts in a perceptual *gestalt* is totally different than just the accumulation of percepts.[44] There are, of course, some central percepts around which the *gestalt* may be organized (like on a scaffolding), but even then every percept is interrelated with the others and one perceptual *gestalt* is dynamically related to all the others so that, as Asch rightly stated in relation to his perceptual model, "The final impression is more than the sum of its parts".[45] Our contention, however, is that the bio-psycho-cultural processing of the sense impressions by the individual into a single percept is permutated and augmented by a corresponding ontogenetic and phylogentic processing of the interacting percepts within the perceptual *gestalt*. Consequently, there is a continuous twisting and biasing built into the perceptual process of the individual, starting from the sense impressions forming into percepts, through those interacting to form perceptual *gestalts*, to those being processed within the cognitive system of the individual as described above in the previous section. It means that the perceptual process increases the uniqueness of our cognition of the object and decreases the possibility of sharing it with other people and communicating it to them.

We stress again what we already mentioned in the introduction, that we know nothing about the object "out there". Our discussion is confined to the relationship between the proximal stimulus, which actually impinges on our senses and its processing by the bio-psycho-cultural components of our personality until it becomes a percept.

The first stage of the processing of the proximal stimuli is their actual reception by the organism. This depends on the RAS, which is the arousal system located within the brain below the cerebral cortex. Without a certain level of arousal the organism will not receive the incoming proximal stimuli, not unlike a television set that has to warm up before it starts receiving and projecting images. The importance of this premise to our present context is that the arousal system varies from person to person, so that a perceptual threshold peculiar to every individual is embedded within the human organism.[46] In other words, the arousal level of each human organism necessary to trigger and start the process of perception varies with each person, *independent* of the nature and intensity of the proximal stimuli impinging on the senses. Moreover, the perceptual threshold is not constant and may vary with each specific individual depending on his emotions and motivations.

Freudians claim that all human behavior is defensive, but even if most or even part of it, depending on the school of thought, is affected by defense mechanisms, then perception as a mode of human behavior is bound to be distorted by them. Indeed, defense mechanisms such as displacement (that shifts meanings and symbols to surrogate sources), repression (that shields ego from painful experiences by repelling them from consciousness), or projection (that imputes ego's forbidden wishes to others), are bound to distort and divert our perception. We shall deal later in more detail with the barriers against communication inherent in defense mechanisms. At this stage we wish to point out the distorting and biasing effects of the defenses on the reception of the proximal stimuli, that is, on its processing, until it becomes a percept and on its storing by the organism. Most of the defenses are believed to be subconscious dynamisms, so that ego cannot be aware of the distorting effect on his perception. Also, the nature, form and potency of the defense mechanisms vary from person to person, so that their biasing effects on perception are peculiar to a given individual and cannot be communicated to others because ego is not even aware of their operation and dynamics.

A dialectical process among conflicting vectors activates the personality core. The form and contents of these vectors vary from person to person, depending on the bio-psychogenic and sociogenic factors comprising their personality. Perception, being part of experience and processed by the dialectics among these specific vectors, is bound to result in percepts peculiar to ego and incorporated within his psyche in a unique and unshareable manner. An initial empirical anchor of this premise is provided by experiments with subjects wearing aniseikonic lenses, which magnify a single dimension of the image of one eye. Cantril reports that a subject sees himself less distorted by the aniseikonic lenses than he sees others. Also a high status person will appear less distorted than a low status one.[47] Fisher reports that the amount and nature of distortion of different body parts, appearing through the aniseikonic lenses, vary according to the viewer. Women who care more than men about the shape of their legs would see their legs less distorted by the aniseikonic lenses than men.[48] When the proximal stimuli are distorted, and hence become ambiguous, perception turns into a projective technique as the personality components are, to varying degrees, projected onto the object. This demonstrates, initially at least, that the personality of the perceiver is related to the form and nature of the percept independent of the proximal stimuli.

The process of perception is not initiated randomly. Ego's bio-psycho-sociogenetic structure, as well as his *ad hoc* interaction with his surroundings, makes him more attuned and hence more receptive to some stimuli than to others.[49] Thus right from the outset we are attuned to perceive objects and other people selectively. This selectivity of perception manifests itself in a wide range of instances. If ego were motivated to find or sense something, he would perceive everything related to the target object in bold relief, whereas other objects would be relatively faint in the background. In some pathological states, especially paranoia, a person selectively perceives the stimuli that support his paranoiac sensitivities, whereas the stimuli contradicting them would be relatively barred from the perceptual *gestalt*.[50]

A large variety of perceptual defenses have been recorded throughout the field of psychology. Bruner and Postman reported that taboo words projected through a tachistoscope took longer to recognize than neutral words.[51] Sullivan notes the selective inattention to stimuli that raise anxiety and the dissociation (i.e. the suspension of awareness of painful experiences).[52] Cancer patients develop virtual blindness to stimuli that point at the obvious symptoms of their disease. If these symptoms pass the perceptual barrier and are recorded by the patients they are liable to be misinterpreted as signs of a temporary sickness. A bereaved parent tends to avert his gaze from the picture of his dead child hanging on the wall. Israeli communists tend to develop a perceptual block against the anti-Israeli policies and the anti-Semitism of the power elite in Soviet Russia.

After the stimuli have been processed, there is a selectivity of recording and storing the percepts. Interesting percepts are better recorded and remembered more vividly and longer than dull or routine percepts and experiences. Finally, Dember states, "every object can be assigned an information value, or a 'complexity value' . . . if an individual is free to choose, he will prefer to encounter objects of a complexity level that matches his own ideal complexity level".[53] Thus each individual has his own selectivity of perception and complexity level of awareness determined by his specific personality structure, and this cannot be shared by others or communicated to them.

It seems that we are not only selectively attuned to perceive stimuli, but also selectively exposed to stimuli by the specific situation in which we interact within a given setting of objects and other people. Vision, for instance, is anything but static and is very much affected by ego's interaction within his field of vision. Vision is influenced by ego's spatial relationship with the object, and the acuity suffers if ego's body is in an unusual but not necessarily uncomfortable posture.[54] Also, the visual perception of form varies according to the area of the retina that has been stimulated.[55]

The subjectivity of perception has been demonstrated by the now classic experiments of the Hanover Institute. Of special interest to our present context is the oak-leaf demonstration. There are no standard sized oak leaves, unlike, for instance, standard sized playing cards. Oak leaves vary in size from very small to very large. When three playing cards, one oversize, the second standard and the third undersize, are placed at the same distance from the viewer in an apparatus which lacks cues for size and distance, the larger cards seem closer and the smaller card seems farther away. However, when oak leaves are placed in the apparatus each person seems to have his own standard sized oak leaf. "In the ambiguous situation he sees any oak leaf, whether large or small, according to his preconception as to how big a standard oak leaf is. Then he places it perceptually at a distance that fits this preconception".[56] This subjectivity of perception makes for a dynamic process in which ego not only perceives selectively the cues and *gestalts* which suit his needs at a given situation, but he provides his own cues when these are missing in the stimuli set.[57]

The classical experiments of Stratton demonstrated that when vision was inverted by means of prisms worn day and night, the subjects' vision reverted back to normal after a few days. The reversal to normal vision was enhanced by the subjects' active involvement with his environment.[58] Kohler, who used distorting lenses, replicated Stratton's experiments in the 1960s. After wearing these distorting goggles for several weeks, the subject's vision adapted itself to the distortion and he saw the world as normal.[59] Thus we adapt our perception to our *ad hoc* needs independently of the incoming stimuli. The latter are a reservoir of raw material to be structured and molded by our psyche into *gestalts*, which serve our needs at a given time and place. The process of perception is, therefore, dependent on the perceiver. It varies from one perceiver to another, and with the changing needs of the perceiver at different situations.[60] Furthermore, as each new perception is a new experience that is absorbed by the personality, influencing it and sometimes changing it, the ever-changing personality is attuned to perceive a different *gestalt*, independently of the flow of the incoming stimuli that is also bound to change constantly. This raises the probability that each percept is a unique event, which is quite unlikely to happen again in the same or similar perceiver stimuli configuration. This might lend a new meaning to Heraclitus' seemingly ambiguous statement, "one never steps twice into the same river".

The value judgment, the emotional loading of a percept and its meaning to ego, colors heavily the whole process of perception. All of us know from experience that there is no one London, Paris or New York. Cities change for us with the change of our companions, moods, motives and age. The gist of our argument is that each individual at a given situation perceives a set of stimuli in a unique manner so that, "there are as many realities as there are perceivers".[61]

The implications of this premise to the possibility of dialogue are that the subjective nature of perception makes a value-free and disinterested assessment of a situation quite unlikely. The value and emotionally laden judgment of a situation by ego is bound to differ from the subjective judgment of the very same situation by alter. The more emotionally involved ego is in a situation, the more he is bound to twist it to fit his bias, and the further his perceptual stance moves away from alter's. Consequently, any perceptual common denominators with other perceivers, who are bound to be less or differently involved with the target object as a basis for dialogue, are liable to be quite unlikely.

It has been established that a wide range of personality parameters influence, distort and bias perception. The more ambiguous a set of stimuli are, the more the perceivers' personality parameters are projected on them. Indeed, projective personality tests such as the Rorschach inkblot and the Thematic Apperception tests are based on this premise. Tolerance or intolerance of objective ambiguity is in itself a personality factor, which is linked to other personality parameters. When people are exposed, for instance, to ambiguous figures such as the Necker Cube, the psychologically more rigid find it more difficult to discern the ambiguity in the figure than the psychologically less rigid, who seem to be more tolerant of perceptual ambiguity.[62] In a like manner, the autokinetic movement of a point of light in a dark room has been utilized as a projective test to measure conformity, rigidity and prejudice.[63] Personality para-meters were also found to be related to the "fusion threshold" in the flicker test. Persons requiring a higher speed of the rotating shutter before they cease seeing the light coming through it as a flicker, and perceive it as a continuous light, are more discriminating and have a stronger ego. Subjects of a weaker ego cease perceiving the flicker at a lower speed.[64] Finally, personality tests such as Witkin's Rod and Frame Test, Petrie's Augmentation and Reduction Test, and Klein's Leveling and Sharpening Test, all mentioned in the previous section of this chapter, are built on the premise that core personality characteristics are manifested through different modes of perception.

Needs, wants, motivations and emotions affect both contents and mode of perception.[65] McClelland and his associates reported that when vague blots were projected on a screen, hungry subjects were more likely to perceive in them food and food related objects than a control group of well-fed subjects.[66] Bruner and Goodman reported that poor children, more than rich ones, tended to overes-timate the size of coins.[67] Franklin reported the effects of six months of semi-starvation on thirty-six men. The subjects bought cookbooks, kettles and frying pans without being able to explain why they bought these seemingly unnecessary utensils. They also lost interest in sex with a corresponding decrease in the perception of sex related objects.[68] Perception is also improved by success and reward and deteriorates with frustration and anxiety.[69] McClelland's review of the relevant studies points out the curvilinear relation-ship between the intensity of motivation deprivation and perception of "reality". At a low level of motivation the individual's imagery is of goal objects. As the motivation increases, the individual tries to find "realistic" ways to satisfy his wants. However, when the want increases the person might seek refuge in fantasies and bizarre imagery.[70]

We have surveyed some illustrative instances in which personality factors, needs, motives, affects, moods and experience influence and distort perception to fit a given personal cultural and situational configuration. Our interim conclusion is that every perceptual *gestalt* seems to be unique in the person-situ-ation context. It cannot be replicated, and even less shared or communicated.

We propose now to examine in more detail some of the dynamics of percep-tual distortions. According to Piaget, distortion is inherent in the process of perception insofar as focusing on one part of the perceptual field relegates the rest of it to relative inattention.[71] Perceptual distortion is also inherent in the fact that our exterocepters are very much affected by cues from our interocep-tors and proprioceptors. Consequently, as we already mentioned, when we are tired, hungry or tense, things appear very much different to us than when we are relaxed, fed and rested. There is also solid evidence that perception changes with age.[72]

However, the most basic distortions inherent in the process of perception irrespective of age, sex and culture are the perceptual constancies. We tend to imbue our stimuli with constancies of size, form, hue and shade, which they do not possess because they never change with time, distance and context. The wall of our summer home on the Mediterranean, which is flaming red by sunset, is still perceived by us as white because we "know" that we whitewashed it the other day. The size constancy of objects is affected by distance and perspective cues although their retinal images vary enormously. Perceptual constancies are learned and therefore vary with different personalities and cultures. The extroverts' perception of size constancy is presumably more consistent than the introverts', and a pigmy out of the forest for the first time in his life sees a herd of buffaloes five miles away as tiny insects.[73]

Another distortion inherent in perception is what the Gestalt theorists call *Pragnanz*. We tend to see symmetry, regularity, continuity and unity even if they are absent in the stimuli. We see chariots in the flaming evening clouds. We see a complete circle even if the circumference line is dotted and has gaps in it. We see the figures of an overlapping ellipse and a square as entwined together, undivided at their areas of interaction.[74] The Gestalt theorists take the *Pragnanz* principle as given. They describe and investigate its effects but they do not try to account for its etiology. The *Pragnanz* principle, however, fits into our theoretical scheme. It stems from ego's congruity based efforts to organize and regulate his surroundings gaining, thereby, a certain measure of inclusionary control over them.

It is our hypothesis that the *Pragnanz* effect is more apparent with the separant object manipulating personality type than with the self-effacing exclusionary participant. This has yet to be tested empirically, although the *Pragnanz* effect has been shown to vary among individuals when measured by certain basic personality parameters. Some closure, organizing and regulating mechanisms, which are related to the *Pragnanz* principle, also have a distorting effect on perception. The proximity principle, for instance, arranges spatially close objects into patterns. Also, when objects are similar by certain conspicuous parameters (e.g. size, shape, direction and color), we tend to group them together.[75] This assimilation principle, which was utilized by Heider to develop far-reaching theoretical systems,[76] is also a congruity based distorting dynamic. This dynamic is related to the quest of the object by our personality core vectors, by organizing it within and by our perceptual system. Contrast provides the reference points or anchors for the assimilation effect by helping to define the "ins" and exclude the "outs". Sherif and his associates demonstrated the distorting effects of assimilation and contrast not only on perception, but also on judgment and social attitudes.[77]

Other relevant perceptual distorting mechanisms are the primacy and the recency effects. The primacy effect, as described by Asch and studied by Luchins, occurs when initial information influences subsequent information.[78] A passage describing a person, for instance, when read first would provide a set, an *einstel-*

lung, which would color and bias subsequent descriptions of the same person. Asch describes the primacy effect as follows:

> When the subject hears the first term, a broad, uncrystallized but directed impression is born. The next characteristic comes not as a separate item, but is related to the established direction. Quickly the view formed acquires a certain stability, so that later characteristics are fitted – if conditions permit – to the given direction.[79]

The recency effect, which is diametrically opposed to the primacy effect, makes the immediate past information more influential on the impression formation than more remote information. It seems that the processes linked to the primacy effect are attention decrement, due to distraction and fatigue and discounting (i.e. "explaining away" subsequent contradictory information). The processes favoring recency effects are recall readiness, which depend on the time lag between the first impression and the subsequent ones, and the relevance of the latter to the former, the greater contrast between the first and subsequent information, and the marked contents and context discrepancies between the two.[80] It is inherent in the nature of the factors that enhance primacy or recency effects that they would depend on the personality of the perceiver and the situational context of the perception.

A fascinating phenomenom, albeit surprisingly scantily researched, is that when people are exposed to subliminal stimuli (often for a very short time) they have no conscious awareness of its taking place or its effect. The influence of these subliminal stimuli on perception has been solidly established.[81] The implications of this phenomenon to our present context are enormous. We are engulfed by a constant flow of stimuli such as ultraviolet rays, radio and cosmic waves as well as sub- or ultrasonic sound waves. The effective range of our senses, however, is pitifully narrow. Consequently, an unknown number, form and configuration of subliminal stimuli operating subconsciously might well affect our perception in a manner that cannot be known to us. The effects of the subliminal stimuli at large on our perception cannot be the subject of even our wildest hypotheses. We simply have no way of knowing about them. Apart from these subliminal stimuli being a proper subject for a macabre science fiction saga, or the means of our metaphysical programming by the powers above, they add a vast residual unknown to the twisting of our perception and decrease further its shareability and the possibility of its communication.

Perception may also be affected and biased by suggestion, hypnosis and sensory deprivation.[82] The nature and form of the perceptual distortions would, naturally, depend on the perceiver's susceptibility to hypnosis and suggestion, and to his vulnerability to sensory deprivation.

Some pathological states of the senses, and especially of the eye, may distort and twist perception. In visual object agnosia, a person is unable to identify certain objects although he can see them. Some neurological and psychological anomalies may cause microposia when objects appear smaller than they are, macroposia when objects look larger than they are, and teleoposia when they appear farther than they are. Squinting may sometimes cause disturbances of spatial perception as well. In the group of disturbances denoted as visual spatial agnosia, a patient is unable to translate objective space into bodily space. He may thus be able to grasp his nose but not point at it, and he can scratch an itch but not point at the part of the body that itches.[83] In constructional apraxia, the patient is unable to construct two or three-dimensional figures. In strabismus, objects appear to be an indeterminate position in space. They seem to be in continuous motion without getting anywhere. In hemianopia, a person cannot estimate correctly distances, with a resultant disorientation of action.[84]

Functional mental abnormalities, notably the neuroses and the psychoses, have been related to perceptual distortions. Polarization of perception, for instance, has been noted with neurotics.[85] Hysteria has been manifested by the contraction of the visual field, temporary functional blindness, night blindness and cortical blindness.[86] Schizophrenic patients may not see the whole person but only parts of him. There is also a reduction in the perception of schizophrenics of the size and shape of objects, and in their perception of distance constancy.[87] The time perception of the schizophrenic is sometimes segmented; he stops perceiving it as a flowing duration, but as discrete sequences of pictures that he tries to fit together.[88] Visual and audile hallucinations are quite common in schizophrenia, and a wide range of perceptual distortions has been noted with manic-depressive patients and among some types of mental retardation.[89] Changes and twists of perception are also inherent under the influence of drugs. Such changes have been well documented.[90] Masters and Houston describe the four levels characteristic of the depth of the subject's experience.[91] The first stage is predominated by sensory experience, causing altered awareness of body and body image, spatial distortions, and a wide range of perceptual changes that ordinarily occur. During the second stage, the content is predominantly introspective and especially recollective-analytic. Personal problems, particularly problem relationships and life goals are examined. Significant past experiences are recalled and may be revivified (lived through) with much accompanying emotion. On the third level, the symbolic level, through historical, legendary, mythical, ritualistic and archetypal imagery, the subject "may act out myths and legends and pass through initiations and ritual observances often seemingly structured precisely in terms of his own most urgent needs". On the deepest level, the integral level, "ideation, images, body sensation (if any) and emotion are fused in what is felt as an absolutely purposive process culminating in a sense of total self-understanding, self-transformation, religious enlightenment and possibly, mystical union".[92]

Cultural factors bias perception because many times people see what they are conditioned to see and because all perception is value-laden. There is a favorable perceptual bias towards the familiar and a negative bias towards the non-familiar. Consequently, perceptual prejudices are as inevitable as human in and out groups. Perceptual halo effects stemming from cultural factors or previous experience color and twist our perception. A person we met in a painful context is initially repugnant to us when we meet him again. "Good" deeds are attributed to "good" guys and a "bad" guy can never do any good. People of high prestige are usually attributed, many times erroneously, with a wide range of positive qualities. Otherwise they wouldn't be where they are. Roles such as father, employer, minister, judge, also tend to color the perception of a person's behavior outside of his role. Consequently, a person may, many times, become imprisoned by a perceiving alter in a single fixed role. A possible variation on Sartre's theme in *No Exit* is that one person is liable to construe a perceptual prison for another.[93] One of the most striking value laden biases of perception may be witnessed in car accidents. Each of the participants usually sees the evidence for the culpability of the other driver but not for his own.

We sum up our present section by agreeing with Blake and Ramsey, "that no perceptual discrimination is correct".[94] So many biological, psychological, cultural and situational factors seem to intervene and interfere with the proximal stimuli, that they really have no chance of being represented correctly in the percept. This was brought home to the author by an exposition in Paris at the *Musée des Arts Decoratifs* of some striking anamorphic pictures by Hans Holbein, Samuel Van Hoogstraeten and Jean Francois Hecoron. The author realized how much our senses, and hence ourselves, are prisoners of perspective and perceptual conditioning and convention. A peephole made some neutral smears of paint appear as a skull. Some random logs, when seen from the proper angle, appear as a table set for dinner, and wheelbarrows turn into ladders. The author realized how vulnerable and shaky our perception is, and if some simple tricks of perspective can upset it, what havoc is bound to be wrought on it by the shattering pressures of our drives, needs, motives and emotions.

Our second conclusion is that perception is biased and distorted according to the specific bio-psycho-cultural configuration of each person and the situation in which he is involved at the moment of perception. Our core personality vectors, drives, needs, desires, wishes, psychological defenses and fantasies, all twist our perceptions to fit the specific configuration of our personality as it interacts with its surroundings. The twisting of perception thus becomes an adjustment dynamic, which is complementary to the needs and expectations of each given individual. The perceptual dents and biases serve as a protective shield to the needs of each individual. Each individual forms a unique configuration when he interacts with and within a given situation. He adjusts his surroundings, by twisting their perception, to suit his specific needs. These needs are related to the personality core vectors and the personality type of the perceiver. A participant Tantalic type tends to efface himself *vis-à-vis* the object so that his perceptual twists of it would augment. *Per contra*, the complementary perceptual biases of the separant Sisphean personality type serves his needs to overpower the object and control it. Therefore, his perceptual twists would reduce the object so that it appears more manageable.

Once again, we state that the perceptual biases of a person are as unique as his personality. The perceptual *gestalt* of an individual within a given situation is as peculiar to himself as his finger prints. It can neither be shared nor communicated. Our perception does not provide a basis for dialogue but constitutes a most formidable barrier against it.

The Misperception of People

If indeed the model of perception is Stimulus Trait → Impression → Response Inference,[95] then the intervention of the impression, which is determined by the bio-psycho-cultural configuration of each individual, would make for a different perception of the target person by each individual.

The ingenious studies by Asch,[96] which were later replicated and developed by Wishner,[97] point out our tendency to label people by central traits. These tend to serve as a scaffolding on which our whole impression of a person tends to be arranged. Some central traits are more potent than others, and Asch found the warm–cold dichotomy to be the strongest of them all. The importance of these central traits to the formation of our first impressions of a person are tremendous. Recommendations for jobs, higher studies and acceptance into an organization are usually in the form of a list of commendable central traits. *Per contra* the gossips, tabloids, critics and political opponents, utilize to the hilt the extraordinary smearing effect of a few derogatory tags on the whole social image of a person. What actually happens is that the vast intricate mesh of core and peripheral personality characteristics of an individual are squeezed, twisted and reduced into a few simplistic and shallow labels. What is more, we tend to accept these labels as a basis for our daily impressions of people. Indeed, the whole labeling and stigma theories in criminology and social deviance are based on our tendency to reduce the personality of the criminal or deviant as a mere appendage to a few derogatory tags.[98] Moreover, the form and contents of this labeling reduction of alter into a few, or sometimes even a single central trait, depends on the personality and its cultural setting of both ego and alter and on the situational interaction between them. The chances of even a similarity of these labeling processes among different people is, therefore, quite remote.

Interpersonal perception involves interpersonal expectations. Ego expects alter to behave in a certain way within a given set of circumstances. Alter's image is colored by ego's expectations of him. When an audience in an experiment was told that the subjects were a submarine crew, they appeared to the audience as other and outwardly directed, but when the audience was told that the subjects were astronauts, they were perceived as inner directed.[99] The audience did not perceive an "objective" image of the subjects, but how they expected certain persons in given situations to sound and to act. People also like a person who complies without perceptual expectations.[100] If he does not, we may feel upset or uncomfortable, and in a conflict situation end up disliking the person who "let us down" by not complying with our expectations. The process here leads to cognitive dissonance about which we shall deal later. At this stage, however, we have to point out that ego's perceptual expectations from alter depend mostly on ego and very little on alter. Ego's needs and motives stemming from the dynamics of his core personality vectors, cultural imprints and situational orientations, cast on alter a set of expectations that he cannot be aware of, and if he is, he can rarely comply with. The conflictual interaction between ego and alter, which is more the rule than its exception, begins from this disjuncture between ego's perceptual expectations from alter and alter's behavior. Of greater importance to our present context is that the perceptual expectations from a person stemming mostly from the needs, motivations and perceptual defenses of the perceiver are bound to differ from person to person, so that alter is confronted with as many perceptual expectations as the number of perceivers he is exposed to. Our contention is that, except for the partial and mostly ineffective verbal communication, there is no way for one perceiver to share his perceptual expectations with another perceiver and with the perceived person.

Piaget's developmental psychology envisages the egocentric child who "cannot take the view-point of another".[101] When the child matures, he is more able to see things the way others see them. However, he still sees them through his eyes and not through the eyes of others. Furthermore, we have pointed out earlier in this work, ego never loses his ontological sense of uniqueness of being chosen to be the seat of awareness, and hence the original perceiver of things and others. Ego can only infer alter's forms and contents of perception, whereas his own perceptions are direct and immediate. Consequently, the perceptions of ego and alter can never be on an equal footing. Ego's perceptions of others are inevitably biased by his sense of ontological uniqueness. It is not suprising, therefore, that ego's own personal dimensions (constructs) are more meaningful to him than those constructed by other persons.[102] Also, ego tends to describe himself in more laudatory and complementary adjectives than he tends to describe others.[103] This is linked to ego's egocentric attitudes towards others as he tends to attribute to others his feelings towards alter. "If I love John I expect all the world to love him". Conversely, if "I hate John I take it as a personal affront if all the world does not hate him too".[104] This assimilative projection was found to be linked to cognitive simplicity, which assumes a similarity between ego and others based on an incomplete differentiation between the self and the external world.[105] We suspect that this projective assimilation is due to ego's feeling of choice and uniqueness and that it would be more pronounced with the separant personality type who aims to control his environment by imposing in an inclusionary matter, his point of view on others. This, however, would have to be confirmed by a properly controlled study. It is important to note that actual similarity of attitudes between ego and alter was found not be significant to the formation of ego's projective assimilation.[106] This shows that ego's perception of alter is determined more by ego's own needs and projective defenses than by the stimuli transmitted by alter towards ego.

Another finding relevant to our present context is that if alter expressed similar attitudes to those of ego, he was rated more positively by ego as well as better liked. This positive rating took the form of being considered more desirable as a work partner, more intelligent, more moral and better adjusted. When alter expressed views which were dissimilar to those of ego, he was rated more negatively by an ego with a high need affiliation than by an ego with low need affiliation.[107] This again shows that ego's needs, in this case his desire for affiliation, biases his perception of alter. Also, ego covered alter with a halo effect of commendable qualities if alter expressed attitudes similar to his.

Jones and Nisbett expound, in somewhat understated terms, the differences in perception between actors and observers:

> Because of the difference in the availability of personal history data, actors and observers evaluate each act along a different scale of comparison, different aspects of the available information are salient for actors and observers and this differential salience affects the course and outcome of the attribution process.[108]

We conceive it rather more bluntly, as an inevitable rift between the actor who perceives his experience through his sense of choice and uniqueness, and the observer who perceives the actor through the stereotypes and clichés of the modal experience of the generalized other, as well as his own defensive biases and projective distortions. Jones and Nisbett bring evidence to support their contention that an actor tends to attribute his behavior to situational constraints, whereas an observer tends to attribute the very same behavior to the dispositions of the actor.[109] This is more or less the case of the student explaining to his tutor that he did badly in his examinations because it was hot and he had a headache while the tutor thinks, but rarely says that the student failed in the examinations because he was just plain dumb.

As for the actor communicating his own self perception to an observer, we must be sure first of all that he is able to perceive himself properly. Bem, in his review of the relevant literature, agrees with Skinner that ego must learn and train himself to perceive his attitudes, emotions and other inner states properly.[110] If this is so, ego's learning to perceive himself is subject to all the twists, biases, selectivity and defensiveness inherent in any other perception. Further, it has been demonstrated that ego can be misled by false internal cues to misattribute to himself some emotions and hence misperceive himself. Valins showed semi-nude pictures of females to male subjects and then misled them as to the state of their arousal by false feedback of their heartbeats.[111] Davison and Valins administered electric shocks to subjects and then gave them a placebo, which they were told would change their skin sensitivity and hence their pain threshold. The subjects were then able to withstand twice the intensity of the previous shocks.[112] This means that misattribution and misperceptions of ego's internal states are not only possible, but they also should not be confined to experimental circumstances. In all probability we misperceive our internal states quite often. Moreover, ego perceives his own actions differently than others. We hear and see ourselves differently than others hear and see us. Ego's internal states, however partially and erroneously they are perceived, are felt directly and immediately by him in a manner alter could never be able to perceive. The perceptual disjuncture between ego and alter is, therefore, apparent on all possible levels. Ego many times misperceives his own internal states, yet he is in direct sensory link with these internal states in a way that alter can never be. There is also a basic rift and difference between the way ego perceives his behavior and the way alter sees it.

Ego's perception of alter is clearly biased by alter's power position. Ego is more attentive to a powerful alter than to a powerless one.[113] Also, ego's attitude towards alter's power will affect his perception of him. Consequently, if ego does not impute legitimacy to alter's power he will be less attentive to him. Alter may quite plainly deceive ego through facial expressions, smiles, gestures and general demeanor, which are contrary to his actual moods, feelings and emotions.[114] Most people do some play-acting, but some are better actors than others and hence are more skilful deceivers.

Ego may be biased in his perception of alter if he defines alter's attitude towards him as favorable or negative. The halo effect of ego's perception of alter as negative is more pronounced if his attitude towards ego is hostile, threatening or negative. If alter's attitude is favorable ego's perception might still be ambivalent or undecided. This stems from ego's uncertainty as to whether alter wants to flatter him in order to gain something from him, or he really admires him irrespective of his wealth, power or social position. These biases of interpersonal perception, which have been denoted by Jones and Davis as Personalism, are relevant to our conception of ego's sense of ontological choice and uniqueness.[115] Anyone who intends to injure it would be met by ego's indiscriminate and engulfing hostility, whereas a friendly alter smiling widely would evoke a suspicion in ego, "Does he really think I am special or is it my money he is after?"

Primacy and recency effects are at least as forceful in biasing our impressions of people as of objects. Our first impressions of people color our subsequent attitude towards them, and it might take us a long time or a dramatic turn of events to lose this primacy bias. The recency effect operates in the opposite direction. A recent success of a film or a sports star makes us forget his previous failures. *Per contra*, a recent flop of the star would make all his previous triumphs evaporate from our memories.[116]

Some relevant distortions of person perception have been demonstrated in controlled experiments. Some subjects, for instance, were told that a speaker was addressing a hostile audience, whereas another group of subjects were informed that the same speaker was addressing a friendly audience. The first group judged the speaker to be more sincere than the second group.[117] If a lower status person rated a higher status colleague in a complimentary manner, he was perceived as a flatterer, but if the higher status person rated the lower status person in a similar complimentary manner, his rating was judged as a sincere evaluation.[118] When subjects' views were to be judged in order to award them prizes, the more favorable judges were perceived by the subjects as more powerful than the judges who evaluated them less favorably.[119]

Contextual factors and inevitable analogies may also serve as distorting effects of person perceptions. Two girls, identical twins, known to the author, used to stroll on the Sabbath afternoon together with their husbands, down the main street of the village. One seemed like an enormous giantess where the other looked a midget. This distortion was caused by the fact that one husband was husky and six foot four, whereas the other husband was thin and stooped. Contextual distortions also induce us to perceive the dirt of an artist as eccentricity, whereas our dirty neighbor would be perceived by us as just plain sloppy.[120] The contextual meaning of the perception, which is crucial in the cognitive transformation from the proximal stimuli to percepts, is defined by the perceiver in a way which is bound to differ from one individual to another. Allen aptly states, "Responses which are phenotypically identical may differ in terms of their meaning for the individual, in the psychological processes which produced them, and in consequences for future behavior".[121] Consequently, the same behavior of a person would elicit a different meaning, and hence a different perception by every individual observer.

The above induces us to reject the Jones and Davis theory of Correspondent Inferences, which attempts to explain how a perceiver can infer the meaning of a given action and what the actor was trying to achieve by his action.[122] They give an example of silent observers watching two people working on a task, while ego gives orders to alter showing displeasure with the quality and quantity of his work. If ego and alter agreed to work together out of their own free choice, ego is judged by the observers as arrogant and domineering, but if ego was an appointed foreman he is so judged. The authors construct a systematic theory of perceived meanings of actions in given contextual frameworks. Our first objection is that they make assumptions concerning the roles of the actors and then make their perceptual inferences. In real life situations, unlike the experimental settings of Jones and Davis, we very often can make no assumptions as to the roles and intentions of actors because we have insufficient information, or because our perception of the actors and their actions is biased by our own needs, projections and other defenses.

Jones and Davis theorize that if the actors' behavior is more extreme than the modal or average behavior of this actor, the perceived significance of the action increases. The author's immediate reaction to this part of Jones and

Davis's theory was to recall a popular Israeli film, in which two representatives of the ruling party were sent to select the local leader of the party in an immigrant town. The representatives went to the town's bistro and saw a man being carried on the shoulders of some youths and a crowd dancing around him. The representatives immediately offered the local party leadership to the man on the crowds's shoulders. Later they discovered to their dismay that they had given the party's leadership to the town's clown. The moral of the story is that any inference on the meaning of an action, however extreme and deviating from the modal behavior of the group, is bound to be erroneous if the perceiver can make no assumptions as to the meaning of the action to the actor. In most cases, perceivers have no clue as to the contextual and subjective meaning of an actor and any perceptual inference as theorized by Jones and Davis is unwarranted. Their example of Dr. Smedley's choice to accept a position at Harvard rather than at Yale and the possible inferences of observers for doing so is pitifully simplistic. Jones and Davis's theory assumes that as Harvard and Yale are both in the Ivy League and equally prestigious, then Dr. Smedley's choice must have been motivated by the better psychology department at Harvard. This, to say the least, can only be partially likely. For all we know Dr. Smedley might have a girlfriend at Harvard or that his maternal grandfather postulated in his will that if any of his offspring ever preferred Yale to Harvard they would never receive a penny. Finally, Jones and Davis illustrate their theory by Miss Adams's choice of a husband. The perceivers are given data about the wealth, social position and physical attraction of Bagley, Caldwell and Dexter, the three suitors, in order to predict Miss Adams's choice. Jones and Davis rule out sexual enjoyment as well as many other variables which the perceivers have no way of knowing. However, the predictive power of the observers, as well as the value of Jones and Davis's theory, is close to zero if Miss Adams knows from personal experience, which the observers do not know, that Bagley is impotent, Caldwell is a premature ejaculator and Dexter is a homosexual.

If the apparent motivation of an actor's behavior is hardly perceptible, and hence not likely to be shared or communicated, the perception of emotions is even more problematic. First of all, ego himself has many difficulties in identifying his own emotions. The ingenious experiments by Schachter and Singer showed that internal cues of arousal and excitation from the interoceptors and proprioceptors were not sufficient for ego to identify his emotions. He had to have some external cues to help him label his own emotions. Moreover, if these external cues were twisted on purpose by stooges, ego would readily be taken in by the stooges' performance and label his emotions according to their misrepresentations.[123] By some amusing coincidence, the author's secretary was told while typing this manuscript that the humidity had reached 84 percent, and only then did she start complaining. If ego has severe problems in identifying his own emotions, even though he has a direct and immediate knowledge of them, ego's ability to perceive alter's emotions correctly, the nature of which ego can only infer vicariously, is consequently sadly meagre.

There is a fair amount of consensus that most of the cues for the interpersonal perception of emotions comes from facial expressions, and these, according to the cultural relativists with whom we fully agree, have different meanings in different cultures.[124] We agree with Labarre that "there is no 'natural' language of emotional gesture",[125] and with Birdwhistell that, "there are probably no universal symbols of emotional states".[126] The function of culture-bound display rules, such as the loser displaying happiness, is to cache, disguise and distort emotions in a manner peculiar to each culture and group, so that they consitute a formidable barrier against the effective sharing and communication of emotions.

Even if alter's expression is not a culturally sanctioned display role, downright deception or play-acting, his facial expressions and gestures can only display a gross façade of an affective stereotype, which can hardly represent the articulate nuances and subtle intricacies of his emotions. It is hardly surprising that almost no significant links were found between demeanors and actual emotions. The intervening variables are so many and intricate, the nexus so grossly obscure, twisted and severed, that any resemblance between alter's facial expression and his actual emotions is bound to be random.

Many claims have been made for eye contacts as the poetic encounters between "the windows of the soul", yet the meaning of eye contact seems to vary from culture to culture, from one group to another and from ego to alter. Laing reports that some people wish to have as much eye contact as they can in order to overcome their inner feelings of inadequacy.[127] But how can ego know if alter catches his eye by chance, out of curiosity, because he tries to make a pass at him/her, or because he practices some of Laing's reaction formations. Many times ego interprets eye contact in a different manner than it was intended by alter that ego should interpret them. The author knows a very beautiful girl with a strict upbringing who used to think that something was wrong with her dress or hairdo whenever a male tried to meet her eyes. Sartre and Laing spoke of Medusa's stare, the petrifying gaze of alter which stultifies ego, depriving him of his authenticity.[128] Some people are averse to eye contact and in some cultures there is a taboo on direct eye contacts.[129] The meaning of eye contact between ego and alter are notoriously diverse. Cartoonists, being many times rather sophisticated social scientists, depict in many variations the man–woman encounter with the man visualizing a voluptuous nude body ready for sex, while the woman reflects in her stare a wedding ring or a wad of bills. One of the author's most memorable experiences was the first encounter with a person who eventually became one of his best friends. We sat in the student restaurant, and he looked at the author who decided at the time that the gaze was arrogant, domineering and haughty. After a while the man came to the author's table and asked permission to sit down. He subsequently told the author that he was a new immigrant from England, that he was very lonely and would he mind if he talked to him for a while. If the person had not approached the author, no lasting friendship would have developed and the last and the only memory the author would have had of his friend would have been what looked to him a cold and arrogant stare. In view of all this, Simmel's statement, "The mutual glance between persons signifies a wholly new and unique union between them . . . By the glance which reveals the other, one discloses himself", describes eye contact as the best communication between human beings; it should make us wonder what is the worst.[130]

One of the attempts to systematize interpersonal perception within a dyad was attempted by Laing and his associates.[131] This was done in the style of "I think that you think that I think that you think etc., *ad infinitum*". The Achilles' heel of this type of analysis is that it assumes ego can perceive alter's experience of ego. This assumption is unwarranted and the authors themselves realize that its validity is quite problematic. Indeed, by calling a projection an action and not a state of mind, they don't make it more perceptible to outsiders. Consequently, Laing and his associates do not describe interpersonal or dyadic perceptions at all, but they try to build a model, very ingenious, no doubt, of what goes on in ego's mind when he perceives alter. This is a model of ego playing a game of solitaire replete with his fantasies, illusions, elusions and projections. Laing's basic concepts of metaperspective (ego's view of alter's view of him) and metaidentity (alter's view of ego as internalized by ego), are all constructs of ego's mental processes happening solely within ego's psyche. There is no interaction or an interperception here between ego and alter. Laing and his associates, contrary to their original intentions, have devised a useful way to describe the inevitable misperception of one man by his fellow man.

The Errant Ego and its Errands

. . . the one magnification persisting as a capital refers to the one person still remaining in a depersonified world: I. Only I and God, one to one, and some say God is dead.

James Hillman: *Revisioning Psychology*

The foundation for our conception of ontology has been stated by the Talmud Sanhedrin as follows, "Every coin resembles the other, but God made Man in the image of Adam yet no man resembles his fellow men. Therefore, each one of us has to say for me alone has the world been created".[1] This is also an apt phrasing of ego's existential sense of his choice and uniqueness that he does not share with others.

Ego's sense of choice and uniqueness may account, partially at least, for his inevitable conflicts with the relevant others around him. Ego comes first to himself, both because of his separant quest to persevere, develop and compete with others over scarce commodities, and his sense of being the sole and unique seat of the cognition of the world. However, the relevant others surrounding ego are also imbued, alas, with a similar sense of choice and uniqueness. Consequently, the initial disposition of ego towards his relevant others is for conflict, strife and disjuncture, and not for dialogue. Many times ego looks around him, sees the misery and squalor in which some of his fellow human beings live, and asks himself why their lot is so much worse than his, though he is not a better person than they are. This question is rational, but deep down, subconsciously and ontologically, he feels that he is chosen and unique, and therefore his better lot in life is justified. Conversely, ego feels a certain feeling of security that he is kind of immune to real disaster. His sense of choice and uniqueness provides, so to speak, an ontological protective force field. Ego feels that "it cannot happen to me". But when it does happen, he feels betrayed because the disaster crushed his basic sense of ontological security, and his intrinsic psychological rehabilitation cannot take place unless he regains his feeling of choice and uniqueness.

Physically, this sense of choice and uniqueness makes for a sharp dichotomy between what is within the personal space of the body image and the ego boundary, and everything and everybody that are outside it. Ego's feeling of choice and uniqueness engulfs all the body's tissues, bones, fibres and juices, but once they leave it they become profane. This sharp change of attitude may be witnessed by each one of us towards our saliva when it is in our mouths and when it lands as spittle on the pavement. The whole significance of the Freudian anal stage of development is bound to change if it is reconsidered in the light of the feeling of choice and uniqueness, which is imbued in everything within the confines of our body, but changes to revulsion or dread towards the substances that are excreted, removed or cut off from it.

The infringement of injury of our sense of choice and uniqueness may well be related to our feelings of shame and guilt. We are ashamed if our feeling of worth related to our choice as the seat and channel of the world's cognition is being infringed by outside events. If the "it cannot happen to me" befalls ego he feels betrayed, deeply hurt, but mostly ashamed. The guardian forcefield has been taken away and ego is exposed to injury and humiliation. A family known to the author lost a son in the war. After some months the father also passed away. When the author came to visit the bereaved mother and wife, he asked about the causes of the father's death. The wife answered, "He died of shame. He didn't believe that his son would die. It couldn't happen to him and when it did he couldn't take it". Guilt may also be related to the injury of our sense of ontological uniqueness, or rather to our tendency not to be true to our "true" self. This is highlighted by the Hasidic story of Zusya of Hanipol, as told by Buber. "Before his death Rabbi Zusya said, 'In the coming world they will not ask me why were you not Moses? They will ask me why were you not Zusya.'"[2] Ontological guilt is inherent in not being oneself and especially in ignoring the call of our *Ani*, the innermost self.

The Ensnared Inner Self

One of the basic tenets of our personality theory is that our inner self (*Ani*), which is the structured embodiment of our participant personality core vector, ever longs to unite with its surroundings. This participant quest of the *Ani*, which includes dialogue with other people, is countered by the separant pressures of the *Atzmi*, the interactive component of the self. Consequently, the very dynamics of our personality contain a built-in barrier against dialogue. For the *Ani*-skewed self, the rift that is necessary to pass in order to communicate with alter seems to him too wide to cross to begin with. His inner life is so direct and immediate that in comparison the outside objects and other people seem to be light years away. The *Ani*-skewed self needs no reinforcement of his ontological sense of uniqueness, as he feels it directly. However, his sense of choice and worth has to be reinforced by his relevant others. Being participant and inner directed, the *Ani*-skewed self is not attuned to gain, on a competitive basis, the appreciation of others. Consequently, his approval-seeking communication with the relevant others is liable to be frustrated, and his interaction with the outside world might suffer some disorientation.

The *Ani*-skewed self is immersed in ideas. He is fascinated and sometimes obsessed by absolutes. He tries to "do his own thing" and being sensitive (averse or vulnerable) to too many stimuli he shuns objects and people when he encounters more than he can be comfortable with. The participant *Ani* self is also rarely bored because he is not hungry for stimuli. Most of the time he is exposed to more stimuli, including other people, than he can cope with. Although the *Ani*-skewed personality craves for a meaningful dialogue, he is not disposed to reach out towards other people in order to achieve it.

We demonstrated in the previous chapter that our moods influence our perception. When we are elated we selectively perceive exhilarating objects, and when we are depressed the glass previously perceived as half full is now perceived as half empty.[3] Consequently, ego cannot have an objective perceptible mood for dialogue based on an objective set of favorable or unfavorable settings. A bright, sunny day that makes ego happy may cause sadness to alter. Ego's moods, which are not necessarily related to the objective surroundings, yet determine his willingness to reach towards alter in quest of a dialogue, narrow the possibilities that ego's readiness for dialogue at a given time and place would be shared by alter. Ego cannot help but impose his cognitive, normative and affective terms for dialogue on his potential partners in the dyad, who have their own preferences, moods and hence their own subjective terms, which cannot be shared by ego nor communicated to him.

In J. P. Sartre's criticism of Albert Camus' *The Stranger* he says, *inter alia*, "Camus shows off a bit by quoting passages from Jaspers, Heidegger and Kierkegaard, whom, by the way, he does not always seem to have quite understood".[4] This is a typical Sartrean projection, because Sartre himself has written some definitive misinterpretations of Heidegger, Genet and Camus. To our mind, *The Myth of Sisyphus*, as well as the figure of the Camusean Sisyphus, is the most lucid interpretation of the Heideggerean notion of the authentic *Geworfenheit Zum Todt*. If we are constantly aware of our existential "thrownness" embodied in the scriptures as, "For dust thou art, and unto dust shalt thou return", we shall have a better perspective of the time span between our birth and our death. If every moment we are aware of our death we have a keener sense and hence a more authentic awareness of our life. The Camusean Sisyphus is fully aware of his galloping downhill with the stone-burden of his life, yet his rebellious awareness of his plight gives him a sense of purpose in experiencing to the hilt every second of the drudgery of his diminishing life. The dialectics between his daily chores and his rebellious quest of purpose should make Sisyphus happy. This is the message of Camus' *Myth of Sisyphus*. Camus' Mersault goes to the guillotine with a sense of a boundless wonder, which imbues with ecstatic authenticity even the last minutes of his life. Yet, this existentialist authenticity is totally within the domain of the self. Mersault-Sisyphus gallops to his doom confronted by a silent universe, totally alienated from his environment, without any hopes for being understood and with no one around who is even remotely open for dialogue. The Heideggerean "thrownness towards death", as interpreted by Camus, calls for a reassessment of our priorities. The competitive rat race would be less appealing as well as less ominous. The dialectical strain between the daily routines and our quest for the impossible lends our life a Camusean authenticity. The Heideggerean notion of freedom is inherent in our awareness of the limits of our "thrownness unto death". Paradoxically, ego's realization of the limitations of his possibilities, including the possibilities of dialogue, awards him a measure of subjective freedom.

Our conception of existential freedom is wider. It involves, first of all, ego's recognition of the extent to which his authenticity is curbed, leveled and stifled by the expectations of alter. Secondly, it calls for ego's realization that his participant quest for dialogue cannot be met and reciprocated by alter.

Heidegger's conception of the freedom inherent in the "authentic thrownness towards death", as well as the Camusean rebellious Sisyphus, are not directly related to our *Ani*-skewed personality type anchoring on his objectless self and preoccupied with participation in Unity. The main problem of the *Ani*-skewed type is to free himself from the tyrannizing yoke of the other. We shall examine later the socializing pressures to conform the child's wish "to be like all the others", and the separant adult joiner's urge to drink beer with the boys and to be a member of Rotary International. The *Ani*-skewed self is basically harassed by the pressures to conform. His inner sense of purpose becomes apparent only after he discovers how to "do his own thing", irrespective or in spite of the pressures to conform exerted on him by the relevant others. This is neither easy nor simple. The participant *Ani*-skewed self still has some competitive components of the activist *Atzmi* in his personality structure. These components urge ego to impress others, subjugate and overpower them, or at least to explain away their success in order to sustain his achievement based sense of worth. Once the *Ani*-skewed ego asserts his own sense of ontological uniqueness he achieves a measure of freedom from the relevant others internalized within his personality, but at the same time he diminishes further the possibilities of dialogue with these others.

This liberation of the *Ani*-skewed type from the tyranny of the generalized other may never be achieved, because it necessitates a very strong *Ani* component of the self, as well as a lot of stamina and willpower. However, once a considerable measure of freedom from the necessity to comply with the expectations of the generalized others has been achieved, the *Ani*-skewed ego regains an inner sense of strength and direction.

The subsequent resignation of the *Ani*-skewed ego stems from his relative disregard of the outside world, social positions, as well as his own animal comfort. Being immersed in himself, the *Ani*-skewed ego finds it difficult to communicate with alter even in routine matters. The sheer reaching out towards alter to effect a communication even on a shallow level of encounter seems to ego as an insurmountable task. Very often it becomes a self-fulfilling prophecy, where the *Ani*-skewed self regards the routine communication with alter as too difficult to carry out and consequently impossible. Ego mumbles some incoherent noises and alter does not understand or decides not to pay attention. In extreme cases, the *Ani*-skewed type reduces his interaction with others to a bare minimum, being convinced that any communication on a deeper level of encounter is a self-defeating venture.

The authentic *Geworfenheit Zum Todt*, as well as its Camusean interpretation, entails the living to the hilt of every existential experience be it pleasant or painful. The force of the experience becomes then more important than its being happy or sad. "Am I happy or unhappy?" asks Albert Camus. "It's not a very important question", he answers, "I live with such frenzied intensity".[5] Ontological freedom is inherent in the certainty that our quest of ultimates and everlasting triumphs is a mirage, and that the only source of partial, alas, fulfillment lies in the impact on us of the dialectics between our longing for our perfect and blissful ideals and the daily vicissitudes of our existence. What it comes down to, is that for the extremely *Ani*-skewed self who rejects the judgment of others and measures his experience mostly by his inner criteria, there is no objective calamity or objective happiness. Experience, and especially the most important events of his life are perceived, felt and judged subjectively. Consequently, the meaning of these events for the *Ani*-skewed ego cannot be conveyed to alter. Also, ego's reactions to the events would rarely be understood by alter, because the criteria for ego's judgment are not likely to be shared by others. He would therefore be judged strange, bizarre and "obviously not like you and me".

The *Ani*-skewed self is less dependent on his social roles. Unlike the other-directed *Atzmi*-skewed personality, which nearly collapses when it is forced to leave by retirement his institutionalized roles, the *Ani*-skewed type seems almost glad to retire. He spends hours upon hours in his garden or at the sea shore, and is quite reluctant to leave the sparkling foam of the breaking waves for the small talk at a cocktail party, or to exchange his contemplation of the breaking sun rays from water drops hiding between rose petals with the pompous verbiage of the senate meetings of his Alma Mater. The *Ani*-skewed type feels out of place in public ceremonies and in group reunions, in which he is expected to feel solidarity with the group and express his emotions collectively in the proper institutionalized ritual. He thinks and feels in his own unique manner the group's expectations, which he feels collectively are either incomprehensible or repugnant to him, or both. However, we stress again that pure personality types do not exist. Even the most extreme *Ani*-skewed type has some covert components of the opposite type within the framework of his personality. This might explain the frantic bouts of activism of a predominantly resigned participant. The frantic activism of the *Ani* type is usually ineffective or takes the form of day dreams *à la* Walter Mitty, and a reaction formation might take place. Harry Stack Sullivan, for instance, the maladroit recluse based his whole clinical *Weltanschauung* on the crucial importance of interpersonal relationships. Also, a very reserved and timid person might try to compensate for his shyness by being loud and boisterous at social gatherings usually with disastrous results. This momentary shift to the opposite personality type might also cause some guilt feelings, due to the *Ani* type realization that for a short while he "was not himself". A literary instance for his premise was provided by G. K. Chesterton, where one of his characters was seen by the narrator to give a sizeable alm to a beggar. When the narrator approached the donor and commended him for his generosity, the donor denied vehemently giving anything to the beggar.

The Futility of Involvement

The ancient Greek storytellers recount the meeting between Alexander the Great and Diogenes. Alexander praised the philosopher and told him how much he wanted all his life to meet the great and wise Diogenes. "Tell me what you want", offered Alexander to Diogenes, who was crouching in his barrel, "and your wish will be granted". "Please move away from the sun", replied the sage.

The activist, domineering, carnivorous Alexander had a deep admiration for the participant *Ani*-skewed Diogenes. This was presumably motivated by the covert participant components of his personality. Diogenes, the resigned recluse, on the other hand, pondering his inner self, is not interested in Alexander's handouts and is not tempted to have a dialogue with him. The admiration of the resigned participant, relaxing in activist separant societies, is again related to the covert participant components in the activist social character. The author recalls that the best compliment one of the most ruthless power-hungry executives of the United States administration could give to the Israeli high command was that "they are a very relaxed bunch of people". The norm in our competitive, industrialized societies is that, "One is more effective in getting one's wishes if one is more relaxed". In a separant competitive society one has to play-act, to misrepresent oneself as disinterested, in order to raise the chances of getting what one wants. This widespread technique of deceitful, covetous disinterest naturally does not enhance dialogue, because the interaction here starts with a false façade. Some corollaries of this least interest principle are, for instance, that if ego seems to be too eager for a dialogue with alter, alter will be more likely to back out of the dyadic interaction altogether. The heated, emotional involvement of ego will make his company less pleasant and desirable for alter. Also, ego's deep involvement with his desire for a dialogue with alter will make him less flexible and willing to compromise for a more shallow level of encounter with alter. His emotional involvement would lend him into an all or nothing impasse. Another corollary of the separant least interest principle is the less emotional involvement in interpersonal relationships the better, because familiarity breeds contempt. The "good executive" is rarely seen by his subordinates, as distance means power. Finally, we have the person who is so sure of his worth that he cannot wish to have any dialogue with what he regards as a non-person. An extreme case is Marie-Antoinette's undressing in the presence of her gardener, because to her he was not a man.

The *Atzmi*-skewed person, attuned most of the time to his significant others in order to find out their all important expectations from him, is liable to find himself quite often in a bind or an impasse. The other-directed ego aims to glean the deep inner motives, emotions and expectations of alter from his overt behavior but this, alas, is impossible. There are no necessary links between alter's overt behavior and his underlying motives.[6] Also, the feedback ego receives from his surroundings as well as from other people about his own behavior is liable to be twisted, erroneous and biased. We mentioned in the previous chapter that ego is very often confused by his recorded voice and inverse image in a mirror. Alter may also mislead and give him false feedback cues in order to abuse, ridicule or take advantage of him for material or status gains. Alter's verbal feedback cues may even be more misleading. Flattery, false modesty and fake concern set as a trap by alter for the vain or naïve ego have been described *ad nauseam* by novelists and playwrights, but hardly dealt with by the behavioral and social sciences. It has been noted that very often wise and cunning people are easy prey for flatterers. It seems that ego's need to reinforce his separant sense of worth and choice is stronger the more skewed his self is towards the *Atzmi* pole of the personality type continuum. The *Atzmi* ego is not only dependent on alter for the feedback cues on his behavior and possible range of expectations, but he also needs constant reinforcement. This opens a whole gamut of mutual subjugations, exploitations and deceit. Alter may make the right noises to reinforce ego's sense of worth because he needs him or wants something of him. The rather alarming disconnectedness between ego and his surrounding alters was demonstrated empirically, showing that the more superlative the laudatory terms used by ego to describe himself, the more derogatory the adjectives used to describe his behavior by the independent judges were in the experiment.[7]

The extreme *Atzmi*-skewed type, the ruthless manipulator of his environment and other people, very rarely weighs his behavior with internal measures. He is rather blind to ethical considerations and will probably be classified by clinicians as a psychopath. James Bond is probably the fantasied projection of the perfect separant activist who always manages to manipulate the elements, men and women (especially women), according to his needs and wishes. Yet even the most earthy activist and manipulator of the object is prodded and motivated by the opposite polar component of the self, however minute, which is structured within his personality. This might explain, for instance, why some very tough, down-to-earth and ruthless Jewish businessmen all over the world display an ethereal longing for Upper Jerusalem, and many times show a keen interest in the ideals of Israel and Jewish spiritual values.

The separant *Atzmi* type often has a hard time guessing the expectations of the relevant others. His whole being is centered on his ability to be attuned to the others around him, and to guess their expectations and intentions so that he is better able to manipulate them. However, intersubjective communication does not exist and the separant's social antennae may sometimes be blunt, his empathy erratic and his guesses unreliable. Consequently, the separant may often find himself in the position of a circus *jongleur* or a tight-rope walker who always has to adjust and readjust his precarious balance, otherwise he topples over with disastrous consequences. The separant must also develop a defensive self-deception as to the attitudes of the relevant others towards him, because they are the source and the anchor of his sense of worth. Max Nordau, in his brilliant but forgotten masterpiece, *The Conventional Lies of Our Civilization*, describes the *Atzmi* type as an ambitious artist and scientist who seeks reinforcement of his sense of choice by the highest separant authority of them all, the King of Men by the Grace of God. The good artist who just completed a *chef d'oeuvre* asks for nothing less than a visit to the king. From the supreme elation of creativity he plunges to the childish vanity that his art be recognized by the king. Yet he knows that the king understands nothing of his music, his painting or his sculpture. His ear is deaf, his eye is blind, his soul is closed to beauty. The king's aesthetic sensitivity is on the level of a Slovak vendor of rat traps and yet the artist's heart pounds with excitement when the king rests his absent-minded lead-grey eyes on his art or hears his music with polite patience.[8]

The king is replaced in modern society by other powerful *arbiter elegantiari* equally disinterested in the arts and sciences, yet the modern separant artists and scientists would do their utmost to gain their praise and approval. Many artists known to the author have manipulated the political power hierarchy of some municipalities in order to be awarded one of their art prizes. The artist would beam with pleasure and self-importance at the award ceremony. Moreover, after a while he would believe that the award was proof of his excellence and not the result of his political string-pulling. This patent self-deception of the separant *Atzmi*-skewed types stems from their vital need of approval from others, because it is the basis of their being. This might explain the hordes of camp followers, lackeys and flatterers surrounding every celebrity who needs the flattery to reinforce his sense of worth although he can see through it. The *Atzmi* type is also power hungry, because the feeling of power he can muster within an institutional setting also reinforces his sense of choice and brings him somewhat closer to his coveted inclusionary goal of being able to manipulate as many people as possible. *Per contra*, the participant *Ani* type is either bored or annoyed by power because he anchors on knowledge and not on power. He is immersed in his inner self and tries to relate himself *vis-à-vis* the absolute.

In a separant society, the pressures towards conformity are enormous and the rewards for compliance with the expectations of the power structure are an integral part of society's system of upper mobility. This accounts for the inner conflicts, black moods and sometimes outright depression suffered by the *Atzmi* type when he feels that his upper mobility is blocked by people in authority. His conflict is that he legitimizes their position and authority because being other-directed they are the natural source for reinforcing his sense of choice. However, one of the core parameters of his Atzmi type personality is that he tends to be extrapunitive, that is he blames others in case of frustration.[9] This resentment bind leads the *Atzmi* type to ambivalence towards the power elite, and to a petrifying conflict betweeen his all important sense of statistical excellence and the derogatory attitude of the relevant authoritative others.

It seems that for the *Atzmi* type separant activist, the temptation prodding him through the suppressed participant component of his personality is to seek failure. Such a seeking serves a dual purpose. First, the covert participant components of their selves identify with the dejected resignation of the losers and failures in the gutters. Second, after their retreatist fantasies and identifications have pacified their participant urges, they can revert back to their true selves and assert their worth by comparing their affluence and social status with the misery and squalour of the slum dwellers.

The need of the *Atzmi* type to be attuned to his relevant others in order both to comply with their expectations and to manipulate them, many times makes for a one-dimensional inner life. The separant culture heroes and success symbols often suffer an inner misery and squalor worse than the most deprived slum dwellers. Marilyn Monroe was driven to suicide by the constant need to comply with the image of a super sex bomb which seems to have been contrary to the inner grain of her personality core. Howard Hughes, the embodiment and fulfilment of the great American success dream, died of malnutrition surrounded by sterile boxes of Kleenex tissue and some empty boxes of "a great American ice cream". Elvis Presley, who more than anyone else symbolized the American pop music idol, died a junkie hooked on tranquilizers. That he gorged himself to death on hamburgers, another symbol of American culture, is a fitting irony.

In an achievement bound separant culture, failures are more vividly remembered than successes because fear of failure is even greater than the quest of success. In a separant society, there is no place for failure, and the sanctions for failures are relatively worse than the rewards for success. The achievement obsessed individuals are, therefore, equally motivated to either advance themselves or to bar others from succeeding. Both are a relative sign of worth and act as a reinforcement of their statistical sense of choice. The empirical anchors of this premise are, *inter alia*, that "the deterrence value for failure exceeds the attraction value of gains from success in affecting risk taking. People weigh negative aspects of an object more than its positive (ones)". "Potential losses exert more influence on gamblers' attractiveness than potential gains of the same magnitude". "Criticism affects us more than praise".[10] Kanouse explains these findings by our tendency to expect good experiences. When bad ones occur we are painfully disappointed, whereas when good things happen to us they do not deviate from our expectations and therefore do not upset us.[11]

We attribute less optimism to Man's *Weltanschauung*. Our explanation, in keeping with our general theoretical orientation in this volume, is quite different. We claim that our greater vulnerability to failure and negative experiences stems from their being part of our inevitable deprivational interaction with our environment, which characterizes the process of our developmental separation. This separant process is being forcefully imposed on us as a manifestation of our "thrownness unto death". Pleasant experiences are in keeping with our quest for participant bliss and hence do not disturb us, but negative experiences reinforce our ontological amiety because they constitute an empirical demonstration of our *Geworfenheit*. This is the reason for our very quick adjustment to pleasant experiences and our taking them for granted after a while. These experiences are built in, fulfilling partially our ontological quest. We are therefore attuned to accept them after a while as a matter of course. But a negative experience further deepens our basic sense of exile inherent in our deprivational interaction with our surroundings. This means that our negative experiences seem to influence our life in a positive feedback cycle much more than our positive experiences.

The classical experiments by Miller and Dollard, in which the avoidance curve proved to be much steeper and forceful than the approach curve, provides a partial support for the above premise. Consequently, the frustrating, separating forces of conflict, frustration and hence severance or lack of communication, which are either a corollary or a result of our painful relationships with people, dominates our life much more than the pleasant experiences of harmony and rewarding encounters with people. It seems that we are bio-psycho-socially "programmed" by our developmental processes more against than for interpersonal communication and dialogue.

The Miscommunicating Self

One of the basic tenets of our personality theory, which also underlies our present exposition, is that the goals of the interaction of any given individual at a given time and place are determined by the interplay between the opposing vectors within his personality as dialectically coordinated by his *Ity*, the personality synchronizer. The personality core vectors and their dialectical interplay differ from person to person. Consequently, at any given time or place, ego is bound to be attuned to a different communication pattern than the one to which alter is attuned. Also, the hold which the coordinating *Ity* has on the personality is quite precarious and volatile, so that even if it sets some course for ego's communication at a given instance it may be disrupted by a sudden jolt or subterranean pressure from one of the core personality vectors.

The socialization of ego, as well as his experience, changes him to the extent that he reacts differently to the same or similar stimuli. Consequently, the mutual expectations for communication at a given time or place change with socialization and experience. Usually socialization and experience "close" a person and narrow his openness for communication. This is so because socialization is mainly a separant process, which embeds the individual in a normative cocoon and isolates him within a mesh of social responsibilities. A child in his early developmental stages is more open and trusting, and is prompted by his more potent participant personality vector to seek immediate contact, encounter and dialogue with everything and every person around him. However, when his early innocence is gradually but inevitably raped by his experience and deprivational interaction with his environment, ego tends to be less and less attuned and amenable to spontaneous open and immediate communication.

The *Atzmi*-skewed self is not immersed in whatever he is doing, but glances furtively at the relevant others in order to guess their expectations so that he may adjust his own expectations and behavior to better achieve his separant goals. This, however, makes him totally dependent on the relevant others, their changing expectations and moods. As ego can very rarely guess with a fair margin of error the expectations and moods of alter, he usually treads on thin ice whenever he has to adjust his relationships with his surroundings, in line with the ever-changing inclusionary goals of his separant personality. And yet this adjustment to his surroundings is the essence of the *Atzmi*-skewed self. The lot of the *Atzmi* self is, therefore, much more precarious and labile than the greater stability of the *Ani*-skewed type who is anchored on his inner self.

One personality type is also prompted by the covert components of the opposite personality type within the self to seek, in fantasy at least, exploits which are in line with the vectors of these suppressed components. Thus Marcus Aurelius, the warrior king philosopher, writes stoic, meditative and self-effacing participant essays, whereas Nietzsche, the feeble scholar, dreams of the omnipotent superman. After bouts of activism, the separant type has an urge to "run away from all this and be alone", whereas the participant recluse would like to leave for a while his secluded hideout and spend some time in the urban turmoil "right in the midst of things when they happen".

We pointed out in the previous chapter that because ego twists the incoming stimuli in a manner peculiar to himself (determined by the bio-psycho-socio components of his personality which are bound to differ from the corresponding personality components of alter), there can be no common basis for dialogue concerning stimuli between ego and alter. These stimuli include the interpersonal perception between ego and alter. Here we shall add some additional barriers to communication and dialogue, which stem first of all from the different *Anschauungen*, expressing a central "executive directive" of the ego-control system, which shapes an adaptive solution.[12] This executive organization is mostly the function of our coordinating *Ity*, which sets different hierarchies of *Anschauungen* and different orders of priorities for each individual, so that communication becomes more difficult because it has to take place on different conceptual planes and different levels of encounter. Furthermore, each individual tends to twist, condense and selectively record events according to his specific socio-cultural *gestalt*.[13] As communication depends on memory, this differential recording of experience also impedes the chances of communication and dialogue. We have already mentioned that communication between the polar personality types is hardly possible, and whatever verbal communication takes place is usually misunderstood and twisted by both parties to the dyad. The *Atzmi*-skewed person cannot grasp the soaring inwards of the *Ani* type.

We may add that the covert opposite polar component within the structure of the dominant personality type may also hamper communication. A resigned self-effacing participant ego may thus suddenly burst into a fit of activist aggression, which may seem to alter to be out of context and indeed would be so that a barrier of embarrassment and even hostility may set in and cut off the encounter altogether. On the other hand, a usually outgoing, garrulous social mixer may be momentarily subdued by a sudden need for detachment and resignation, having the same effect of terminating the encounter and severing off any initial communication that might have taken place between ego and alter.

The Veiling of Emotions

Our emotions seem to influence our attitudes much more than we are willing to admit to others and especially to ourselves. Many studies assert that our affective responses precede our rational responses.[14] Man, the rationalizing animal, prostitutes his rationality to his emotions. After he complies with the prodding of his affects he musters his reason to justify, *post facto*, his emotion-based attitudes and decisions. However, similar facts, which presumably give rise to similar emotions, might have different effects with different people. For instance, bereaved parents in Israel whose son died in war are entitled to buy tax-free cars. Some parents buy these bargain cars and feel that their son continues to help them even after his death, whereas other parents feel that any material advantage gained by the death of their son is a profanation of his memory.

Emotions are notoriously hard to repress, yet some individuals are more adept in repressing them than others. However, these repressed emotions, when stored in the subconscious, have a tendency to erupt unexpectedly and unpredictably. These irrational emotional outbursts or coloration of attitudes are hardly predictable or understood by ego, and even less by alter. Consequently, these emotional effects on behavior and subterranean influence on attitudes confound any mutual prediction of behavior and attitudes in a dyad and contribute to the thickening of the barriers against communication and the severance of any encounter that has taken place.

There seems to be a fair amount of agreement in contemporary psychology following the work of Schachter and Singer, that emotion is a configuration between physiological arousal and psycho-social labeling by ego of the arousal as conveyed to him by his interoceptors and proprioceptors.[15] We may be aroused, for instance by alcohol and drugs, but the "high" we feel may be labeled by us as love or desire for the woman or man we happen to be with at the moment. If we are sexually aroused we may label this arousal as omnipotence. The classic Italian anecdote illustrating this premise is the priest counselling the poor peasant, who complained that he could not support his large family, to practice coitus interuptus so that he would not have any more children. "When the time comes my son", advised the priest, "you should retire so you would not have every year a baby". "But Padre", retorted the peasant, "when the time comes I feel I can support the whole world". In a similar manner, if people are artificially aroused without their knowledge they might infer that they had strong feelings about a person or a subject.[16]

The pioneering experiments by Schachter and Singer revealed that the physiological arousal of the subjects was disparately labeled, ranging from euphoria to anger depending on the external cues directed towards them, the physical setting, the social context and even the verbal instructions given to them by the experimenter.[17] Consequently, ego can feel his arousal but needs his surroundings to help him label the arousal. Alter, as part of ego's surroundings, may provide the cues for the labeling of ego's emotions, but he can have no first hand feeling of ego's arousal. The paradox here is that although ego and alter collaborate to create the bio-psycho-social configuration of ego's emotions they have no common basis for communication in relation to it. Furthermore, ego's cognitive processing of alter's cues is colored by his personality before he utilizes them to label his emotions so that they become a different product from the original cues transmitted to ego by alter. The result is that both ego's biological arousal and its psycho-social labeling are peculiar to ego's personality and are not communicable to others.

Ego's physical arousal is also dependent on many of his bio psychological parameters. These are, *inter alia*, higher and lower neural thresholds, and different neural vigilances (e.g. a doctor wakes up from the sound of the ringing telephone and his wife will wake up only if their baby cries). There are also different levels of optimal arousal for different people. We should also add here ego's hunger or aversion to stimuli as measured by Petrie's instrument (mentioned earlier) as an indicator for his higher or lower capacity for neural arousal. These and many other parameters place ego on one point on the bio-psychological arousal continuum. The chances of alter being on the same point, or on a point close to ego's, are quite meagre, as are their chances of reaching an emotional rapport. This is one of the reasons why we are so reluctant to accept advice given to us by others. Our stance is colored by our emotions, including the physical arousal transmitted to us by our intero and proprioceptors. Alter is not hooked to our interoceptors and proprioceptors and he cannot be aware of the tremendous pressure and affect that our bio-psychological state of arousal and our emotions as a whole have on our attitudes. If alter's advice is against our stance we *feel* (we wish to stress the emotional component) that "he doesn't understand". What we actually mean is that alter does not feel what we feel, which is undoubtedly true. However, we cannot separate our attitudes from their emotional coloring, and what seems to us a perfectly logical argument is many times a rationalization of our affective arousal. Our unwillingness to accept advice may be, therefore, more a measure of our lack of communication with our counsellor than a sign of our hard-headed stubbornness.

Emotions drastically change one's attitudes and states of mind. On the other hand, the constancy of emotions makes for constancy of moods and attitudes, even if the physical and social conditions have changed drastically. This is forcefully portrayed in Jack London's autobiographical novel *Martin Eden*:

> It was the first time in his life that Martin had travelled first class. On ships at sea he had always been in the forecastle, the steerage, or in the black depths of the coal-hold, passing coal. In those days, climbing up the iron ladders from out the pit of stifling heat, he had often caught glimpses of the passengers, in cool white, doing nothing but enjoying themselves, under awnings spread to keep the sun and wind away from them, with subservient stewards taking care of their every whim, and it had seemed to him that the realm in which they moved and had their being was nothing else than paradise. Well, here he was, the great man, on board, in the midmost centre of it, sitting at the captain's right hand, and yet vainly harking back to forecastle and stoke-hole in quest of the Paradise he had lost. He had found no new one, and now he could not find the old one.[18]

The application of the least interest principle is quite universal. As a simplistic rule of thumb, the more involved we are in a subject and the more aroused we are emotionally, the less intelligible we are to others. Emotions are the least structured and most subjective component of our attitudes and hence the least communicable. Consequently, the more emotional ego's attitude is, the less communicable it is to alter. Ego's intense emotional involvement makes him less predictable and also less able to manipulate effectively his environment. He becomes thus more exposed and more vulnerable to the vicissitudes of interpersonal interaction, and the emotional severance of encounter or relationship becomes altogether more imminent. If ego becomes cross with alter or decides not to have anything to do with him anymore, it is because of his emotional involvement with alter, and not because of the lack of it. Ego's emotionally loaded behavior is liable to unsettle and harass alter and make him avoid further contact with him. On the other hand, a relaxed non-involved ego makes a pleasant companion. This is one of the most painful paradoxes of human inter-action. The more emotionally involved ego is with alter and the more he longs for a dialogue with him, the less is he likely to achieve it. There seems to be a built in negative feedback cycle within the human psyche against a dyadic dialogue. This self-defeating mechanism is a special case of the least interest principle, which seems to be so universal that it could be a core dynamic of our personality. The more emotionally involved we are with a girl and the more ardently we woo her the less she is likely to be attracted to us. Sexual impotence is many times a combination of strong emotional attachment coupled with an equally strong fear of failure. The manager who is emotionally attached to his job might be too involved with the issues of employees and in this way create conflicts and management problems. The cool and sleek executive is more effec-tive because he is emotionally detached from his subordinates so that he can be more rational and objective. Our separant core personality vector seems to have ingrained in us a programming countering our core personality quest for emotional participation, rapport and dialogue. The separant "programming language" seems to be that if you wish to get your girl, be promoted, make a good bargain, or be a much sought after cocktail guest, one must be aloof and be detached. The second best way to achieve your separant goal is to disguise your emotions, but the best is not to have any. The longing for dialogue seems destined not be fulfilled. The quest for a rewarding dyadic encounter is a Tantalic *fata Morgana.*

Involvement and Interaction

They had started off on the wrong foot, not only when they had firstmet, but from the day they were born in their separate corners of the Universe.

Alan Sillitoe: *The Widower's Son*

Encounter and Discord

We discussed earlier that social norms are a separant by their very nature.[1] They engulf the individual in a mesh of proscriptions and barriers, and make for a structured formality of human interaction. These are bound to be in constant conflict with the participant longing of our inner self, for a total exposure and the melting of the partitions between ourselves and other people (some of them at least), so that a direct intersubjective dialogue ensues. Consequently, the strength of the social norms structuring and stereotyping the modes of interpersonal relationships is universally related to the depth of the encounter between people and the authenticity of the contact between them. This is presented schematically as follows:

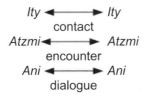

Figure 7.1   Separant social norms

The paradigm indicates that the more formal and socially structured the encounter is, and the more controlled and regulated it is by social norms, the shallower is it liable to be. The daily *Ity–Ity* contacts are the most formally regulated interactions, and any infringement of the normative distance between ego and alter in these impersonal routine contacts is sanctioned most severely. Ego, for instance, may stand in a bus near a very attractive lady dressed scantily in a thin summer dress. Noticing his furtive hungry glances she may even provoke him coquetishly and raise her arm to straighten a lock of hair thus lifting her bust line. If he smiles at her and tells her how beautiful she is, she is quite likely to freeze her smile and tell him to shut up. If he goes as far as helping her to stroke her hair she is liable to scream and call a policeman. Another normatively highly structured *Ity–Ity* relationship is between employer and employee. Georges Duhamel, in *Scène de la Vie Future*, describes an employee who brought some papers to his manager's office. The employee suddenly was seized with a desire to touch the manager's ear. When he did the results were disastrous.

The *Atzmi–Atzmi* encounter is characterized by a ritualized togetherness with formal initiation ceremonies, fairly strict rules of interaction, and an established yet mostly unwritten code of behavior. To be accepted by the boys, one need not necessarily be very good at one's professional or social vocation. Excellence is most likely to raise envy and hence a *resentiment* rejection of T.H. Lawrence and C. O. Wingate. To be accepted by the boys at the officers' mess, it is far more important to tell a good joke, order as many rounds of drinks as possible, and when walking, to throw one's legs loosely from the hip as befits the gait of an officer and a gentleman. Yet each member of the group expects it to be much more than a social meeting place, and he expects his friends to be more than drinking partners who appreciate his jokes. In this, he is in for a surprise. He becomes furious when his request for a loan from his "brother" in the masons' lodge, after he had some publicized financial difficulties, is politely but firmly rejected. He may also slump into a depressive despair when he is not invited to any more parties thrown by his dear buddies because his name was mentioned in a rather unpleasant scandal. Our poor solidarist *Atzmi*-skewed ego does not understand that he expected much more than his *Atzmi–Atzmi* encounter with the boys could ever offer.

The quest for an *Ani–Ani* dialogue is masterfully portrayed by Albert Camus in *The Misunderstanding.* Jan, the brother in disguise who returned home after a long time abroad, longs for a deeper rapport with Martha, his sister, who does not recognize him and plans to murder him for his money. Jan asks his sister, "isn't your life here a bit dull at times? Don't you and your mother find it very lonely?" But his approaches for a dialogue are curtly rejected by the sister who says:

> I decline to answer such questions. You had no business to ask them, and you should have known it. I can see I'll have to warn you how things stand. As a guest at this inn you have the rights and privileges of a guest, but nothing more. Still, don't be afraid, you will have every attention you're entitled to. You will be very well looked after and I shall be greatly surprised if you ever complain of your reception here. But I fail to see why we should go out of our way to give you special reasons for satisfaction. That's why your questions are out of place. It has nothing to do with you whether or not we feel lonely; just as you need not trouble yourself whether

you cause us inconvenience or ask too much of us. By all means stand upon your rights as a guest. But do not go beyond them.[2]

Jan tries again and beseeches his sister not to be so remote from him. "I beg your pardon", he says "Nothing was further from my intention than to offend you; I only wanted to show my good will. I had a feeling that we weren't quite so remote from each other as you seem to think; no more than that". But Martha puts him in his place. The roles of guest and innkeeper are clearly defined and one should not infringe the social norms which define each one to himself and the proper distance from others. Martha says:

> I can see I must repeat what I was saying. There can be no question of offending me or not offending me. Since you seem determined to adopt an attitude that you have no right to adopt, I prefer to make things clear. I can assure you I'm not in the least vexed. Only it is in our interest, yours and mine, that we should keep our distance. If you persist in talking in a manner unbecoming a guest, there is no alternative; we must refuse to have you here. But if you will understand, as I cannot doubt you will, that two women who let you a room in their hotel are under no obligation to treat you as a friend into the bargain, all will go smoothly.[3]

However, all does not go smoothly, because in the macabre setting of Camus's play any longing for a deeper encounter between human beings other than routine relationships is a *hubris*, which is liable to lead to disastrous results. The son then goes on to beseech his mother and sister, without revealing his identity, so that the element of the later surprise is not spoiled, to show some warmth to their lost son. He longs to regain the grace he has lost when he left the family fold. The mother is on the verge of giving in to her stranger son and allowing some grace to permeate into their relationship, but the sister cuts her brother short and catapults him back to the bleak realities of life. "Remember", she warns him, "you are in a house where the heart isn't catered to".[4]

They then carry out their plan to murder the son, which leads to their own death. But before she dies, the sister Martha hurls at Maria, her dead brother's wife, some harsh truths. "But before I go to die, I must rid you of the illusion that you are right, that love isn't futile, and that what has happened was an accident. On the contrary, it's now that we are in the normal order of things, and I must convince you of it". Maria replies, "What do you mean by that?" To which Martha says, "that in the normal order of things no one is ever recognized".[5]

The message of Camus' play, oozing through its blood curdling replicas, is that in the normal course of human interaction there can be no dialogue.

Inclusion of the Object and Exclusion of the Self

The main characteristics of our polar personality types are also apparent in the manner, direction and style by which they seek dialogue. The separant

Sisyphean *Atzmi* type aims to manipulate alter into a dialogue with him as pace-setter and senior partner in the dyad. The participant Tantalic *Ani* type wishes, on the other hand, to achieve dialogue even at the cost of giving up his personal preferences and comfort. In extreme cases, he is even prepared to degrade himself in order to reach the coveted encounter with alter.

The separant aiming to effect a dialogue by inclusion would mostly avail himself of projection, identification, and empathy in order to "win over" or "gain the heart" of alter, so that the encounter is conducted under his terms and according to his *mise-en-scène*. The participant, on the other hand, tries to intro-ject whatever actions or advances alter makes towards him. His ardent wish to partake with alter in a *dialogica* union induces him to impute an inner meaning for himself to alter's behavior.

All interpersonal relationships are based on a complementarity of give and take, which involves, according to Laing, "a definition of self by other and other by self".[6] In our context, it means that if ego and alter were both separant object manipulators trying to overwhelm each other through inclusion, they would soon find themselves in conflict and at each other's throats. In a like manner, two self-effacing participants both trying to reach each other through an effort to efface themselves and partake in the other are bound to be frustrated at the outset. If their relationship continues in a formal framework like marriage, they will soon start torturing themselves in an exclusionary fashion. Even if ego and alter do belong to opposite and hence complementary personality types, their complementarity has to be symmetrical in order to reach a mutually satisfying dialogue. This borders on the miraculous, and statistically its possibility of occurence is somewhere near zero. Consequently, most of the attempts to achieve dialogue are variations on the theme of Laing's following description which is rather extreme but none the less typical in its essence:

> Jack is potent. Jill is frigid. Jack does not want to ejaculate alone. It means nothing to him. Or rather, he feels he has been rejected. He wants to give her an orgasm. She does not want to be frigid because she would like to give him her orgasm; it would be a present. But if he forces her to have an orgasm it would be a defeat. He would have won and she would have lost. She would, however, like to be defeated, but he does not seem to be able to beat her. Meanwhile, if she is not going to come, he is damned if he is, so he now becomes impotent. It usually takes several years of marriage to arrive at this position, but some people can work through the stages in a few months.[7]

The interim summary of our present premise seems to be that the separant inclusionary efforts to reach a dialogue are bound to end in Sisyphean frustra-tion, and the participant longing for dialogue by self-exclusion is liable to lead to Tantalic despair.

Our quest of dialogue forms in us a set of expectations from our prospective partner in the dialogue. The more we are emotionally involved in the encounter (i.e. the deeper we wish the encounter to be), the greater our expectations from alter, as well as our anxieties as to the nature of his response. Consequently, we tend to perceive selectively both alter and his reactions to our quest for encounter in order to bring them nearer to our expectations. We also protect ourselves with perceptual defenses in order to reduce our anxiety in case alter's response does not seem to fit our expectations. We hypothesize that the more emotionally involved ego is in the encounter, the more he is liable to twist his perception of alter and augment his perceptual defenses against the anxiety as to alter's possible response.[8] However, the more twisted ego's perception of alter is, and the greater his perceptual defenses against alter's unfavorable response, the greater the likelihood is that a sudden or an unexpected turn of events will not allow ego to perceive alter selectively any more, or his perceptual defenses are not strong enough to gloss over alter's unequivocally negative or rude reaction to ego's overtures of dialogue. Then the veil is torn and ego sees alter "as he really is". The bitterness of ego's disillusion is proportional to his emotional involvement in the encounter with alter and his expectations from it. As the saying goes, "the higher one flies on the wings of drink at night the harder one falls on one's head in the morning after".

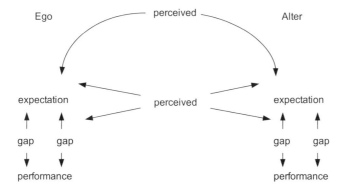

Figure 7.2 Gaps between expectations and performance

The possible disjunctures between the mutual expectations of ego and alter as to their depth of encounter is further complicated by the gap that many times exists between ego's expectations as to his own capacity for dialogue and his actual performance. A proverbial example is the Latin Lover whose promise of his heart, the moon and the stars is quite sincere when made, especially when kindled by guitars and tequila, but when the time comes to deliver the goods, the emotional reserves seem to be empty because most of them were spent on words, gestures and fantasies. Alter may also believe that he is capable of euphoric emotions and great love, but when the time comes he realizes that he is unable to take in so much emotion. He is overwhelmed by the intensity of the encounter, and consequently terminates it by escaping from it. The give and take aspects of the dyadic expectations are related to the separant active engulfing (taking) and the participant passive giving. The gaps between expectations and performance may, of course, be both in relation to the participant and separant components of the personalities of the parties to the dyad. To take account of this our model envisages dual cycles of disjunctions between the expectations of the parties to the encounter (figure 7.2, page 151).

The disjunctions between the expectations of ego and alter from the encounter, including the depth of it, are compounded by the gap between ego and alter's own expectations as to their potential for depth of encounter and their actual performance as perceived by themselves and by their partners to the dyad. This is why our model is not readily reducible to a computerized model of dyadic interaction like R E L A T E, which essentially envisages a single cycle of expectations and interactions within a dyad.[9] The implications of our dual cycles of expectations model to the possible disjunctions of communications within the dyad are crucial. There is an intrinsic difference between a Danish blonde in a bikini who smiles an open and wide smile at a Bedouin boy on the sea shore at Sinai, not knowing that her smile might be interpreted by the boy as an invitation for an amorous encounter, and an Israeli blonde clad in a similar bikini and smiling a similar smile but *knowing* the cultural context in which her behavior might be interpreted by the Bedouin boy. The Danish girl is not aware of the potential of her behavior, whereas the Israeli girl is aware of it. In the first possibility there is a rift between the expectations she transmits and her actual intentions, whereas in the second possibility there is a concordance between the transmission of expectations and actual intentions. However, in both cases the behavior of the girl was the same and the Bedouin boy is ill equipped to discern the actual intentions of the girls from their outward behavior. These are not hypothetical cases but an account of actual cases from police records following the amorous advances of Bedouin boys made at bikini clad girls.

The dual cycle model accentuates the pitfalls in the dyadic encounter, which are a combination of rifts between the expectations transmitted by the parties and their actual intentions and the gaps between the expectations as perceived by ego and alter.

One important aspect of the longing for a relatively deep level of encounter is the mutual desire of the parties for exclusiveness. This desire for exclusiveness and the accompanying jealousies is a proper measure for the intensity of the involvement of the parties in the encounter. Once ego or alter do not desire the dyad to be exclusive, their involvement in it is not so deep or is over altogether. This desire for exclusiveness also makes the parties neglect many of their other social and emotional liaisons so that when the encounter breaks down they find themselves in relative loneliness.

One important aspect of dyadic interaction which is relevant to our present context is Laing's development of the theme of confirmation and disconfirmation following Buber's exposition of "distance" and "relations".[10] Laing says:

> Thus, we can think of confirmation as partial and varying in manner, as well as global and absolute. One can think of action and interaction sequences as more or less and in different ways, confirmatory or disconfirmatory. Confirmation can vary in intensity and extensity, quality and quantity. By reacting "lukewarmly", imperviously, tangentially, and so on, one fails to endorse some aspects of the other, while endorsing other aspects. Modes of confirmation or disconfirmation vary. Confirmation could be through a responsive smile (visual), a handshake (tactile), and expression of sympathy (auditory). A confirmatory response is relevant to the evocative action, it accords recognition to the evocatory act, and accepts its significance for the evoker, if not for the respondent. A confirmatory reaction is a direct response, it is "to the point", or "on the same wavelength" as the initiatory or evocatory action. A partially confirmatory response need not be in agreement, or gratifying, or satisfying. Rejection can be confirmatory if it is direct, not tangential, and recognizes the evoking action and grants it significance and validity.[11]

Laing's treatment of the subject is uni-dimensional because he does not differentiate the need for confirmation according to the type of personality. The separant is more in need of outside confirmation to reinforce his sense of choice, whereas the participant anchors on his sense of inner uniqueness which needs less outside confirmation. Because the separant is more of a taker and the participant is more of a giver, a separant needs to "take" confirmation from his partner to the dyad who may induce the latter to lie and flatter him. This pseudo confirmation may nonetheless reinforce the separants sense of worth because it is dependent on outside confirmation. The separant's sense of choice and worth is liable to be inflated by the false confirmations of his partner to the dyad to grotesque or unbearable proportions so that ultimately the partner is bound to have enough of the "egocentric egomaniac", and the dyad is liable to be disrupted. Again, there is a built-in mechanism of disruption within a dyad, which operates more against the separant, who is more dependent for confirmation from his partner to the dyad, than the more self-sufficient participant. This need for confirmation, operating like a negative feedback cycle on a dyad, is another dynamic which seems to have a function of disrupting the dyadic encounter by augmenting the expectations of ego to dimensions which cannot be met by alter.

Sisyphean Inclusion

The separant aims to incorporate the object within his sphere of power and realm of control. Short of achieving this optimal goal he aims to mold and recreate the object in his own image. To cast wood, steel and clay in the structured frames of his ideas and his dreams, to educate children and implant them with his *Weltanschauung*, and to train disciples so that they spread the word and proselytize the uninitiated to embrace his ideas. The minimal aim of the separant is to reach out towards the object and achieve, at least, a subjective feeling or revelation of a dialogue with it. Merleau-Ponty echoes this quest for dialogue with the object when he says:

> When I glance at the objects surrounding me in order to find my bearings and locate myself among them, I can scarcely be said to come within reach of the world's instantaneous aspect. I identify here the door, there the window, over there the table, all of which are the props and guides of a practical intention directed elsewhere, and which are therefore given to me simply as meanings. But when I contemplate an object with the sole intention of watching it exist and unfold its riches before my eyes, then it ceases to be an allusion to a general type, and I become aware that each perception, and not merely that of sights which I am discovering for the first time, re-enacts on its own account the birth of intelligence and has some element of creative genius about it . . . [12]

This is also the goal of the Hasidic "worshipping in the concrete", when the Hasid aims to reach the sacred spark within the object and unite with it.[13] It is interesting to note that the Judaic traditional sources envisage a mental link between Man and object. For instance, the rules concerning finds and losses postulate that the finder of a chattel does not gain ownership of it unless there are reasonable grounds to assume that the original owner has lost hope of finding it again. The mental element of ownership here binds owner and chattel until it is severed by the owner. Not the physical possession but the spiritual umbilical cord between chattel and owner seems to be the essence of ownership in Judaism. The rules of conversion in the Talmud state that if someone steals wood and makes utensils out of it, or steals wool and turns it into clothes, he is liable to pay only for the value of the stolen raw material. The utensils and clothes become his because by changing the essence of the raw material and imbuing it through his work with his personality, he gains possession of the end product.

Separant inclusion in its extreme form aims to devour and swallow the object in the manner expounded by Melanie Klein.[14] The separant ego feels as if his possessions and whatever he owns or controls are included in the realm of his self.[15] This primary quest for separant object-cathexis, so heavily relied upon by Freud,[16] evolves into more vicarious and less direct forms of inclusion, like George Kelly's theory of Personal Constructs, which tries to project order and predictability on Man's surroundings and gain thereby a measure of control over it.[17] In science the intention of control and manipulation actually comes later. For example, the Manhattan Project utilized Einstein's breakthrough in theoretical nuclear physics and genetic engineering, which is bound to follow the recent discoveries of DNA transplants.

Failure of our inclusionary efforts may lead to a "sour grapes" rejection of the rebellious object. Sherif and his associates, for instance, demonstrated that if we cannot "stretch" a category to include a divergent object, we shall not only reject it but compress the range of the applicability of the category away from the divergent stimulus.[18] Freud hypothesized another alternative to the failure of a separant object-cathexis. If one has lost a "love-object", he said, "or has had to give it up, one often compensates it oneself by identifying with it".[19] We claim that identification is a participant exclusionary deference to a rule-setting figure. The mechanism described by Freud envisages the participant alternative of identification to a failure of a separant object-cathexis inclusion. It is a psychological resort to the folksy defense, "if you can't beat them join them".

Some empirical referents and measurements will serve, initially at least, as an anchor to our rather abstract theorizing on the processes of separant inclusion and participant exclusion. The Schutz FIRO-B scale enables one to determine the subjects being high or low in their orientation towards controlling others in their environment.[20] Consequently, those who described themselves as wishing to control others more than they wished to control themselves would be our inclusionary separants aiming to control their surroundings, whereas those who wished to control themselves more than others are more likely to be self-effacing exclusionary participants.

The measures developed by McClelland and Atkinson measure the strength of the achievement motive and may serve also as measures of the inclusionary tendencies of an individual to control, overpower and manipulate his environment.[21] The various measures of the affiliation motive, especially those based on the pioneering work of Schachter, might measure, initially at least, the self-effacing exclusionary tendencies of an individual to be accepted, praised, controlled, dependent or patronized by some relevant others and membership groups.[22] Some of the ingenious experiments of Exline on visual interaction provide us with an initial vindication of our inclusion–exclusion dynamic continuum. He praised his groups of subjects and asked them to look into each others eyes for seconds:

> A few seconds pass and some begin to fidget, others giggle, or unsuccessfully try to suppress laughter. Smiles and nervous grimaces can be observed, and though some pairs sit silently boring deadpan into each other's eyes throughout, many more break contact before the half minute is up.[23]

The subjective reports of the subjects ranged from a loss of the sense of self, which is precisely the aim of participant exclusion, to the awareness of the other, which is the reaching-out-towards-alter characteristic of separant inclusion. It is important to stress that a certain measure of complementarity between the subjects was needed to effect the subjective feelings of inclusion or exclusion. If ego aims to overpower alter and alter submits to him, ego can feel an "inclusionary awareness of the other" and alter feels an exclusionary "loss of the sense of self". Exline cites Sartre's dictum, "Either the other looks at me and alienates my liberty, or I assimilate and seize the liberty of the other", and brings Norman Mailer's following account of a battle of glances with an American Nazi:

> . . . They were interrupted by the insertion of the next prisoner . . . a young man with straight blond hair and a Nazi armband on his sleeve. He was installed in the rear . . . but Mailer was not happy, for his eyes and the Nazi's bounced off each other like two heads colliding . . . Standing in the truck, a few feet apart from each other, all prisoners regarding one another, the Nazi fixed on Mailer. Their eyes looked like magnets coming into line, and for perhaps twenty seconds they stared at each other. Mailer looked into a pair of yellow eyes so compressed with hate that back of his own eyes he could feel the echo of such hatred ringing . . . Mailer could feel violence behind violence rocking through his head. If the two of them were ever alone in an alley, one of them might kill the other in a fight – it was not unlike holding an electric wire in the hand . . . After the first five seconds of the shock had passed, he realised he might be able to win . . . now he could feel the hint of force ebbing in the other's eyes, and could wonder at his own necessity to win . . . the thought of losing had been intolerable as if he had been obliged not to lose, as if the duty of his life at that particular moment must have been to look into that Nazi's eye, and say with his own, " . . . you know nothing, my eyes encompass yours. My philosophy contains yours. You have met the wrong man". And the Nazi looked away and was hysterical with fury on the instant. "You Jew bastard", he shouted, "Dirty Jew with kinky hair".[24]

Mailer's vignette seems to be the living embodiment of Sartre's position. "Either the other looks at me and alienates my liberty . . . " wrote Sartre. "My eyes encompass yours. My philosophy contains yours", exulted Mailer as he sensed the Nazi giving way. Exline, and for that matter Sartre, disregard the all important dimension of complementarity. The Nazi was giving way because deep down his covert participant exclusionary inclination wished to give in to Mailer's inclusionary visual assault on him. This did not last very long and the Nazi regained his outer façade of a bully and hurled in a reaction–formation rage, anti-semitic curses at Mailer. We envisage, therefore, a two stage model of encounter in which the first stage necessitates an initial complementarity (i.e. that ego tends towards separant inclusion and alter towards participant exclusion, or vice-versa), otherwise no encounter will take place. The encounter breaks into conflict at the outset, or ego and alter avert their gaze from each other because both are participant or separant and thus have no complementary basis for encounter. Yet, even if they do complement each other in their polar personality types, there is bound to be a cognitive and affective distance between them related, as we have demonstrated earlier, to their different bio-psycho-social configuration. This is when the second stage sets in, and an illusion of encounter prompted by the complementary craving for it by the parties makes the partners to the dyad feel as if the gap between them closes. However, these illusions of encounter are also subject to the differences in the bio-psycho-social configuration of ego and alter. Consequently, even the illusions of encounter are bound to be fragmentary and short-lived. Our two stage model of encounter is presented schematically as follows:

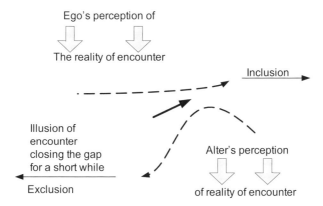

Figure 7.3 The illusions of encounter

The implications of our model are many. We claim, for instance, that Buber's miraculous short lived dialogue is precisely our illusion of encounter disrupted after a while by the separant pressures of reality.

The inclusion-seeking separant is basically an egotistic bully. He tends to attribute to himself actions of other people that are consistent with his interests.[25] Being an achievement motivated *arriviste*, he tends to attribute successes to himself and failures to others. In a separant achievement motivated society, successes seem to have many parents, whereas failures are orphans. A director of an institute known to the author, who is quite near to the extreme separant pole of our personality continuum, expects all the employees of the institute to behave like him. Whatever he does is the law. If he plays tennis all his subordinates have to play tennis, not only for their own well-being but for the better functioning of the institute. The employees have to imitate his eating habits and "to know how to eat well" as part of the ultimate good. If the guru hates somebody, his name should be anathema for everybody in the institute, and if he loves a person everybody should adore him. This demand for totality and exclusiveness inflated *ad absurdum* by the institute director is one of the main characteristics of separant inclusion.

Laing introduces his ingenious mechanism of collusion to describe a double play-acting, which according to him may serve as a basis for a lasting relationship.[26] We take issue with Laing's exposition because we claim, as we have explained in the presentation of our double-stage model of dyadic encounter, that ego and alter must be of opposite personality types, and hence complementary, in order to be at all predisposed to enter into a double illusion, which will award them a short-lived and make-believe encounter. Laing's disregard for this complementary predisposition to the dyadic encounter made him illustrate his argument with the wrong examples. Genet's play *The Balcony* does not portray "a game played by two or more people whereby they deceive themselves", but clients in a brothel who play-act and deceive themselves by being judges, bishops and generals, and those who do not deceive themselves at all but know exactly what they are doing for the money they get. We also expressly chose to denote the second make-believe stage of short encounter in our model as a double illusion because we do not believe in a prolonged collusion of self-deception. Again, Laing uses the wrong example. Sartre's *No Exit* has Garcin state "Hell is other people" as a sudden revelation, implying that the attenuating and comforting double or triple illusions cannot last long, and the illusory hopes for reciprocal understanding ever revert to the harsh realities of discord and alienation.

To conclude this part of our analysis, we point at a mechanism that, probably more than any other single factor, defeats the inclusionary aims of the separant. This is his lack of concern and interest in the objects he succeeded in achieving, and the people he managed to gain over. These are "in his pocket" so that he does not have to worry about them. He concentrates his efforts to win more assets, to subdue his adversaries and gain over to his side more dissenters. Eventually, he spreads his resources and efforts too thin and cannot control even the assets and people that were within his original fold. Finally, everything starts rolling down the slope, and in a true Sisyphean manner he has to run down the hill and start collecting his marbles all over again.

Tantalic Exclusion

The participant is gripped from time to time, and sometimes continuously, with a longing to extricate himself from the absurd and meaningless spatiotemporality, which for him sometimes loses its sense of solid reality and seems to waiver. In exclusionary moods, we keep looking with Proust for the graces of time lost, or seek to escape the discrete vicissitudes of time on the undulations of the Bergsonian *Durée Reel*. We suspend our frantic involvement in spatiotemporality with Husserl, and reveal ourselves to it without complicity (*ohne mit-zumachen*) and with a sense of wonder as paraphrased by Merleau-Ponty:

> Reflection does not withdraw from the world towards the unity of consciousness as the world is basis; it steps back to watch the forms of transcendence fly up like sparks from a fire; it slackens the intentional threads which attach us to the world and thus brings them to our notice . . . [27]

Finally, we may *crave* with Jack London's *Martin Eden*. We stress *crave* because there is evidence that Jack London's death from an overdose of morphine was a suicide, so that he might have projected his suicidal longing on the hero of his novel to annihilate the pangs of life by partaking in the archetypal womb of the ocean. Even if the ultimate goal of participation in the object and with other people is unattainable by definition, the process of exclusion often involves many times a liberation from the yoke of the generalized other, who exercises a big brother like external and internal control over our behavior. This liberation awards us many times with an exhilarating sense of freedom.

The participant bent on self-effacing exclusion is always apologizing in an intropunitive manner. He takes great pains not to be conspicuous. If somebody looks at him he quite often takes it as a cue that something is wrong with him. Many times he tends to project on alter his own self-effacement, so that even if alter was a separant and an initial complementarity could have facilitated an encounter, ego's projection makes him expect alter to be also self-effacing. If this does not happen ego tends to back away from the encounter in a depressive mood because he tends to blame himself for the failure of the encounter.

Exline's data on visual interaction provide us with a partial anchor for the exclusion behavior of the participant although Exline himself does not interpret his data in this manner. The less controlling subjects in the experiment, which would be our participants, gave significantly more visual attention to their dyadic partner in the experiment if the partner withheld his gaze from him.[28] This is the exclusionary quest of the separant participant to be controlled and accepted as a passive partner in the dyadic encounter.

Deprivational Interaction

The existentialist angst fear as inherent in the Heideggerean *Geworfenheit Zum Todt*, envisages anxiety and fear as an essential element of human interaction:

> Heidegger's bizarre use of the word "freedom" is rather misleading. What he actually means is that man is thrown into this world, and he is propelled in free fall towards an ontic certainty – his death. It is the freedom of one galloping down a steep road. One falls towards one's end without the cushions of comforts and illusory purposes because there aren't any. What remains, then, is a thrownness (Geworfenheit) propelled towards annihilation with the accompanying moods of amiety and despair. This grim freedom is expounded by Heidegger with characteristic teutonic heaviness in the following words: "anticipation reveals to Dasein its lostness in the they-self, and brings it face to face with the possibility of Being-Itself, primarily unsupported by concernful solicitude, but of Being-Itself, rather in an impassioned freedom towards death – a freedom which has been released from the illusions of the "they" and which is factical, certain of itself and anxious."[29]

It is interesting to note that Sullivan, who based his psychological orientation on interpersonal relationships, regarded anxiety as the prime mover of human interaction. This lends an existentialist hue to Sullivan's psychology. Indeed, our personality core model regards the deprivational interaction of the developing ego with his surroundings as the main characteristic of human existence. The newborn is catapaulted from blissful self-sufficiency in the womb to the strife, pain and conflict outside it. Sometime in the middle of the oral stage, the infant is expelled from the pantheistic, omnipresent early orality to form a weak separate self, which is harrassed by objects and people around him. Finally, at puberty the youth is initiated by cruel and painful rites of passage into the burdens of responsibility, and thrown out of the forgiveness of the family fold into the loneliness of adulthood.[30]

We hold that the amiety, pain and fear inherent in ego's deprivational interaction with his surroundings constitute factors that impede and hamper his dyadic relationships with alter. Festinger and Schachter have shown that ego's affiliative tendencies are a function of his insecurity in his relationship with the object and a general amiety concerning his motivations.[31] In our context, this means that ego's exclusionary self-effacing and emotional ability induces him to seek refuge by affiliation with a protective separant type. Yet his fear from interaction prevents him from carrying out his intentions. Eventually this fear, coupled with his exclusionary wishes of affiliation, lands ego within the petrifying clutches of an approach–avoidance conflict. On the other hand, a separant ego bent on inclusion within an achievement bound culture is trained to be fearless and suppress his amiety. The ideal of the western hero and executive is a "fearless, cool operator". However, fear and amiety are defense mechanisms against the dangers inherent in ego's interaction with his surroundings. His fearlessness in the wrong place and time might expose the separant ego to the dangers of his deprivational interaction with his surroundings, and in a Sisyphean manner his inclusionary efforts to overpower the object are frustrated, accompanied perhaps by injuries to his status and personality. Freud writes in his autobiographical study:

> Only a few instances on the expression of anxiety in infancy are intelligible to us; we shall keep to these. Thus, the three situations of being left alone, being in the dark, and finding a strange person in place of the one in whom the child has confidence (the mother), are all reducible to a single situation, that of feeling the loss of the loved (longed-for person). From this point forwards the way is clear to an understanding of anxiety . . . anxiety thus seems to be a reaction to the perception of . . . separation from a highly valued object . . . The most basic anxiety of all . . . arises in connection with separation from the mother.[32]

All three cases of anxiety mentioned by Freud are but instances of the basic deprivational interaction of the developing self with his surroundings. Moreover, for us amiety is not only a corollary of separation from the beloved object (i.e. the mother or her surrogate), but constant fear from any further developmental separation. These developmental separations are the "thrownness" of birth, the expulsion from oral pantheism and the painful rites-of-passage from the family fold to the loneliness of adulthood, all of which are invariably registered by the growing self as catastrophes. This is why basically Man has a built-in fear of change, because he has been conditioned by his developmental traumas that all changes were for the worse as they augmented his deprivational interaction with his environment. Another major source of amiety is ego's fear that he is not making as much progress towards partaking in the object and towards as deep an encounter with others as he expected. Consequently, anxiety dominates Man's deprivational interaction with his environment both inanimate and living. The centrality of amiety in our conception of human interaction is as basic as the concept of *Angst* in Heidegger's philosophy of Man. It is in keeping with our conception of the centrality of amiety in human interaction that the proven most forceful reinforcer of human behavior is the reduction of amiety.

The conflicts, clashes and frictions between ego's longing for participation with the object, and his separant developmental reaching outwards constitute the pain and misery of his deprivational interaction with his surroundings, which has been depicted in literature and drama as the rape of innocence by life. This was summarized by Kazantzakis in Zorba the Greek's aphorism that, "to live means to look for trouble".

Indeed, the prevailing folksy convictions, experiences and philosophy are that human life is a continuous chain of misery and squalour sparsely spaced by occasional short lived sparks of pleasure. Religions, both theistic and secular, have readily profited from Man's anxious "thrownness-unto-death" by offering him a blissful ever-after and the millenium of Utopia provided he follows their body of dogma. This exploitation of Man's misery by false promises with him as a willing victim is one of the most sinister corollaries of his deprivational interaction with his surroundings. Further, the belief voiced by some advocates of social welfare and progress (whatever that means), that human interaction becomes less harsh and mellowed in the course of history is thoroughly unfounded. More people have died violent deaths and suffered hideous torture in the twentieth century than in any other century.

Man's extant deprivational interaction with his environment usually makes him expect "problems" from people he is dealing with. If these are pleasant and accommodating he might be taken by surprise, and momentarily at least, he is liable to be disoriented. But if the environment feels hostile, ego, especially if he is separant, is bound to feel that he is in his element. Whenever Theodor Herzl, the founder of Zionism, felt antagonism from the people he had to convert to the cause, which was most of the time, he worked himself into a rage so that he mustered enough energy and eventual composure for the ensuing battle of wits.[33]

One of the most painful paradoxes inherent in the deprivational interaction among human beings is embodied in the saying that "familiarity breeds contempt". The scenario being that ego longs for a deeper encounter with alter.

When he feels (most of the time erroneously) that he achieved this longed-for encounter, he may feel free to treat alter and especially express himself towards him without reservations or reins.[34] This eventually is bound to hurt alter and indeed breed contempt, which cools the dyadic relationship and eventually disrupts the encounter. Similarly, when ego is so sure of alter's loyalty and affection that he hardly pays attention to him, this may also breed contempt and ultimately disrupt the encounter. The self-defeating element in human interaction is that the closer and deeper individuals wish their encounter to be, the greater the chances are of its disruption.

Creative Involvement

Nietzsche envisaged the creative process as a dialectic interplay between two opposing personality components.[35] Although our personality types are totally different from Nietzsche's Dionysian and Apollonian duality both in form and content, we also envisage creativity as the cathexis towards the object. We denote the dialectic product of the interplay between the Sisyphean and Tantalic components of the self as the Tantalus Ratio.[36] Man's need to grapple with the continuous conflicts of the polar core components within his self when structured logically, intuitively or aesthetically in his relationships with objects, flora, fauna and people, constitute the essence of creativity. As the dialectical tension necessary for creativity needs our two vectors to interact conflictually with varying amounts of force, one vector should not be overwhelmingly more potent than the other. The extreme *Ani*-skewed self, for instance, has to immerse into his inner self to interact aesthetically with his surroundings. *Per contra*, the extreme *Atzmi* separant lacks the ideational inner depth in his relationship with the object so that his creativity is bound to be shallow. The extreme *Ani* participant, even when creative, has difficulties in distinguishing between himself and the outside world, so that his creativity tends to be more of an autistic delusion than a structured creation. On the other hand, the extreme separant activist is exclusively concerned with overpowering and "swallowing" the object. Because he has no wish to interact with it aesthetically, the range of the separant's creativity is bound to be narrow. The separant's creation tends to be more cerebral, whereas the participant's creativity is more intuitive. In drama, for instance, the dramatic tension is related to the dialectic interplay between separant and participant conflicts. Growth and decay, mastery and submission, salvation and annihilation, the quest of encounter and dialogue, and the tragic breakdown and absurd despair, are good examples of such conflicts. Indeed, the artistic triumphs of some of Bunuel's and Bergman's movies is in their superb dialectic interplay between beauty and ugliness, love and hate, growth and decay, God and the Devil, life and death.

Creativity feeds on ego's craving to seek union with the object and the latter's reluctance or inability to oblige him. Whatever ego's expectations from the object may be, separant–inclusionary or participant–exclusionary, his Sisyphean or Tantalic dialectical involvement with it is the kindling fuel of creativity. A contented complacent ego in slumbering peace with himself is rarely creative. One often hears creative people declare that they "need to recharge their batteries". This usually means that they need a new love affair, or they want to meet new and "exciting" people, "let themselves go" on an African safari, or they long for some new revelations while journeying into the inner selves. These would replenish the interacting personality core vectors with new dialectical vigour and enable ego to resume his creativity.

The relevant dynamic in creativity is the conflictual interplay between ego's idea or construct, and its execution through an inclusionary or exclusionary involvement with the object. Our conception of creativity as a dialectical object involvement is, therefore, not very different from the structuralist's conception of art as the relationship between the projected human thought on an object and the design-contents of the ensuing artifact or work of art. A recent structuralist interpretation of the paintings on the Sistine chapel ceiling states as follows:

> I assume that any human creative act starts out as a mental operation which is then projected onto the external world. These projections can take all sorts of manifest forms; they include speech utterances, written texts, functionally useful material constructions such as houses and bridges, performative constructions such as plays, ceremonials and religious ritials, and purely symbolic material objects such as carvings, paintings and so on. All such creations are "designed" by the creator; they have a structured order which, in part at least, is built into the product intentionally. In some respects the structure of such human creations is determined (or at least delimited) by the nature of the object and by the materials of which it is made. For example, in the case we are to consider, the Sistine Chapel and its very awkward vaulted roof already existed before Michelangelo set to work on it. Comparably, when an architect designs a house, there has to be feedback between his mental operations, the requirements of his clients, and the limitations set by what is technically possible . . . "[37]

This similarity between the structuralist and our conception of creativity is not random because structuralism, as expounded by Claude Lévi-Strauss, is very much concerned with ego's involvement with the object by projecting his mental constructs on it.[38] Our quest of creative involvement with the object also entails the projections of our expectations on it.

The creativity of the participant is marked by revelations through misery and exclusionary renunciations. Gauguin and Van Gogh renounced the separant bourgeois havens of security, money and status, while Petrach and Kierkegaard renounced their hoped for nuptial love. Such creative revelation through the exclusionary renunciations of one or more aspects of worldly existence should not be confused with the "romantic agony". This is mostly supplied as a consumer good for vicarious identification with the trials of a fictional hero. After the movie or the weekly installment of the serialized novel the housewife goes back to cook her dinner and the salesgirl resumes her place behind the counter, their eyes aglow and their cheeks radiating freshness from the bath of tears. The psychological mechanism here is that the subdued participant vector acting as an "internal saboteur" and having visions of glory amidst apocalyptic annihilation, induces the separant ego to dream of the partaking in a romantic agony so that the vicarious experience may release some of the tension generated by the repressed craving of the participant internal saboteur. This is not unlike many of us watching a crime movie or reading the exploits of our favorite private eye. Our repressed aggression and deviant tendencies identify subconsciously with the "bad guy", cleansing ourselves thereby of our pent up anti-sociality.

The participant component in the creator's self provides the revelatory element in the act of creation. It is the moment of "dawning" when it comes to the artist that a certain idea of his can be structured into a work of art. The creative revelation sprouts forth from the participant dynamic of the personality core and interacts dialectically with the separant component of the self to mold and to present the creation to the outside world. This need for an audience seems to be inherent in the process of creativity. Even the reclusive Nietzsche-Zarathustra, who gorged himself on the rarified heights of revelation, confessed to the need to descend to Man and share with him his wisdom:

> When Zarathustra was thirty years old, he left his home and the lake of his home, and went into the mountains. There he enjoyed his spirit and his solitude, and for ten years did not weary of it. But at last his heart changed – and rising one morning with the rosy dawn, he went before the sun, and spake thus unto it:
>
> Thou great star! What would be thy happiness if thou hadst not those for whom thou shinest!
>
> For ten years hast thou climbed hither unto my cave; thou wouldst have wearied of thy light and of the journey, had it not been for me, mine eagle, and my serpent.
>
> But we awaited thee every morning, took from thee thine overflow, and blessed thee for it.
>
> Lo! I am weary of my wisdom, like the bee that hath gathered too much honey; I need hands outstretched to take it.
>
> I would fain bestow and distribute, until the wise have once more become joyous in their folly, and the poor happy in their riches.
>
> Therefore must I descend into the deep; as thou doest in the evening when thou goest behind the sea, and givest light also to the nether-world, thou exuberant star!
>
> Like thee must I go down, as men say, to whom I shall descend . . . [39]

The raw unstructured revelations or emotions are totally incomrnunicable. *In extremis*, they may be likened to the shrieks and groans emitted by Antonin Artaud in front of an audience in a theatre especially invited for his "performance".

The extreme separant artist is totally attuned to his customers-masters in the audience, in order to cater to their artistic tastes as he perceives them. His work is planned, structured and programmed according to the latest market research as to the modal whims of the public. The extreme participant artist, on the other hand, lets the revelatory dreams and longings gush outwards in uncontrolled outbursts. His creation is quite likely to be misunderstood and rejected by the public. The artist himself is also liable to be stigmatized and encounter the resistence against innovators suffered by them from time immemorial. As a wild hypothesis, we may offer our hunch that the great contemporary artistic successes are a separant catering for the public taste. The taste includes its faddish quest of novelty spiced by some smatterings of participant authenticity, to give the public a feeling of elation as it lifts itself temporarily by its own bootstraps from the quagmire of the commonplace. The hypothesis does not apply, of course, to the creative innovations which withstand the faddishness of a given time, and proved their durability outside the vested interests of a given place.

Prima facie art seems to be a prime medium of communication. Yet, the music conceived and created by the composer is bound to be perceived differently by each individual depending on his mood and his psychosocial configuration at a given time and place. The constructs projected by the creator and incorporated in the work of art are not likely to be shared by the perceiver. The latter is bound to perceive the work of art selectively, colored by his perceptual biases and the projection of his mental constructs. The paradox lies in the dynamic we have mentioned earlier, namely that the participant component of the self lends the artist the sense of authentic immediacy towards his creation, yet this component of the inner self is the least communicable. On the other hand, the wide promotion and commercial success of a work of art depends on its being attuned to the broadest common denominators of the public taste. These are catered for by the interactive, separant, public opinion bound efforts of the artist, which he incorporates in the work of art to enhance its circulation and sales value. Consequently, the more authentic a work of art is and the more it is a sincere expression of the artist's inner self the less is communicable. The elegiac result is that creativity, which is the prime expression of man's uniqueness and inner self, is least communicable when it is most true to itself.

The Absurd Revisited

We envisaged the Absurd value breakdown as a failure of involvement with objects and people. Our deliberations there lacked depth in some areas and suffered some lacunae, which we have tried to provide in the present work. Before proceeding to the next chapter we shall take time to summarize our position *vis-à-vis* the ideas set forth in this text.

First, we introduced the three levels of encounter sought by ego with the object and other people ranging from mere routine contacts to dialogue to the quest for inner-core union.

Second, we provided a whole bio-psychological theory to account for ego's quest for deep encounter with the object and others.

Third, we expound the full-fledged dynamics of the inclusionary process, by which ego tries to bridge the rift between himself and the object by overpowering or controlling it, and the process of exclusion through which ego aims to efface himself and partake in the object.

Fourth, in case of a cognitive dissonance between previously internalized information and new dissonant experience, the separant would try to twist, in an inclusionary manner, the perception of the incoming information so that it fits his previously internalized experience; whereas the participant would try by self-effacing exclusion to adjust his previous information to the contradictory new experience.

Fifth, we hold that ego's efforts to achieve a deep encounter with the object or with people cannot be fully realized because ego's expectations for the form, contents and depth of encounter on his terms are going to conflict with alter's sense of choice and ontolological uniqueness, and his terms for encounter. Further, an exact complementarity between ego's separant quest for inclusion and alter's participant longing for exclusion, which is a condition precedent for a perfect encounter, are statistically so remote as to be practically non-existent.

In the following chapter we shall try to trace some of ego's efforts to communicate with other people, and the modes of the frustrations of these efforts.

Personality Type
The Medium Controlling
the Message

The extreme separant personality type tends to be authoritarian in so far as he legitimizes people in authority and their actions because he tends to utilize, if he can, the authoritarian institutions to achieve his expansive separant aims. He might not be infatuated with power, but being a manipulator he knows its instrumental value, so that whenever he can he will try to find himself on the right side of power. The separant's chase after property, money, power, social status and the external rituals of one-upmanship is an expression of his separant wish to extend the realm of his personality over as many objects and people as possible. The author heard one of the right-wing members of the Knesset in Israel expounding his view that the occupied territories should not be given back to the Arab states. He described his relationship with the land of Israel and its soil as being "part of his body" and giving some of it away like "cutting off of a limb".

The separant ego, whose sense of choice can be reinforced only by signs, facts or events indicating his successful manipulation of objects, always needs to inflate his sense of worth by more things, more status symbols and more power over people. Indeed, his need to inflate himself is directly related to the poverty of his participant inner self. The separant scientist and artist tend to be eclectic, trying to include as many topics, issues and concerns within his research or art. All means are justified to serve the separant's expansive aims: power politics in academia, intrigue in art circles and plagiarism if he thinks that he can get away with it. The separant ego, who is very much attached to spatiotemporality, tends to be a physical coward because to expose himself to danger would threaten his wordly possessions as well as his ability to use them. The separant also finds it very difficult to live by himself. He always needs company, more people and a larger audience because he is under the (erroneous) impression that everybody has the same or a similar interest in his experiences as his own egocentric preoccupation. Naturally, the separant ego would have little to say to the participant alter, whose sense of ontological uniqueness is reinforced by inner awareness, and whose interest in knowledge and art is through their significance to his quest for the "Absolute", and whose constant prodding into his *Ani* and inner self makes him very often oblivious to other people and his own animal comfort and well-being.

The separant looks for the place where the action is, but being stimulus hungry he usually feels that he is not getting enough action. Also, the action almost never seems to take place where he is at the moment, but in other places, so that he is almost constantly and frantically looking for these places. The participant, on the other hand, feels that the blue bird must be somewhere between the porch he is sitting on and the synapses of this brain. He is harassed by outside stimuli, which are always too many for his comfort. Travelling is a chore and he expects the world to come to him if it needs him. A Diogenes sits there contemplating in the sun even if an Alexander is around, and a Heidegger expects his visitors to climb to a secluded hut on top of the Black Forest Mountains, not out of megolomania, but because with the participant the discourse with himself comes first and only then, quite far removed, comes the outside world.

The problems of communication encountered by the participant type are because he wishes to be consistent with his inner self, but also to be accepted by his relevant others. This is impossible, because his sense of ontological unique-ness cannot be shared nor understood by other people. It is the dilemma of the outsider who wants to remain an outsider, and yet be accepted by the pace-setters and power elites of the various groups in society. If he wishes to remain true to his inner self he may renounce the approval of others *à la* Kierkegaard and all his cosy social affiliations like Camus's judge-penitent. To get along in society, he must go along with the small talk of cocktail parties, be a pillar of the community, sit as a member of the local chamber of commerce and serve as deputy-secretary of the annual charity ball. The participant's predisposition to be a social outsider, and his suppressed separant vector's dreams to be the local nice guy, loved by all the boys in the bar, is a typical internal saboteur constel-lation pregnant with intrapsychic and interpersonal conflicts.

The separant ego tends to judge and evaluate alter by his wealth, power, social position and group affiliations. Alter, as a person taken out of his social context and roles, is of little interest to the manipulative ego. Yet, even the most sophisticated and otherwise shrewd alter in a position of power is be vulnerable to the separant ego's flattery and manipulative deception that he is interested in an encounter and discourse with him as a person. Alter's selective decoding of ego's messages, and in extreme cases, his downright self-deception, is induced by his need to reinforce his sense of choice. Being a separant power manipu-lator, alter tends to identify and hence confuse his social roles and his person. The separant ego's attunement to his relevant others tends to make him a reactor and a responder to the expectations of these others. He is more of a joiner to an established institution or movements, in order to manipulate them from within. The inventors of the idea or the initiators of the movement tend to be participant innovators and outsiders. There are usually conflicts and a lack of communication between the ideological pioneers who start a movement and the manipulating "apparatchicks", who take over once the movement is established and the project becomes a going concern.

We have provided many illustrations of our premise, that a discourse between a separant ego and a participant alter is rife with obstacles and barriers. However, a disconnection of a discourse and a disruption of an encounter may be related to an *ad hoc* or continuous discord between the personality core vectors of ego or alter, or both. Ego, for instance, may initiate an encounter with alter through the prodding of his separant vector, but then the repressed participant vector may take over the initiative, or rather the lack of it, and sever the encounter. This sudden upsurge of the opposite personality vector in a dynamic, which we have described earlier as the internal saboteur constitutes a built-in programming for disrupting interpersonal communication. The internal saboteur within the personality is an over repressed personality vector that surges out when the dialectic interplay between the opposing vectors within the personality permits it, and plays havoc with the person's behavior and personality dynamics as determined by the predominant vector within the self. Consequently, if the separant ego starts an active involvement with alter and the relationship, as viewed from ego's angle, develops into a frantic pace, ego's subdued participant vector induces him to make a counterproductive move, which will cease the frantic involvement of ego or induce alter to sever the encounter and thus pacify ego, temporarily at least, into a relatively passive state in line with the participant vector's aims. On the other hand, a participant's ego's meditative concentration on an object or a longing for a deep exclusionary encounter with alter may be disrupted by the sudden outburst of ego's subdued separant vector into an explosive bull-in-a-china-shop activity.

Apart from the subjective decoding of emotions by ego, he also tends to react emotionally to alter. Ego's attitudes towards alter are imbued with emotions, even if he may not think so, and emotions are not only subjective and scarcely communicable, but they change with each of ego's moods. A separant ego more than a participant ego, will tend to rationalize his emotions and moods and believe that his attitude towards alter is objective and logical, yet this in itself constitutes an additional barrier to dyadic communication. Moreover, ego tends to perceive his own social role as well as alter's role in a subjective manner. Consequently, when ego tries to discover the real alter behind his social roles and appearances, he projects his own subjective interpretations of these roles on him, and expects him to comply with them which alter is naturally unable to do. This constitutes another blocking dynamic, which may both twist and disrupt dyadic communication. The subjectivity of attitudes makes it difficult for ego to convince alter of the logic and veracity of his point of view, especially if they are of divergent personality types. The selectivity of perception, the differences of accentuations both formal and content-wise and the divergent vested interests make for equally credible, even if diametrically opposite presentations of the same facts by ego and alter. With the proper touches of psychopathy or hysterics, ego, alter or both will even believe à la Rashumon, in their own lies. One may encounter a similar phenomenon in courts of law, where the parties and their lawyers present their cases in a very often equally credible manner. This reminds us of the following Jewish anecdote. A Rabbi hears the pleadings of the parties to a case. The plaintiff presents his version and the Rabbi tells him, "I think you are right". When the respondent presents his version of the facts the Rabbi reacts by saying, "It seems to me that you are also right". Then the Rabbi's wife comes out indignantly from the kitchen and reproaches her husband, "How can they both be right if each one says the complete opposite of the other?" "You know what", the Rabbi replies, "I think that you are also right". We claim that the inevitable subjectivity of perception of facts and attitudes lends a rather realistic hue to this anecdote.

Laing points out that a fair part of our behavior is based on pretence.[1] As pretence is by definition a façade, which caches ego's non-pretentious intentions and motivations, alter cannot usually see through ego's pretences, especially if ego is a good actor. More complicated are the cases in which ego believes in his own pretences, so that any hint by alter questioning the authenticity of ego's presentation of himself will be rejected by ego with a reaction–formation furor.

Elusion in Laing's terms is an introjection of a fantasy and imputing reality to it.[2] Through this double fantasy ego not only believes in his illusions, but acts as if they are real in their consequences. Ego may project his elusions onto alter and expect him to comply with them or at least to react to them, but alter has no way of recognizing ego's illusions and certainly not their recycling as elusions.

Collusion, as denoted by Laing, pertains to alter's readiness to confirm ego's pretences.[3] There is, however, no communication or dialogue here because ego uses alter for a consideration, to play-act as if he confirms his fantasies. The prime example of collusion presented by Laing is in Genet's play *The Balcony*. The whores there are paid to comply with and cater to their clients' fantasies of being judges, generals and bishops, but they themselves have no illusions about their clients or about themselves. The relationship between the false judge, phoney bishop, fake general and the whores is not a dyadic encounter but a purchase of a commodity – a temporary illusion. When the characters in Sartre's play *No Exit* try to reach a collusionary concord with each other they fail because each one wants the other to reinforce his own illusion but is not prepared to reciprocate. Collusions in real life are rarely consummated, and when one has a temporary illusion of having reached a collusionary dyad the illusion is usually brusquely terminated by a harsh awakening. The Madame of the whore house in *The Balcony* sends the audience, at the end of the play, to their homes where life is even more phoney than in the brothel.

Illusions, elusions and in many instances collusions are formidable barriers to communication, because ego has almost no means to surmise alter's fantasies and alter can rarely have access to ego's illusions. Laing, in the appendix of his book *Self and Others*, provides some symbolic models for dyadic communication and miscommunication. We prefer to envisage dyadic miscommunication within the following paradigm of disparities of expectations between ego and alter as to their desired level of encounter:

Expected level of encounter by ego	Expected level of encounter by alter		
	Ity	Atzmi	Ani
Ity	X	Uncouthness	Assault
Atzmi		X	Nuisance
Ani			X

Figure 8.1   Dyadic miscommunication in expectations between ego and alter

Ego is bound to judge alter's behavior as uncouth and gauche if he expects a routine *Ity–Ity* encounter and alter responds with an *Atzmi* level familiarity. This happens when ego (a woman) asks for some information from alter, a telephone operator, who starts flirting with her and asks her for a date. If while sitting by herself in a coffeehouse, ego greets a male patron who interprets her friendly smile as an invitation to join her (and in no time gives her a kiss), ego will scream and call the police. The third instance of miscommunication may occur when a playboy-about-town invites a girl for an evening of wining and dining. If in the morning she declares her eternal love for him and her matrimonial intentions he is bound to add an "N" for nuisance beside her name in his telephone notebook and decide never to see her again.

Miscommunication may be intentional, and ego may wish to deceive alter. Depending on the situation and ego's proficiency in inhibiting, simulating and faking information, he may be fully or partially successful in convincing alter of the veracity of the falsehoods he is presenting to him. Even if the deceiving ego emits what Ekman and Friesen call "deception clues and leakage" (some telltale items in ego's behavior revealing his intentions of deceit), ego's "real" intentions are not disclosed to alter. This is because, as Ekman and Friesen rightly note, deception clues in ego's behavior tip alter off that deception is in progress but do not reveal to him the concealed information.[4] A very common form of deception is what Goffman calls Mystification.[5] Ego may surround himself with an aura of secrecy and drop hints and obscure allusions about his person and occupation, so that alter himself would make the deceptive inference without ego expressly stating it. The author has encountered many instances of successful deception by mystification, two striking examples in particular. One was an army filing clerk who managed to convince his civilian friends and acquaintances that he was engaged in top secret intelligence work by dropping nonsense syllables within the context of stories about elaborate espionage schemes. This gave the impression that the nonsense syllables were technical terms relating to intelligence work. When asked whether he was engaged in intelligence, the person denied it vehemently and added with an all-knowing smirk that he was just a filing clerk. This seemingly outward upholding of his "cover" strengthened his audience's conviction that the filing clerk was a master spy. Another instance was that a president of an American scientific organization who used to hint vaguely about his landed Irish ancestry and his ties with the IRA. The truth was that he grew up in a Tel Aviv suburb in an Eastern European Jewish family.

Ego may also surround himself with Byzantine layers of deceit because he has been caught in a vicious circle of lies. One lie needs another to present detection, and a third one to gloss over the deception clues of the second lie, and so on in a geometrical progressions *ad infinitum*. Lies may also twist and encumber communication, even though they were intended to protect or help their recipient. One such instance known to the author was the case of a husband who tried to protect his sick wife by concealing the fact of their married daughter's death in a car accident. This necessitated a formidable maze of lies to account for the daughter not visiting her mother. The husband's well meaning lies to this wife further complicated communication between them and added additional burdens to their strife ridden life.

Cultural Barriers to Communication

Different cultures attune the individuals socialized in them to experience different segments of their environment.[6] Consequently, individuals from different cultures tend to perceive the objects around them differently, as well as the social roles of themselves and other people. "In every culture", says Frank, "the individual is of necessity cribbed, cabined and confined within the limitations of what his culture tells him to see, to believe, to do and to feel".[7] Ecological conditions and demands on a group have also been found to influence both the form and contents of socialization practices.[8] Consequently, both culturally determined selective cognition and differential patterns of learning constitute massive barriers to intercultural communication. Hudson has reported several studies in which pictorial conventions and rules of perspective perceived by Europeans were absent among Africans.[9] The effect of cultural backgrounds on selectivity of perception have been tested, *inter alia*, by means of binocular rivalry.[10] Also, the susceptibility to visual illusions, and hence to perceptual biases, has been found to be related to basic modes of acculturation.[11] Cultural differences have been observed in more sophisticated stimuli such as the

Rorschach inkblots as well as the ink blot test assessments by clinicians. As a common baseline of perception is necessary for effective communications, the cultural differences in the perception of the same or similar stimuli constitute an impediment to cross-cultural communication.

On the personality level, Wober found significant differences of field dependence/independence between Nigerian and American subjects as measured by the Rod and Frame Test.[12] This is especially valuable for our present context, because field dependence measures a subject's separant dependence on the object, whereas field independence shows the subject's participant detachment from it.[13] The cultural differences, as measured by Wober, add another dimension to the perceptual variance related to our separant–participant personality continuum. Both personality and cultural differences of perception constitute cumulative obstacles to interpersonal communication. The cultural barriers to communication are especially insurmountable in the area of aesthetics. Indeed, culture has been found to a determine to great extent aesthetic judgment and taste.[14] Arab torch singing is as bizarre and distasteful to the occidental ear as an Italian opera is shrill and repugnant to the ears of a Saudi Sheikh.

The class barriers to interpersonal communication have been researched *ad nauseam* by social and behavioral scientists and documented by endless works of fiction and drama. There seems to be an initial devaluation of the views of individuals from lower social or organizational strata. "The wisdom of the downtrodden is scorned", say the traditional Judaic sources. Better than any intercorrelation matrix, this sums up the bias inherent in inter social-strata communication. Individuals of different social aspirations find it difficult to communicate, and there is "not so much to talk about". This might stem from the fact that an achievement oriented individual, for instance, would be interested in different reinforcement, and hence in different feedback cues from his relevant others than an affiliation oriented individual. The former is bound to design his communication strategies in a totally different manner than an affiliation oriented individual whose focal concern is solidarity with the members of the group and being accepted by them.[15] Of special interest to our present context are the cross-cultural studies of "proxemic behavior". Proxemics, as defined by Hall, is "The study of how man unconsciously structures microspace – the distance between men in the conduct of daily transactions, the organization of space in his house and buildings and ultimately the layout of his towns".[16] Watson and Graves compared the "proxemic behavior" of Arabs and Americans and reported, "Highly significant Arab-American differences emerged in the direction expected with the Arab students confronting each other more directly than the Americans, moving closer together, more apt to touch each other while talking, looking each other more squarely in the eye, and conversing in louder tones".[17] Proxemic behavior may serve in many instances as non-verbal communication. Cross-culturally, differences in the meaning of non-verbal communication may serve as a barrier to communication.

Moreover, the differences in the connotation of proxemics across cultures may even contribute to the disruption of encounters because proxemic behavior that is deemed commendable in one culture may be downright offensive in another culture.

Indeed, the whole range of non-verbal communications is replete with cultural overtones and undertones that may confound, impede or prevent altogether cross-cultural communication. Ekman distinguishes between what he denotes as the neural determinants of the facial expressions of emotions and their cultural components. The neural determinants control the relationship between a specific emotion and the "firing" of a particular pattern of facial muscles, whereas the cultural determinants identify the events that elicit a given emotion – the rules that control its manifestation and its consequences.[18] We hold that the neural "universals" in facial expressions are on a basic physiological level so that their communicative value is minimal. However, once ego tries to express and convey his emotions through his facial expressions and alter attempts to decode and interpret them, they resort to their learned experience, which is culture bound and hence varies cross-culturally. There is really no solid evidence to suport Ekman's claim that there are universal facial expressions of emotions of fear and anger.[19] Even if there are some "universal" neural triggers for specific emotions (which, on a very basic neural level they are bound to be), there are so many layers of intervening cognitive processes, as Ekman himself notes, which are socially learned and are certain to influence both the encoding and the decoding of the facial messages. In some cultures "macho" masculine behavior decrees the suppression of any expression of pain or fear and the "Strong American Man" should never show any emotion altogether. A person in these cultures is supposed to cache, disguise and suppress the non-verbal cues, facial or otherwise, which may reveal his emotions. Here again, cultural mandates provide an additional screen dividing between encoders and decoders of non-verbal communication. "Display rules" also govern ego's presentation of emotions and constitute a battery of learned dynamics, by which his raw emotions are transformed into socially acceptable behavior, which of course varies from one culture to another.[20] Ekman's video frames for instance, which are supposed to convey disgust in the facial expression of Japanese and American subjects,[21] looked to the author as conveying fear or strain (in the Japanese face) and surprise or curiosity (in the American face). The expression of women in the height of orgasm may easily be interpreted, judging from a snapshot of their faces, as unbearable pain. Indeed, the most pronounced expression of male orgasm witnessed by the author was on the face of the chief of the Rome Carabinieri receiving a ceremonial salute from the uniformed guards at the gates of the Roman city hall.

An interesting study by Cole and his associates, utilizing Piaget's premises of the egocentrism of children, revealed first that Kpelle adults were as egocentric as Genevan children. On closer examination, however, it appeared that the

Kpelle cognitive orientation was so different from the European that the application of Piaget's egocentrism hypotheses to the Kpelle culture was untenable.[22] The implication of Cole's study to our context is that many times the differences of cognitive orientations of different cultures are so basic that the transfer of conceptual frames of reference from one culture to another is virtually impossible. Moreover, in some cultures people use intentional conceptual ambiguity as a form of defensive communication. A classic example is the *sanza* of the Zande, which is an ambiguous double-talk that may be interpreted in many ways with the speaker holding the option to fall back on the more harmless interpretation. Evans-Pritchard describes the successful *sanza* as an ambiguity that enables the speaker "to keep under cover and to keep open a line of retreat should the sufferer from our malice take offence and try to make trouble".[23] Naturally, someone who is not familiar with the fine points of the *sanza* will misunderstand the whole message in which a particular *sanza* is employed. Evans-Pritchard was aware of this when he remarked, "It [*sanza*] adds greatly to the difficulties of anthropological inquiry. Eventually the anthropologist's sense of security is also undermined, his confidence shaken. He learns the language, can say what he wants to say in it, and can understand what he hears, but then he begins to wonder whether he has really understood . . . he cannot be sure, and even they (the Zande) cannot be sure, whether the words do have a nuance or someone imagines that they do".[24]

The Distorting Tags

Like cognitive dissonance, stigma (i.e. derogatory tags branded on a person) twists and biases ego's communication with his surroundings. His behavior may then be viewed as a defense of his sense of existential choice. In *The Mark of Cain* we presented an aetiological model of stigma on various levels of analysis.[25] In the present context, stigma may be envisaged as a devious communication mechanism which does not enhance encounters, but rather alienates and segregates Man from his fellow men.

The main twisting mechanism inherent in stigma is its smearing halo effect generalizing from some patterns of an individual's behavior or even from a single act, to his whole personality. The mass communication media are responsible both for contributing to and reporting many instances of character assassinations by gossips, professional muckrakers, and law enforcement agencies, which extend the label of one act to the whole person of its perpetrator. This holds true even if the attribution of the act to a given person was unjustified to begin with. The author has witnessed many people whose mere detention for initial investigation by the police made the public view their whole person through the twisting lenses of their stigma. In one instance, a successful lawyer known of the author lost most of his practice following his investigation by the police, although he was not formally detained or arrested and no charge was ever filed against him. Some even went as far as to confide that they knew all along that, "deep down he was corrupt through and through", echoing Garfinkel's statement that the work of the denunciation effects the recasting of the objective character of the perceived other. The former identity, at best, receives the accent of mere appearance. The former identity stands as accidental, the new identity is the "basic reality".[26]

Stigma expands some of the stigmatized deeds or characteristics to engulf the whole person. The author remembers with dismay how his first negative impression of a person formed by stigma and gossip lasted for a fairly long time until he realized that he had been led astray by the derogatory labels. He realized that he was eager to accept the stigmatic image of the person. Cataloging and pigeon-holing the person put his mind at ease. He did not look for contrary impressions and other views portraying the person as honest and of utmost integrity, as he turned out to be, but was content to accept the person's stigmatized image without question. The author's sad experience, time and again, is that Man is an eager, voracious and sometimes carnivorous consumer of stigma, yet he is ever ready to rationalize this gluttony by projection, displacement and a battery of other defense mechanisms.

We also tend to brand people with permanent uni-dimensional labels as such as "Tom is bad" and "Dick is stupid", which engulf a whole person with one stereotype along an indefinite span of time. Also, by assigning a given person to a group we label him automatically with the stereotypes of the group to which we have allocated him.

In *The Mark of Cain* we presented the following dynamic process of stigmatization:

The Dynamic Process of Stigmatization
Psychogenic Motives
1. Outlet for aggression
2. Projection of guilt
3. Displacement of resentment
4. The stigmatized as "scapegoat"

Socio-Psychological Pressures
5. The stigmatized as symbolic source of danger
6. Relative powerlessness
7. Vulnerability to the source of stigma
8. "Somebody to look down upon"
9. "Explaining away" alter's achievement

Social Level
10. Social Stigma as an act of power

The possibilities of twisting or disrupting interpersonal communication are inherent in each component of this process.

The outlet of aggression and defensively projecting outwards their guilt and frustrations seems to be the main fuel pushing stigmatizers to besmear their fellow men. Some of the author's colleagues who never added the names of their assistants as co-authors of their papers although they did most of the work, were constantly accusing somebody of plagiarism. Others who were less than honest in their financial dealings had many stories about Professor X and Dr. Y who were appropriating research funds, and one colleague who used to bring his mistress to conferences abroad always had stories of his adulterous dean. In a similar vein, Simmons and Chambers found that people who were more liberal tended to resort less to negative stereotyping (that is to stigma) than people who were more conservative. The latter had to project outwardly through stigma their repressed aggression against the normative system.[27] The stigmatizing projections operate by some of the principles of the projective measurement techniques. In the Rorschach and T.A.T. tests, for instance, one has to keep the objective stimuli at varying levels of ambiguity in order to induce the testee's projections to soar outwards. In a like manner, the projections of stigma would be more prominent in cases where the predisposing factors within the configuration are amorphous and ambiguous. In mental illness, the venting out of aggression and the projection of guilt in the form of stigma usually results in an extremely biased communication because it provides a subconscious basis and a righteously indignant support for our numerous Archie Bunker-like discriminations and bigotries.

The defensive displacement through stigma is apparent in the very common practice of labelers to besmear and slander people they do not know or who could not possibly have had any connection with the facts attributed to them by the stigma. The author has been labeled a nihilist by one person and a paranoid by another. Sometimes a good dose of paranoia in our rat-maze world is a sign of sanity and many times international politics as impinging on the eastern shores of the Mediterranean indeed make the world seem a tragicomic mistake. However, both stigmatizers have admitted not to have read any of the author's books nor attended any of his lectures or for that matter ever met him.

The scapegoating of outsiders, pariahs, the bizarre, the misfits, as well as the creative innovators, usually involves some form of stigmatized ostracism which entails some blocking of communication with the stigmatized. Those who were ostracized in ancient Greece and the "outlaws" in medieval Europe were actually cast out from the community. In modern society, non-communication with the stigmatized may take other forms. For example, the office politician orienting a new man: "Nobody in the office likes Tom so you are better off not having anything to do with him, if you know what I mean". Or through gossip to a hostess: "Dick is such an awkward fellow, he doesn't know how to behave.

He'll just stand in the corner, and stare at your guests embarrassing them. If I were you I wouldn't invite him to the party". In all probability the hostess will not invite Dick to the party even if she usually dislikes and distrusts the gossip because she does not want to take any chances with the success of her party. The gossip knows that all she has to achieve by her stigma is to cast a slight doubt as to the desirability of inviting or of communicating with the stigmatized. The professional gossips know that the effect of casting a doubt on the integrity, propriety or desirability of the stigmatized is rather effective because one of the "reasonable man's" maxims is "if in doubt, out".

The outsiders, the odd, the crazed, the peculiar and the unclassifiable have been perennial objects of stigma. In *The Mark of Cain* we traced Man's anxiety relating to the dissident, the strange and the deviant to his congruity based quest of concordance. In *The Myth of Tantalus* we linked this congruity principle to Man's core-personality quest to regain togetherness with the object. The relevance of this to our present context is that the stigmatized constitute a direct or symbolic source of danger to the stigmatizer so that he evades encounters and avoids communication with him.

The powerless and downtrodden stigmatized are many times unable to communicate freely and openly with people outside their social structure. Very often ethnic minorities and the politically oppressed are notoriously cut-off from the communication channels outside the immediate structures in which they are enmeshed, confined and oppressed. Even if they are exposed momentarily to these channels, they prefer to be silent fearing the backlash which is certain to be wrought on them later by the power structure. Similarly, there can be very little candid communication with creative people within a given structure or group by people outside it if the "in" group people are out of favor with the clique's power elite or not "in" with the current *arbiter elegantiari*. The stigmatized and the downtrodden within a given institution very rarely come to the attention of the official spokesman of the organization, nor are they plugged in to the proper channels by which modern public relations are manufactured. Visitors to countries, organizations and institutions, are towed towards the more desirable scenes and led to communicate with the "right" people. In totalitarian regimes this is done bluntly and rudely, whereas in pluralistic societies trained public relations personnel do it with polished sophistication, but the selectivity of exposure is similar.

Many of the stigma slanted communications are related to what we have denoted in *The Mark of Cain* as "relative achievement".[28] By derogating alter and belittling his achievement ego raises himself by his own bootstraps of stigma. Ego's derogating description of alter is rarely related to a material issue of achievement. Mostly it is in the form of "What? Harry an academy award winner. I went to school with this schnook and his nose was always running". "What? Tom wrote a book? He hardly knew how to sign his name when I knew him". "What? You want to elect Dick to the Chamber of Commerce? He is a raving lunatic! He drinks four martinis for lunch". In academia, "explaining away" a colleague's achievement by means of stigma is a favorite vocation. Smith developed a new field of research, so along comes the campus gossip and assures his eager listeners that Smith did academic market research and ascertained that nobody wanted to deal with that specific area so he decided that was his opportunity to become a lone shining star. If Taylor publishes too much, the labeler's verdict is that he must be shallow. If he publishes too little he is surely sterile. Jones receives an international award, so university politics enter and spread the word that the awards committee heard about the death of Jones' wife and the nervous breakdown of his daughter so that their decision to award him the prize was made out of pity.

The examples given above of "distorting tags" indicate just some of the levels of miscommunication. Stigma slanted communications, or rather miscommunications, have been dealt with fully in *The Mark of Cain*, to which we refer the reader. Before proceeding to the next chapter, however, there is one important aspect of stigma communications that has to be covered – the labeling of mental illness.

The Labeling of Mental Illness

The sociological approach to the genesis of mental illness, with its stressing of the importance of the breakdown of human communication as a predisposition to mental aberration, highlights the importance of stigma in the formation of the self-concept roles and images of the mentally ill.[29] Moreover, some scholars find a close similarity between the core mechanics of social deviance and mental illnesses. Scheff, for instance, regards social deviance as the main dynamic underlying mental illness:

> The culture of the group provides a vocabulary of terms for categorising many norm violations: crime, perversion, drunkenness, and bad manners are familiar examples. Each of the terms is derived from the type of behavior involved. After exhausting these categories, however, there is always a residue of the most diverse kinds of violations for which the culture provides no explicit label.[30]

Scheff illustrates his point by the rather amusing yet apt illustration of ego who insists on gazing during his conversation with alter at the latter's ear. The author has tried it with one of his colleagues and indeed the word was spread that "Shoham has become clinically mad far beyond his usual eccentricities".

In so far as some forms of madness involve a breakdown of the sensory encoding of messages and of interpersonal communication, and infringe a residual mass of social norms, which generates a value laden societal reaction and control, the mechanisms of labeling social deviance apply *mutatis mutantis* to mental illness. The role of stigma in accelerating and deepening mental illness, similar to its role in forming the deviant career, has been pointed out by Scheff as follows:

> In a crisis, when the deviance of an individual becomes a public issue, the traditional stereotype of insanity becomes the guiding imagery for action, both for those reacting to the deviant and, at times, for the deviant himself. When societal agents and persons around the deviant react to him uniformly in terms of the traditional stereotypes of insanity, his amorphous and nonstructured rule-breaking tends to crystallize in conformity to those expectations, thus becoming similar to the behavior of other deviants classified as mentally ill, and stable over time. The process ...is completed when the traditional imagery becomes a part of the deviant's orientation for guiding his own behavior.[31]

Nunnally has demonstrated that the mentally ill are regarded with fear, distrust and dislike. As with social deviance, their whole person is engulfed with a negative "halo" effect. Their public image is that of being "dirty, unintelligent, insincere and worthless". Scheff artfully demonstrated how the patient who is confused, insecure and powerless is totally influenced by the "Great White God", the omnipotent and omniscient therapist.[32] As psychiatrists and clinical psychologists are notorious labellers, the patient is more than willing to oblige "The Great Man" and adopts the labels of mental illness and acts accordingly. Such stigmatizing produces symptoms of mental illness that are even more pronounced than in the covert stigmatization of the young Genet by the peasant family at Le Morvan, and the labeling of the young Jewish North African prostitute by her father.[33]

Of special importance is Temerlin's study, which had psychiatrists, clinical psychologists and graduate students in clinical psychology diagnose a sound-recorded interview with a normal healthy man. Just before listening to the interview, they heard a professional person of high prestige, acting as a confederate of the experimenter, say that the individual to be diagnosed was, "a very interesting man because he looked neurotic but actually was quite psychotic".[34] The results were that the suggestion by the prestigious person had the greatest effect upon psychiatrists biasing them to diagnose the normal person as psychotic.

Rosenhan's study reports the adventures of eight sane (whatever this means) volunteers who gained admission to twelve different mental hospitals by feigning symptoms of mental illnesses. After being admitted they dropped all pretenses of madness yet found it difficult to be released from the institutions:

> Despite their public "show" of sanity, the pseudopatients were never detected. Admitted, except in one case, with a diagnosis of schizophrenia, each was discharged with a diagnosis of schizophrenia "in remission". The label "in remission" should in no way be dismissed as a formality, for at no time during any hospitalization had any question been raised about any pseudopatient's simulation . . . the evidence is strong that once labeled schizophrenic, the pseudopatient was stuck

with the label . . . It is clear that we cannot distinguish the sane from the insane in psychiatric hospitals. The hospital itself imposes a special environment in which the meanings of behavior can easily be misunderstood. The consequences to patients hospitalised in such an environment – the powerlessness, depersonalization, segregation, mortification and self-labeling – seem undoubtedly countertherapeutic.[35]

A recent court case in Israel revealed that a person was institutionalized in a mental hospital for five months by the order of a district psychiatrist (a Government appointee) who never examined the patient, but made his decision on the complaint of the patient's wife who was herself institutionalized in a mental hospital. A general practitioner also wrote a letter stating that "the patient is a sick man who disturbs the family life". When investigated by the judge the district psychiatrist testifed, "Sometimes there is no choice and I have to commit a person to a mental hospital without examining him. Sometimes I issue four committal orders a day and I cannot examine everyone of them". The judge wrote in his judgment against the district psychiatrist, who was sued by the patient for damages, "I am trembling with fright as to what could happen to every one of us if the district psychiatrist is not aware that he has to get clear evidence as to a person's mental illness before he commits him to a mental hospital". But the sad moral of this, and many other cases, is that there are no clear-cut and unequivocal definitions and syndromes of mental illness.

The author recently had a long talk with a very perceptive and intelligent young woman who spent many years in a mental hospital and managed to pull herself out of the vicious cycle of institutionalization, remission, stigma and breakdown by sheer willpower. In conclusion she said, "I received all the so called therapeutic shocks and have been diagnosed by all the diagnoses in the books. I don't believe in any of these. They are just words". One may conduct as many aetiological studies on schizophrenia as one wishes with the same worthless or amorphic results because the dependent variable, schizophrenia itself, is a "blanket", nondescript construct. The most visible and, to be sure, the most concrete aspect of mental illness is the labeling of the patient as ill and his committal to an institution. This is linked to the general dynamics of stigma, the projective nature of which is more apparent with phenomena which are amorphic and ill-defined so that they are more readily tagged by the projections of the stigmatizers.

Some critics like Walter Gove reject the extreme labeling approach to the genesis of mental illness because societal reaction in itself and by itself cannot explain the aetiology of schizophrenia:

In summary, the available evidence on how people enter the mentally ill role indicates that the societal reaction formulation, at least as stated by Scheff, is false. The evidence is that the vast majority of persons who become patients have a serious disturbance, and it is only when the situation becomes untenable that action is taken. The public officials who perform the major screening role do not simply process all of the persons who come before them as mentally ill but instead screen out a large portion. If the person passes this initial screening he will probably be committed, and there is reason to assume the process at this point frequently becomes somewhat ritualised. But even here a number of persons are released either through the psychiatric examination or the court hearing.[36]

Again, the fault lies in the extremity of the labeling approach and the exclusiveness, which its proponents claim for stigma as the main or even sole dynamic of mental illness. As with deviance and crime, the more realistic approach is to see the societal reaction as one dynamic within a configuration, which also includes behavioral disturbances and functional maladjustments as predisposing factors towards morbidity. In the study referred to in Chapter 9, we show the importance of familial double binds in predisposing a child toward schizophrenia, in the same way that conflict situations in the socialization process predispose a child toward deviance and crime. However, the predisposing factors to morbidity are not so readily visible and perceptible as in crime and deviance, so that the role of stigma in the ultimate definition of mental illness is bound to be more pronounced than in social deviance and crime.

The stigma of mental illness is also used as a device of relative achievement. Among the author's colleagues in academia, a scholar's esoteric yet brilliant book is often dismissed as "the hallucinations of a madman". The author was present recently at an excellent lecture by a scholar who was known to be a dull lecturer. The author overheard one of the lecturer's colleagues explaining away the brilliance of the lecturer by the fact that he had undergone intensive psychiatric treatment. "So much treatment and money", winked the friend of the lecturer, "should produce at least one good lecture".

Labeling by madness solves many conflicts. For example, a third party intervening in a fight and pacifying one of the combatants by saying, "Leave him alone, don't you see that he is mad, he'll bite your nose off". The most revolting instance of labeling with mental derangement as a weapon of power politics was experienced recently by a close friend of the author whose two sons were killed in the Yom Kippur War. He tried his hand at politics and his political opponents confided to everybody that he was totally unreliable and should not be elected to the Knesset (Israeli Parliament). "You know, of course the terrible blow he suffered", they whispered with a tragic intonation. "It is a great shame but one cannot vote for him because his lack of mental balance is sure to endanger the party".

The labeling of mental illness involves an extreme disjuncture of communication. The basic assumption underlying some forms of mental illness is that they constitute a severe breakdown of the patient's communication with his surroundings. We shall examine this assumption in detail in Chapter 9. But even in cases where the non-communication of the patient with his surroundings is not so extreme, as in some psychoses, the patient is apparently labeled for infringing residual social norms that he might not even be aware of contravening. In social deviance and crime the infringed norms are more conspicuous and not residually amorphic as in mental illness. Consequently, the patient is often confused, amious, disoriented and totally unclear as to what has happened to him, or what abominations he committed in order to incur his declaration as a mad non-person. It is probable that this total confusion, more than other factors, is responsible for the patient's further retreat into an incommunicado stance *vis-à-vis* his incomprehensible hostile surroundings. The psychiatrists and clinical psychologists utilizing the medical model of diagnosing mental illness are probably not aware that by labeling a certain behavior which infringes some residual conventions and norms by the rather amorphic and ambiguous psychiatric labels of madness, they operate as agents of social control. This aspect of the labeling of madness, which is the subject of the following final section of the present chapter, constitutes another distorting dimension in the interrelationship between the stigmatizing therapeutic staff, the labeled patients and the public at large.

The Stigma of Madness as Social Control

Howard P. Rome, former President of the American Psychiatric Association, declared some time ago, "We appreciate that in a very meaningful sense, society can be sick too . . . Actually, no less than the entire world is a proper catchment area for present-day psychiatry, and psychiatry need not be appalled by the magnitude of this task".[37] Two Australian authors stated last year, "mental health services do in part perform a legitimate social control function (because) some mentally disordered people create intolerable burdens".[38] Nicholas Kittrie expounded in his volume length thesis that the functions of the administration of criminal justice and social control are more and more being invested in the organs and institutions of the modern state.[39] If indeed some, at least, of the custodial and therapeutic measures against the mentally ill are initiated by overt or covert aims of social control, then the stigma of madness attached to these measures also has a function of normative sanction and control. In the West and in other pluralistic democracies the stigma of madness as a means of social control is used covertly, apologetically and many times unknowingly. In the other totalitarian countries, the label of madness and its consequences is an overt and official sanction against nonconformity to the state and party. Sidney Bloch and Peter Reddaway published an account of 200 cases of political dissidents, social outsiders and intellectual nonconformists who were labeled mad and treated accordingly.[40] At the 1977 meeting of the World Psychiatric Association, a former Soviet psychiatrist, Marina Voikhan-Skaya, presented a "white list" of Soviet political victims in mental hospitals and a "black list" of psychiatrists who committed them to these hospitals. She pleaded with the delegates, "to help hundreds of psychiatrists in the Soviet Union who have been drawn into crime only because they lacked the courage to say 'no'".[41]

Psychiatrists, clinical psychologists and the therapists of aberrant human behavior, do indeed aim to tow back the "crazy" individuals to the normative confines of adjustment, to make them function "properly" within the limits of acceptable social standards of a given society at a given time. The pressures of the therapists on individuals to behave in conformity with the normative system becomes apparent if we bear in mind that unless a person seeks treatment voluntarily he may suffer continuously abysmal misery yet not be considered mad or crazy if his outward behavior conforms within some margins to the accepted social norms. There is, therefore, a leveling element in psychotherapy because a "successful treatment" involves the traction back of the patient to within tolerable limits of the mean, mode and median of normative behavior. Many creative innovators whose specific outlook on things was necessary for their novel perspectives and insights, have been victims to the adjustment-based leveling pressures of psychotherapy. A particularly sad instance was the experience of Antonin Artaud, who was virtually reduced to a vegetative existence by a succession of electric shocks. Artaud states:

> A lunatic is a man who has preferred to because what is socially understood as mad rather than forfeit a certain superior idea of human honor . . . a vicious society has invented psychiatry to defend itself from the investigations of certain superior lucid minds whose intuitive powers were disturbing to it.[42]

Psychiatry, as a prime tool of the cult of mediocrity adhered to by the organs of social control, was denounced by Karl Kraus, the *enfant terrible* of Vienna:

> . . . nerve doctors who ruin genius for us by calling it pathological should have their skulls bashed in by the genius's collected works . . . One should grind one's heel into the faces of all rationalistic helpers of 'normal humanity' who give reassurance to people unable to appreciate works of wit and fantasy.[43]

It is of relevance to the present context that ego's striving to assert his ontological uniqueness as programmed by his specific psychosocial *gestalt* will be curbed and stifled if he wanders out and beyond the mesh of normative controls, one net of which is yielded by the guardians of mental health.

There is also a marked element of subjugation of the patient to the therapist because the powerlessness of the patient is almost total in a mental hospital where he becomes a non-person. The therapist is the one who decides when to release the patient and many times his decision is influenced by the patient's family, which has quite often a vested interest that he remain institutionalized. Greenly reports in his study that,

> In the informal interviews, most of the psychiatrists confirmed what the structured-interview data appear to show: patients' families had the ability to effect a discharge

or prevent a release. As one therapist put it, "It's hard to stand up to a family, which is quite funny since we are supposed to be a professional group". Only a small minority of the psychiatrists interviewed denied consistently that families were sometimes more influential in release decisions than they themselves were.[44]

As a far-fetched wild hypothesis based partly on the author's own observation, we suggest that therapists are attracted to and choose their profession because of their own psychic problems and knots which they project, "sell" and steam off by prodding into the patient's mind which "opens up" to them trustingly and willingly. The mechanism of transference enhances this symbiosis, which creates a skewed form of communication and dependence of dubious value to the patient, except that he gets a captive audience to listen (for a consideration) to his troubles. The therapists, however, have most of the trump cards, both lucratively and mentally. The essence of our argument is that unless the patient suffers from organic nervous system damage, relatively minor problems can be "sold" to the therapist. Severe ontological and existential crises cannot be helped by others. These may be coped with by the individual's recognition of his inner potential as determined by his personality core vectors and by trying to implement his quest of authencity by a Camusian revolt against his stifling surroundings including the labels of maladjustment, deviance and madness. We offer no philosopher's stone or cookbook recipes for instant authenticity. We shall however, discuss at length the redeeming nature of ontological revolt in chapter 10 of this work.

Defenses, Rituals and Slanted Congruity

> I had principles, to be sure, such as that the wife of a friend is sacred. But I simply
> ceased quite sincerely, a few days before, to feel any friendship for the husband.
>
> Albert Camus: *The Fall*

One of Freud's major innovations was that all of Man's interpersonal behavior is defensive because the direct expression of his drive is curbed by social norms. When these repressed drives seek expression, they arouse anxiety and the individual defends himself against them through alternative and substitute forms of drive-expressions, which are socially normative or symbolic, and hence non or less anxiety generating.[1] We, however, base our conception of defenses on ego's sense of ontological uniqueness and existential choice, a theory put forward in *The Myth of Tantalus*.[2] If ego is existentially chosen, and other objects and people are competing with his feeling of choice, and he cannot possibly assert realistically this choice in all his object and interpersonal relationships, he tends to defend himself by distorting reality or changing its symbolic meaning so that his sense of choice remains intact. Similarly, if ego's core personality feeling of uniqueness and worth are threatened by his own needs and desires, he defends himself by projecting these outside himself and anchoring them on other objects and people. If indeed most of our behavior, both conscious and unconscious, is defensive, we are bound to distort our decoding and encoding of communications in keeping with our specific needs. Defenses are, therefore, the most formidable barriers to communication, because they not only involve a constant violent distortion of incoming and outgoing information, but also ego's defensive distortions are not likely to be similar to alter's defensive biases or to complement them. We propose to survey some of these defense mechanisms and examine their blocking effects on interpersonal communication and encounter.

Man's sense of separant choice and participant uniqueness, which stem from his bio-psychological phases of development, are reinforced in modern society by its child centred socialization. This leads to another paradox rife with potential for frustrations and anomic breakdowns. The child centred education in

modern society, especially in the formative years, augments ego's sense of security and choice. He grows up with a feeling that "bad" things cannot happen to
him and that "they" (the generalized others) cannot do "it" (injure, betray etc.)
to him. But the ever fiercer competitive modern society makes others "do it to
him" with increasing callousness and cruelty as he grows older and plunges into
the rat race. This necessitates a thicker, heavier and more forceful battery of
defenses to protect his feelings of choice and uniqueness, and in the process
twist, slant and ward off the incoming information, which may injure them.

Arrogance is a separant defense mechanism that helps ego to assert his
choice, whereas meekness is a participant defense which enables a Spinoza or a
Kierkegaard to evade the bullying harassment of the generalized others, to "do
their own thing" and safeguard their sense of ontological uniqueness.

Sarcasm is a competitive separant defense. The sarcastic person derogates
others, belittles their achievement, scorns their art and vilifies their drawbacks.
The sarcastic person is rarely sarcastic to, or about himself, but mostly toward
others. In a similar vein, slapstick is a cherished separant entertainment, the
identification being with the thrower of the cream cake but not with its recipient on his face. The sarcastic person is also a "relative achiever". By derogating
alter, ego aims to relatively raise his own performance to a higher level. Humor,
on the other hand, is largely a participant defense. With humor, ego manages
not to take the spatiotemporal world seriously, including himself. Humor may
be subtle and very personal so that it may not be understood very well by others,
especially if they are extreme separants who are reluctant to laugh at themselves.
The latter usually laugh at the misfortunes of others and mostly their own
heavy-handed sarcasm makes them merry. Humor does not travel well across
cultures. Jokes are notoriously stagnant in translation. Ego may use other
defense mechanisms like reaction formation, or he may counteract his compul-
sive chasing of money by becoming a salon-communist. He may also exchange
his downtrodden reality by the excessive consumption of fantasy-suspense
movies where justice always prevails or science fiction where our rotten planet
usually gets smitten (together with ego's tormentors) by a *Gotterdammerung*
from outer space. However, the master twister of them all is the defense mechanism of projection.

When we repress wishes, affects and behavior because they are normatively
proscribed, we attribute them to objects and people outside ourselves. This is
more than just twisting or slanting communication – it is the complete illusory
and sometimes delusive reversal of the flow of information to us from outside
objects and people, instead of from us outwards to the objects and people.
Despite this radical reversal of the flow of communication, projection seems to
be Man's most common defense mechanism.[3] Projections are many times
accompanied by reaction formations and then the twisting of the flow of information is cumulative. For example, ego loves alter but a normative proscription
has it that he should not love him, so he defends himself by a reaction forma-

tion and hates him. However, often reaction formation is not defensive enough so ego supplements it by a projection, "alter hates me".[4] Finally, "complementary projections" attribute normatively repressed characteristics of ego's relevant others to other objects and people. The crucial point, however, is that we know from the projective techniques of personality assessment that we tend to project more freely if the outside stimulus is ambiguous. The catch is that for ego, alter is always ambiguous to various degrees and extents.

Ego's perception of alter is by necessity vicarious and mediate, and never direct and immediate. Consequently, the radical distortion inherent in projection is the inevitable basis of interpersonal communication and relationship. Some of the vicissitudes of projection are apparent in affective relationships. Ego projects many commendable attributes on the beloved alter, which he does not possess, and develops a perceptual block against many of alter's derogatory attributes. When ego's affective infatuation with alter wanes or slackens he sees alter "as he really is" and this augments his aversion and disenchantment. Ego does not realize that both his infatuation and subsequent disenchantment with alter have less to do with alter "as he really is" than with ego's differential magnitude and intensity of his own projections. Also, when the outside world is unbearably menacing to ego, he tries to overpower it by projecting some delusional control mechanisms on it. Consequently, paranoic projections are a major component of the separant ego's frantic efforts to impose, in an inclusionary and to be sure delusive manner, some order on his ambiguous and chaotic surroundings.

Another corollary of our largely projective dyadic interrelationships is linked to our needs to ascertain the motivations of others in their interaction with us. However, as ego cannot have any clear and comprehensive perception and hence knowledge of alter's motivations, he projects his own motivations for the encounter on alter, very often with disasterous results both for ego and alter and for their encounter.

In a sense, the egocentrism of children, as expounded by Piaget, involves a form of projection because the egocentric child feels that whatever happens to him also happens to the objects around him and to other people.[5] This is more related to the blurred boundary with children between themselves and their surroundings. However, if an adult still clings to his infantile egocentricity it is bound to augment his distorting projections.

The author recently carried out a crude empirical stock taking of the more gross distorting projections which he encountered during one week. The following is a list of the more conspicuous instances of distorting projections recorded by him. A colleague of the author who is not on speaking terms with almost anybody on campus asked the author to have a word with Harry because "his interpersonal relationships had deteriorated lately and he goes around alienating people". Another colleague, a moral Daltonist, gave the author a long lecture on the slackening of morals in Israeli society. A woman lost her temper and shouted shrilly at a bank teller. On leaving the bank she muttered audibly that the people at the bank were hysterical and that she was going to take her business to another bank where the personnel were polite and sober. The author's assistant admitted candidly that when she felt guilty about something she would give her husband hell and point out to him how badly he treats everybody around him. A student known to the author for a long time who is exceptionally cold-blooded and cold-hearted told the author that he broke up with his girlfriend because "she is incapable of having any feelings towards anybody except for herself". A fellow professor, who is notorious for appropriating the papers of his graduate students and publishing them under his own name, asked the author half-jokingly, "How are the ghost writers who have written the book and numerous papers you published last year?"A very disturbed student in one of the author's seminars, who is usually loaded with valium to ease her many tensions, remarked to the author after class that the student who presented the seminar paper, "was very tense, his hands were shaking". An extravagant lady student always dressed in flaming reds, yellows and glaring violets with deep exhibitionistic decolletes, thanked the author coquettishly at the end of term for his interesting lectures. "I have only one remark", she added, "you are such a showman, it seems that you need us as an audience in front of which you can expose your intricate personality".

In all probability, the author was also projecting and the instances were recorded in an exaggerated manner to fit his personal biases. Projection is a prime defense mechanism to project ego's feeling of separant choice and onto-logical uniqueness. The separant projects his personality attributes, moods and *Anschauungen* on his surroundings. The optimist sees only the silver linings of the clouds, whereas the pessimist sees only the clouds. The separant also imbues his surroundings and his relevant others with his own biases, prejudices, anxieties and inadequacies.

A defense mechanism similar to projection, sometimes denoted as assimilative projection, is when ego feels and thinks that his relevant others and his partners in his encounters think and feel like himself. Ego also assumes that all others perceive objects and people the way he does. This assimilative projection is many times fatal to communication and encounters because it creates in ego unjustified expectations. If ego is a good dancer and writes beautiful love letters, he tends to project his proficiencies on alter, a beautiful lady whom he invites to a ball. In the first dance she treads on his toes and when he writes to her in the morning trying to woo her with poetry she answers him in the style of *The Ladies Home Journal.* The most painful assimilative projection occurs when ego expects alter to reciprocate his good attitudes and treatment with inevitable disasterous results because ego's definition of a favorable attitude and treatment as projected on alter is many times diametrically opposite to alter's conception of what commendable attitudes and deeds should be.

In extreme cases, projections may be so far removed from reality that they become escapes. The mythomaniacs, surrealists, science fiction novelists and addicts live their fantasies to varying extents and thereby blot or numb the vicissitudes of their realities. The ultimate in projection, however, is paranoia, where ego's surroundings are assaulted by barrages of projective delusions, hatred and rage.

A variation on the theme of projection is a defense mechanism named by Ichheiser as the Mote–Beam Mechanism. We have denoted this previously mentioned defense mechanism as the Camel Syndrome, from the Bedouin proverb, "the camel sees the humps of his fellow camels but never his own". Ego afflicted with the Camel Syndrome attributes derogatory traits to others, but cannot or refuses to notice the same traits in himself. An old lecher, an acquaintance of the author, complained bitterly the other day about the lax sexual mores of the younger generation. A high government official imprisoned for taking bribes complained to a judge visiting the prisons that law enforcement agencies are not active enough in combatting corruption in government. The crucial point is that people are blind to the mainly subconscious dynamic of projection. Also, the defense mechanisms of projection itself are subject to the Camel Syndrome. Ego is not aware of his projections but is ever complaining about alter's projecting onto him.

Deception, Self-Deception and Double Standards

In a separant culture, alter's success raises mostly envy in ego, and many times anxiety and guilt for not being equally successful. Alter's failure, on the other hand, may fill ego with aversion because failure in a separant achievement bound culture is obscene. Mostly, however, alter's failure will raise in ego a sense of satisfaction or glee at alter's plight or condescending pity. In more participant cultures, people are less impressed by success or failure and they tend to be more fatalistic towards themselves and rather apathetic to the fate of their fellow men. In societies like India, where millions of people are born and die on sidewalks and their corpses are hoisted onto garbage vans, people are bound to gain a less enthusiastic perspective on human endeavor.

Even if dyadic interrelationships in separant cultures are less Hobbesian than we hold them to be, ego will need all the defenses he can muster, and especially rationalization and self-deception in order to counteract alter's spiteful assault and his sense of choice. If things do not work out right, ego will have all sorts of resentment and "sour grapes" rejection of his coveted but rather elusive goals. He will collect bits and pieces of rather crude flattery to reinforce his injured feeling of choice, even from people whom he otherwise despises as Philistines and fools. Or he will engage in chronic self-deception like the author's acquaintance with an enormous behind who confided to him that she was actually very narrow around the hips and after a week's diet she will be as slender as a sylph.

The separant ego's deceptions are mostly geared to dominate alter and get favors or advantages out of him. Even if ego knows that alter knows that he deceived him, ego counts on some of his easy going charm and manipulation to placate him by a smile, a promise or a small favor so that alter agrees to "let bygones be bygones". Another common separant manipulation is that when the aggrieved alter comes to complain to ego and try to right his wrongs, ego baits him with side issues so that when alter delves into these side issues and is absorbed by them, he has less energy to deal with the issue he came to discuss. Also, ego might look at his watch and exclaim hurriedly that they spent so much time together and he has to rush to another appointment. If ego succeeds in provoking alter with these side issues and alter loses his temper, ego takes quick advantage of alter's outburst and throw him out of the room with righteous indignation. Mostly, though, ego counts on alter being participantly passive, detached, not interested, afraid or too timid to fight back. In this way he gets away with his manipulative deceit.

Pity involves both deception and self-deception. Ego deceives himself if he thinks that his pitying alter is purely based on altruism and he deceives alter if he makes him feel that his pity stems wholly from sympathy. Actually, pity is one of the most common condescending dynamics. By pitying alter who grieves or is in pain, or suffered a social and professional downfall, ego asserts his superiority over him because he is still going strong and had the better luck to keep his social position. Many times, sympathy and pity involve a degradation technique by means of which ego imposes his magnanimous condolences on a broken-hearted alter who is writhing in pain. The author remembers with disgust the time he was grieving over a death with unbearable pain. Hordes of people, most of whom he hardly knew, came over to his house and meted out to him their heavy-handed sympathy uttered in pompous tones, which seemed to them as befitting the solemn occasion, a succession of condoling clichés.

After making lamenting noises on various levels of (in)sincerity in alter's presence, ego goes to their common acquaintances and recounts how miserable alter was, how difficult it was to see him in his dejection, and how ego was shocked by alter's sorrow. The partial comforting implication was that the lot of ego and his audience is so much better in comparison to alter's misery. Our present premise might explain the eagerness of some people to attend funerals, visit people in pain and read accounts or watch movies of disasters, because by comparison it makes them feel fortunate and safe. However, alter might be eager to be pitied because he is the self-pitying type and willing to deceive himself that ego's sympathy is real, although he himself was in the habit of spraying his bereaved acquaintances with crocodile tears and false pity. Alter might even declare that he did not want pity and sympathy but usually it would have more than a tinge of grudging resentment implying that he did not get from ego as much pity and sympathy as he deserved. Self-pity may even lead ego to identify with alter's plight, but only up to a point. Ego's need to pity himself may lead him to see himself in the place of the suffering alter, but if alter's plight is too horrid, ego's identification ceases. He "cannot stand the sight of it anymore". Ego can identify with a romantically suffering alter, but if the pain becomes too gruesome, continuous and ugly it is too much even for a self-pitying ego. The self-pitying seeker of pity may also be in for a surprise if his dyadic partner is a carnivorous bully. The miserable self-pitying façade would then not evoke pity but cruelty and further aggression.

One way for the downtrodden to escape the adversity of envy, and for the miserable to avoid the humiliation of being pitied, is for them to stick together. Two ugly spinsters can be good friends without envying each other. Two bums can get drunk together in the gutters on methylated spirits without one threatening the other's sense of choice. Two bereaved mothers can recount to each other their trials without being exposed to the degradations of pity. Equal partnership in misery may sometimes be a refuge from deception, self-deception and double standards.

Another separant device to preserve one's sense of choice even if one is miserable, is to witness somebody who is even more miserable. After visiting a hospital, people are bound to declare something like, "Seeing all this misery around, one should not complain if one is just healthy". A bereaved mother, a friend of the author, developed a strong attachment to a woman whose son was totally paralyzed from a war injury, whose husband had been killed in a road accident and she herself was dying of cancer. A not too clever husband of a wife who visited the author and reviewed the domestic problems of their friends concluded, "My wife and I are so happy by comparison". The author himself was very much involved recently in helping two of his friends who had severe problems, one because he was fired from the university and the other because he had the police investigating his business. In moments of candid introspection the author had to admit to himself that, partially at least, his frantic involvement on behalf of his friends was to counter his guilt for feeling relieved and lucky that the misfortunes befell his friends and not him.

The separant egocentric ego assumes that all the others feel and behave the way he does and if they do not, they should. Therefore, he expects all the others to love the people he loves and especially hate all those he hates. He deceives himself, of course, if he thinks that his relevant others would comply with his separant expectations. They might, however, deceive him because of fear or affection and put up appearances as if they comply with his expectations. A diametrically opposite self-deception is the self-effacing participant who feels "transparent" when he goes into a coffee-house to talk to his mistress over the telephone and cringes with shame because he is sure that everybody around can see what a terrible sinner he is.

Goffman is of the opinion that ego can effectively project his definition of the situation when he enters the presence of others. Subsequent events occuring in the interaction between ego and the others may contradict or disprove ego's projected definition of the situation, which may result in conflict or even in the disruption of the encounter altogether.[6] We claim, however, that Goffman's assumption of the effectiveness of ego's projection of his definition of the situation is unwarranted. The transmission of ego's definition of the situation to the others is subject to all the communication gaps, twists and biases which we have described in previous chapters. Consequently, ego's conflicts with the others in any given situation and the possible disruption of the encounter might well be because he did not transmit effectively to others his definition of the situation, and hence his expectation from the situation and from the present others.

> The others, therefore, could not comply with ego's expectations because they perceived them differently than ego meant to transmit them. Ego may indeed use 'defensive practices' if he feels that something went wrong with his projection of his definition of the situation and try to correct it.[7]

However, these defensive practices are also subject to communicative distortions, which may further compound the conflicts and increase the misunderstandings rather than reduce them. Goffman does not allow for the possibilities, which are crucial to us, that ego may be just play-acting in a given situation, deliberately or out of habitual hypocrisy presenting a false mask – a façade which alter may take seriously and thus further distort the communication process and the encounter.

In a separant culture, self-deception and the deception of others is the double-edged defense to preserve one's worth. Ego deceives himself by indiscriminately consuming ego boosting flattery even from people he knows to be liars, fools and professional lackeys. For the same reason, people are avid consumers of gossip, slander, defamation, scurrility and character assassination. By besmearing and besmirching others and spreading the slander, even if knowing it to be false, ego asserts his relative worth and choice. This is why slander spreads like wildfire, whereas praise creeps like a tortoise.

Ramparts of Choice and Uniqueness

The basic screen dividing, disconnecting and cutting ego off from the communication sources around him, as well as distorting the messages that sift through, are related to his constant need to safeguard his feelings of choice and uniqueness. We have mentioned this need earlier in relation to ego's egocentricity. Indeed, there is evidence that Man's egocentricity goes beyond pre-adolescence, as postulated by Piaget, and stretches in some cases up to the age of seventy.[8] It seems that this egocentricity (i.e. Man's basic difficulties in grasping and comprehending the point of view of other people) is one of the major impediments to interpersonal communication. The author experienced recently some painful proof of this premise, when two of his best friends acted in a way that they must have known could have hurt the author's sensitivities, yet when somebody alerted them to the consequences of their deeds they claimed that they did not realize the author was so touchy. Moreover, the author's expectations that his friends be aware of his sensitivities in these specific matters, which were obviously not complied with by his friends, is another proof for the lack of communication even among the closest of friends.

Some people are virtually incapable of taking the point of view of others. They may be extreme types on our participant–separant personality continuum, as well as being intolerant of ambiguity and closed minded as measured by some socio-psychological instruments.[9] Apart from orthodox religious people and the followers of secular creeds like Communism, there are adherents of other totalitarian systems of thought, such as Ayn Rand elitists, who are incapable of listening and trying to understand points of view that are not in line with their dogma. The author recently had a traumatic experience with an Ayn Randist who refused to hear anything that was contrary to his firmly held views, yet tried to impose his own views with roars of verbal violence.

Ego's egocentricity and his constant need to safeguard his choice and uniqueness makes him vulnerable to encroachments on his sensitivities. If alter treads on ego's sensitivities it is painful and "unfair", yet there can never be any reciprocity and interchangeability of sensitivities between ego and alter. Ego can never be even remotely sensitive to alter's pain, hurt and vulnerability as he is to his own. Consequently, any mutuality of understanding between ego and alter as to their respective sensitivities and vulnerabilities is near impossible. This raises the possibility that ego's inadvertant hurting of alter's sensitivities because he was not fully aware of them is liable to be interpreted by alter as intentional, and reacted to with what seems to alter as justified aggression. Also, the layers and batteries of defenses to guard ego's choice and uniqueness, only a small number of which has been reviewed by us here, makes him present an outward façade of defenses. These are rarely directly related to ego's inner dynamics of thought and affect. Mostly these defenses are deviously and symbolically interrelated with ego's psychic core processes. When one defense proves to be weak or inadequate, another one takes its place so that at no time is ego's psychic system devoid even partially of his defensive armor. Consequently, all encounters between ego and alter are mediated by their façade of defenses and this in itself makes any communication between them vicarious, indirect, blurred and distorted.

We also have some evidence from attribution research that ego tends to attribute his action to the situational requirements of his surroundings, whereas alter tends to attribute ego's actions also to his personality factors.[10] This, no doubt, reveals the basic separant nature of American culture as well as its social psychology. Ego is largely geared and socialized to manipulate his environment, whereas for alter, ego is just another object in his environment which interacts with the rest of the objects in his surroundings. The relevance of this finding to our present context is that ego's point of vantage is, perforce, different from alter's in every phase of their object-relationships, which constitute another hindrance to their dyadic communication. A similar view is expressed by Levy and Dugan who state, "it has long been an accepted tenet of projective psychology that each individual imposes his own unique structure on the world about him".[11] Consequently, there must be a conflict, or at least a disparity between the way the unique ego perceives and encodes messages and the way they are decoded by alter who to ego is not unique (as he is) but just like any other person.

The separant ego's constant attempts to impose himself on his surroundings may land him into conflicts of miscommunication, because he assumes that people around him are aware of what goes on in his expansive ego. He also expects that the people around him support him in his attitudes and opinions without his having to explain them to his relevant others because he assumes (erroneously, of course) that they surely know his feelings about certain issues and his attitudes about specific people. If the relevant others behave contrary to these unfounded assumptions of ego, he is bound to be hurt and complain sulkingly that "nobody can be trusted any more" and that he is "being betrayed in his own house".

Another powerful distorter of communication is ego's need to be accepted by his peers, and by his various membership and reference groups. These social desirability mechanisms may be separant in so far as they help reinforce ego's sense of choice, or participant when ego suppresses his conspicuousness in order to fit into the modal parameters of the group and hence be more acceptable by it. This "ugly duckling syndrome" is especially apparent with children when a child suppresses his higher intelligence and excellence in order to be more acceptable to the "gang". Ego would present to alter and to his relevant others an inauthentic façade in order to avoid their hostility and ostracism, and gain the comforts of acceptance of the group. Later in life, the grown ugly duckling will still have the problems of social desirability. On one hand, his excellence and creative innovation would make him conspicuous and different, yet on the other hand, success and recognition necessitates acceptance by the group. The creative innovating outsider has to present to the group a streamlined façade if he wishes to be accepted and recognized by it. Ego's very common apology, "I am sorry I didn't mean it" might be, on the face of it, an attempt to correct a misunderstanding or a miscommunication. Yet on a deeper level of analysis, it is a social desirability device of acceptance and a surrogate technique of participation to regain the grace of early childhood in the family fold where the magic words "I am sorry" brought immediate and unconditional forgiving acceptance.

However, ego's self-effacing participatory deference to alter as a social desirability device for acceptance or as a surrogate technique of participation is pregnant with a wide range of miscommunications and conflict. A separant, manipulative alter might take advantage of ego's submissive need for acceptance and subject him to continuous rituals of degradation and thus reinforce his amious deference without granting him any acceptance. Also, ego's assistance, support and help might injure the separant alter's sense of choice, because the inference from ego's help was that he could not accomplish the task by himself. Alter is liable to resent and reject ego and not accept him as a consequence of his help. The author's own sad experience in this matter was that when he found a publisher for a friend who had been unable for many years to publish an autobiographical novel, the friendship was terminated.

The flattering ego is mostly a separant manipulator who uses laudatory words, demeanor and behavior towards alter in order to gain from him things, power or favors. Alter is vulnerable to exploitation by flattery because, as we have already expounded, he cannot deceive himself directly the way he presents himself outwardly. He needs ego's feedback in order to reinforce his sense of choice. Consequently, ego is in a better position than alter to know that his flattering praise is unfounded, and yet it is many times the cheapest and most effective means to manipulate and exploit alter. This is why flattery is a prime tool of achievement in competitive cultures and structures. The habitual flatterer is ever attuned to the weaknesses, vulnerabilities and soft spots of the people in power. He then directs his Byzantine flattery in Levantine profusion or Teutonic precision to the strategic areas at the right moments. An apt portrait of the flattering arriviste has been drawn by Toulmin and Janik:

> Redl, who was the son of a poor railway clerk in Lemberg (Lvov), had risen to prominence in the Empire's military machine, by an exceptional capacity to conceal his true opinions and attitudes, an uncanny knack for saying just what his superiors wanted him to say, and for doing just what was expected in any situation. As with so many boys of his generation, his sexual awakening came during his days in Cadet School. (Musil's own partly autobiographical novel "Young Torless", centers on just such a situation and was received as nothing short of scandalous). Redl cleverly hid the truth about his homosexuality as successfully as he had hidden everything about himself. He was a man with but one goal: the status which accommpanied success in the military. He sacrificed everything and everyone to this end, proving that anything was possible in the Empire for a man who did not quibble over means, so long as he kept up appearances.[12]

The inversion of flattery is hurting one's sense of choice, yet it also distorts communication and more often than not disrupts the encounter. If ego hurts alter personally the communication cannot proceed on a factual–material level. The communication becomes skewed with emotional undertones and overtones and is distorted by fastly recruited psychic defenses by both sides to the encounter. As with flattery, one is selectively attuned to injuries to one's sense of choice. Even if ego does not usually associate with alter and he does not value his opinions, he will be hurt by alter's insults to his sense of choice. As ego cannot even be remotely aware of the wide range of alter's vulnerabilities and sensitivities, he is liable to hurt his sense of choice inadvertanly and contribute, thereby, to the defensive distortion of the communication and to the possible rupture of the encounter.

One of the pioneering expositions of the intentional or situationalized misrepresentations in daily encounters is Goffman's study of the presentation of false fronts in order to deceive and defraud.[13] He describes the numerous occasions in which ego presents a "fostered appearance", and alter has no means to ascertain the difference between ego's front and whatever non-simulated affects and thoughts there are behind his performance. Indeed, whole professions are built on the proficiency to present fronts and appearances in the most appealing way to the widest audience, without worrying too much whether there is any correlation between the image presented and reality. The entertainment industry does not usually intend to sell its customers more than aesthetic pleasures, an exciting pastime or fantasies. But the advertisement colossi, the public relations concerns and the political machines profess to sell to the public not images but reality, yet many times the qualities attributed by these image makers to their products are as real as minotaurs. Further, the whole legal profession is trained, geared and employed to present issues in a one-sided and hence twisted and biased manner. Yet, one of the most bizarre paradoxes of the administration of justice is that only people of legal training are appointed as judges in most legal systems and from then onwards they are supposed to be objective.

Goffman describes many varieties of performances that are intended for outward consumption in order to support a front which is advantageous to ego or is in line with the presumptuous roles he plays at a given time and place.[14] The intellectual *poseur*, for example, has leather copies of Spinoza and Nietzsche on the living room table, but keeps the real reading material (Harold Robbins novels) in the bedroom. A friend of the author, a scientist, had a special suit and a trained demeanor for his visits to research funding agencies. Another personal example is when, on a visit to Australia, the author encountered a group of émigre Hungarians who were mostly cab drivers and travelling salesmen. On Sundays, some would sit in coffee houses in Sydney's Bouble Bay quarter and arrange to be paged as barons or colonels. All these are defenses of the feelings of choice or separant devices to enhance success in a competitive context.

We disagree with Goffman that there is a statistical relationship between ego's contrived façade and his "real" intentions.[15] Short of being psychotic, ego does not believe in his false façade. His "sincerity" in performance is a measure of his acting talents and not a function of his belief in the false role which he plays for outward consumption.

Secrets are also obstacles against communication because they give the secretive ego a manipulative advantage over alter who is ignorant of the secret. Goffman speaks of "dark secrets" (which if known to the audience would disrupt ego's performance and façade), "strategic secrets" (which ego may use to manipulate alter in the future), and "inside secrets" (like the secretive façade presented by the groups of Ouspensky followers who give the impression that they possess some universal secrets revealed to them by Gurdjieff, which they are not allowed to divulge).[16]

A large variety of false fronts are presented by people in authoritarian settings who are under the power of their *ad hoc* audience. A mental patient will "oblige" the treatment staff in a mental hospital and display the symptoms which are expected of him.[17] Jean Genet diplayed a deviant front to his foster family as expected from a foundling bastard from the *Assistance Publique.*[18] Young prostitutes who grew up in authoritarian families of North African origin displayed to their relevant others the promiscuous behavior, which they felt subterraneously to be expected of them.[19]

The need to dramatize a certain performance or role also distorts communication.[20] Ego is of the opinion that the meaning of his message will not be clear enough to alter, so he exaggerates its presentation by the dramatization of what seems to him the most expressive core of the message. This is usually at the expense of the connotative nuances and the peripheral penumbra of the message to which less attention is paid or which is disregarded altogether. Ego may also invest so much energy in the dramatic staging and transmission of the message that its material contents are neglected, as is aptly portrayed by a quotation of Sartre by Goffman. "The attentive pupil who wishes to be attentive, his eyes riveted on the teacher, his ears open wide, so exhausts himself in playing the attentive role that he ends up by no longer hearing anything".[21]

Most of human communication in a separant competitive setting is based on double standards. There is a discrepancy of various magnitudes and nature between ego's façade, which he presents to alter, and his covert aim underlying this façade. The smart guy manipulates other people and makes them do what he wants them to do while presenting a façade of related disinterest, sympathetic altruism and a free-floating desire to help everybody and especially his audience, who are quite likely not aware that they are being deceived and exploited. One of the ex-deans of the author's faculty used to deliver long speeches supporting a certain resolution, which he had introduced and claimed to be so obviously for the good of the faculty. When the resolution was accepted, the author discovered that the dean slipped in a proviso that was solely to his personal benefit, and which was the main reason for his introducing the resolution. An old acquaintance of the author telephoned him the other day and expressed his wish to visit him because they hadn't seen each other for so many years. When he came he brought some cherries from his garden and reminisced for two hours about old times. When he said goodbye and was just about to depart he asked "by the way" if I could recommend him for a scholarship to a university in the United States.

The double standards and hypocrisy in sexual matters are legendary and proverbial and have been the topic of endless works of fiction and drama throughout the ages. Yet, even in the presumably liberated and permissive twentieth century, sexual relationships are rife with deceptive façades. A colleague of the author, who runs with amorous intentions after almost everything that moves, lectured the author over a cup of coffee how faithful he was to his wife, not because of a normative duty but because she fulfilled all his needs both spiritually and sexually and he did not desire any other woman.

Most administrators have to have a façade, which is, to varying degrees, different from their underlying intentions. Otherwise they are not able to maneuver themselves among the conflicting interests of the various members and factions in the organization and gloss over the constant tensions in its structure. Most of their statements begin, continue or end with a proclamation that the good and welfare of the organization, association or institution needs a certain decision or that the flourish, and the glory of the Syndicate, the Party or the Nation necessitates a given action. Yet, more often than not they have their own welfare, the power of their clique, or the interests of their faction in mind when they advocate a decision or an action. However, they explode with fury if they are accused of hypocisy and double standards, because the rules of the game are that one should have double standards and behave accordingly, but one should never admit having them.

Manners, etiquette and devices of keeping a social distance are many times used as what Goffman calls "forms of mystification" to assert rank and prevent familiarity that breeds contempt of superiors.[22] This mystification involves, no doubt, fences of various heights and width, which bar communication among the various ranks in a given hierarchy. Blau and Scott have demonstrated that the formal status hierarchy in an organization creates obstacles to the free flow of communication. Specifically, dependence on superiors for formal rewards restricts consultation across hierarchical boundaries.[23] A superior subordinate may not freely discuss a certain matter because the former might show ignorance and lose face and authority, whereas the latter on showing ignorance might risk his forthcoming raise or promotion.

In the Byzantine hierarchies of academia, a junior non-tenured faculty member has very often to weigh and then modify every syllable he utters in order not to offend one of the august professors who are bound to be on his promotion committee and flatter profusely year after year every possible candidate for his tenure committee. Hierarchies also create barriers of non-communication as status symbols, like a superior passing in the corridor and looking through a subordinate as if he was thin air. In a like manner, the pompous boss inflated with his own self importance, and the defensive meekness of a subordinate sitting in front of "The Great Man" with false modesty are very common forms of distorted communication in bureaucratic structures.

The Oblique Rituals

Robert Merton portrays the ritualist as one who relinquishes the cultural goals because he either despairs of achieving them or is afraid of fighting for them.[24] Consequently, he anchors himself on means, rituals and rules around which he structures his anomic existence. We maintain, however, that the separant *arriviste* does not fall back on rituals as a *faut de mieax* last resort anchor, but as the only way he knows to interact with other human beings when he is not busy manipulating them. His separant core personality vectors, as well as his socialization, make him regard social encounters as no deeper than the *Ity–Ity* level of small-talk at a cocktail party and the rites of his weekly meeting of the Lions' Club and bridge games. Unless he is engaged in a business meeting to make a kill, he is quite happy and content to make the opening speech at the inauguration of the neighborhood swimming pool and shake the hand of the mayor while photographers immortalize it at the annual charity ball. Nobody, of course, is uni-dimensional, but if a person is close to the separant pole of our personality continuum, interaction rituals are all that he sees in interpersonal relationships unless he is engaged in competitive go-getting where the only rule is "catch-as-catch-can".

The participant, on the other hand, led by his inner sense of purpose, regards interaction rituals as empty, boring and many times nauseating puppetry engaged by people who do not know what to do with themselves or with their time. The Heideggerean scorn regards these ritualized gatherings for small talk (*Gerede*) as the embodiment of inauthenticity. It is not being with others but chattering with others (*Miteianderreden*).[25]

The rituals of human gatherings serve mostly to ensure that the outward façade of the interaction complies with the prevailing norms of style, fashion and etiquette. That the party, the meeting, the fund raising dinner should run "smoothly", *comme il faut*. The organizers of these gatherings are not so much concerned with the material topic under discussion as with the observance of the rules and procedure. The separant mostly focuses on the form of human interaction, whereas the participant looks for its underlying meaning. If one looks for a deeper meaning in rituals of human interaction than their separant regulatory function one may land in deep trouble. Oscar Wilde, for instance, took the rituals of human interaction too seriously. He confounded form and content with disastrous results. George Bernard Shaw, while eulogizing Wilde said, "Wilde was so in love with style that he never realized the danger of biting off more than he could chew. In other words, of putting up more style than his matter would carry. Wise kings wear shabby clothes and leave the gold lace to the drum major".[26] Greetings are also formal, regulatory devices which have no intrinsic meaning content-wise. One of the definitions of a *Schlumiel-nudnick* is one who asks "How are you?" and responds by reciting his troubles.

There are, however, some functional uses of rituals both for separant and participant ends. Fascists discovered the anxiety-generating effects of a long approach to the leader's desk, behind which the light floods from a window and blinds the visitor. In a like manner, other separant devices such as furniture placement, the differential allocation of Persian carpets and mahogany desks, and the location of the visitor's seat in relation to "The Great Man" are intended to put the visitor in his right place.

Participant rituals like the dances of the Sufi Dervishes and the Far Eastern meditation rites are instrumental to the achievement of the participant *Unio Mystica*. Yet the non-participant observer might not be aware of the underlying meaning of the ritual. A visiting Baptist preacher visited the Sufi Monastery in Acre in Israel, and later described in his report the Dervishes' dance as similar in function to the American Indians' rain dance.

In his studies of human interaction rituals, Goffman concentrates on the nature of the *persona*, the masks that people wear in their interrelationships with other people. We, however, focus on the hypocritic nature of the interaction ritual in the ancient Greek sense of *UTTOKPITOS*, the role-player who puts on a face and the disparity between his façade and its underlying meaning, which cannot be perceived by an outside audience. Consequently, this hypocritic façade which changes with time, place, culture and different people within a culture constitutes a major barrier to communication.

We may state, in conclusion, that the distortions of interpersonal communication due to self-deception, deception and interaction rituals are almost endless. Goffman displays a reserved optimism about ego's ability to see through alter's front and perceive the "truth" behind it.[27] We do not share Goffman's optimism even in its limited form, and our discussions and analyses in the present chapter support our reluctance to do so.

Dissonances

Reducing dissonance is a defense mechanism, which can be done either by ego changing his cognitive stance prior to the dissonant message or changing the cognition of the incoming message so that it is more congruent with the previous cognition. The former mechanism is related to the dynamics of conformity. If ego has undergone a genuine attitude change following his exposure to the dissonant message then it is outside the scope of the present work, which deals with distortions and breakdowns of communication. In the present section, we shall confine ourselves to ego's twisting the incoming messages in order to regain congruence with his previous cognitive stance. Achieving consonance in this manner between two discordant cognitions inevitably necessitates the distortion of ego's communication with his surroundings and with other people. Aronson claims:

Dissonance is a negative drive state which occurs whenever an individual simultaneously holds two cognitions (ideas, beliefs, opinions) which are psychologically
inconsistent. Stated differently, two cognitions are dissonant if, considering these
two cognitions alone, the opposite of one follows from the other. Since the occur-
rence of dissonance is presumed to be unpleasant, individuals strive to reduce it
by adding "consonant" cognitions or by changing one or both cognitions to make
them "fit together" better; i.e. so that they become more consonant with each
other . . . Thus, dissonance theory does not rest upon the assumption that man is
a rational animal: rather, it suggests that man is a rationalizing animal – that he
attempts to appear rational, both to others and to himself.[28]

Many of the defense mechanisms which we have described earlier are, of course,
utilized to reduce cognitive dissonance. If ego, for instance, is a woman-chaser
and this is incompatible with his self-image as a devoted *pater familias*, he may
project and rationalize. "Everybody is running after girls these days, but even if
they don't they would very much like to, only they are just frightened of their
wives and of gossips".[29] The distortion of incoming messages to reduce dissonance is both in avoiding information, which increases dissonance, and actively
searching for information which increases consonance.[30]

The most common defense mechanism against cognitive dissonance is selective exposure. Ego may guard himself against dissonant messages with a wide
series of defenses ranging from the derogation of the source of the dissonant
message, through preparing beforehand refutations of the impending contradictory messages, to distorting the contents of the contradictory message so that
it is more consonant with the existing cognition.[31] A corollary of this premise is
that the greater the dissonance, the greater the defensive distortion of the
incoming messages.[32] It is submitted that ego's definition of himself as being
dissonant *vis-à-vis* an incoming message is related to many personal and
contextual factors. For instance, if ego's cognitive system is a simple-monolithic
one, as far as a given frame of reference is concerned, he is more prone to define
himself in a state of cognitive dissonance in relation to a divergent message than
when his multiplex cognitive system is, to begin with, composed of diverging
stances in relation to a given focal concern.[33] Similarly, if ego is intolerant of
ambiguity or is closed minded as measured by some socio-psychological instruments, he is more prone to cognitive dissonance than if he was tolerant of
ambiguity and open minded.[34] People also differ in their ability to bear cognitive dissonance as well as in the means they use to reduce it.[35] Finally, a message
may be dissonant with ego's relevant cognitive system in one time and place,
and be neutral or consonant with it at other times and other places. The relevance of this to our context is that alter cannot be aware most of the time of
what message is dissonant with ego's cognitive structure, and why it is dissonant with his specific psycho-cultural *gestalt*. Consequently, he is not able to
perceive the meaning and motivation of ego's behavior, which is intended to
reduce the dissonance. Cognitive dissonance and the means used to regain

consonance constitute, therefore, another major obstacle to interpersonal communication.

We note that ego's efforts to achieve consonance by manipulating the divergent incoming messages is basically a separant inclusionary mechanism, whereas the change of ego's cognitive stance to conform to incoming dissonant messages is basically a participant exclusionary dynamic with which we have dealt in earlier chapters.

In his classic exposition of the theory of cognitive dissonance, Festinger points out that the magnitude of dissonance is related to the importance to ego of both the relevant existing cognitive configuration, and the contradictory new messages to which he is being exposed.[36] The importance of this to our context is that the greater the relevance of the conflicting cognitive elements to ego's core personality dynamics, the greater would be his efforts to regain congruence by distorting the divergent messages.

The Balance Theory is linked to Heider's dictum that we believe that "bad" action comes from "bad" people and "good" deeds are carried out by "good" people. We also tend to cluster "good" things with "good" guys (like us) and "bad" things with "bad" guys (not like us).[37] The most relevant instance to our context is when alter, whom ego esteems and likes (a good guy), says something derogatory about ego (a good guy indeed). Ego may achieve congruence by derogating alter. "I don't know what has come over him lately, this excessive boozing of his made him lose his ability to judge people" (i.e. a good guy like ego). Ego may also "interpret" alter's words so that he did not really mean to derogate ego and whatever he said was a constructive and fair criticism of his performance. Finally, ego may disassociate alter from the derogatory statement and the culprit becomes "the SOB Harry who misquoted alter", so that good guy alter is still favorably disposed towards good guy ego.[38]

The further relevance of the various consistency models (the Cognitive Dissonance theory, the Balance and Congruity models) to the present work is in our ability to provide deeper aetiological insight into their congruity based dynamics, as well as into the distortion of communication effected by them. The various consistency models take the congruity principle in human behavior as given or base it on some structural components of the human psyche. We, however, provide in the present work (and in *The Myth of Tantalus*)[39] a bio-psychological and developmental explanation to Man's quest for congruity – namely, the separant ego's efforts to regain dominion over the object which he sensed himself as having during his early developmental phases and the participant's longing to revert back into the omnipresence of early orality. The variability in the potency of the conflicting separant and participant vectors in ego's personality core, as well as the relative magnitude of the Sisyphean and Tantalic cultural components that he has internalized, determine the power that drives him to achieve cognitive congruity. The magnitude of this motivation to achieve congruity determines, in turn, the extent of ego's needs and willingness to distort dissonant information and messages so that they fit a given cognitive stance. Our exposition of ego's feelings of existential choice and ontological uniqueness provide another dimension to his reluctance to accept or to give in to normative transmissions which diverge from his previously internalized cognitions. This, more than some homeostatic mental construct, which some personologists postulate, may account for the entrenchment in attitudes of people and their security bound anchor on stability. The less secure ego is in his social position, and the harder it is for him to achieve it, the more violently he protects his sense of choice from the assaults on it by cognitive dissonances. The author has recently had some business with a high level civil servant of low education and intelligence, but with animal cunning and stubbornness who got his job through political connections and loyalties. He expressed truths as absolute decrees and his justice as unequivocal. Any view diverging from his was rotten, corrupt and a brazen lie. He stuck desperately to the meagre pearls of wisdom he mastered with great effort and which he expressed in basic Hebrew, and fought tooth and nail against any view and anybody who tried even remotely to contradict them. The more embedded we are in our previously held cognitive stances (that are largely based on our participant quest of stability), and the stronger we are motivated to impose our existing cognitive structure on divergent incoming messages in a separant manner, the more we tend to distort the dissonant communication to fit our congruity bound cognitive system.

One of the attractive aspects of the theory of cognitive dissonance is the fascinating study that gave it one of its first empirical anchors. Leon Festinger managed to plant some participant observers in the group led by Mrs. Marian Keech of Lake City who predicted, on the basis of messages she claimed to have received from outer space, that on a certain date the whole continent of America would be submerged by the Ocean. A group of ardent believers gathered around her and awaited the end of the world. When at the set date the prophecy failed a frantic proselytizing activity started by members of the group to spread the Word and the Faith. Festinger stated the conditions, based on cognitive dissonance theory, under which we may expect an increased religious fervour following a disconfirmation of a prophecy:

1. A belief must be held with deep conviction and it must have some relevance to action, that is, to what the believer does or how he behaves.

2. The person holding the belief must have committed himself to it; that is, for the sake of his belief, he must have taken some important action that is difficult to undo.

3. The belief must be sufficiently specific and sufficiently concerned with the real world so that events may unequivocally refute the belief.

4. Such undeniable disconfirmatory evidence must occur and must be recognised by the individual holding the belief.

5. The individual believer must have social support. It is unlikely that one isolated believer could withstand the kind of disconfirming evidence we have specified.[40]

The saga of Mrs. Keech and her group has the aura of the theatre of the absurd – a more fantastic and yet realistic version of Beckett's *Waiting for Godot*. It also served Festinger as a far-fetched yet intellectually attractive matrix for the genesis of religious movements. It seems to us, however, that Festinger's interpretation of Mrs. Keech's movement was somewhat simplistic. Religious movements are never monolithic and they contain a certain division of labor between the dreamer prophets and their *apparatchick* priests. The rather detached participant prophets like Jesus Christ and Shabetai Zevi had their separant "Macher" priests like Saint Paul for Christ and Nathan of Gaza for Zevi, who started to spread the word when the prophets' prophecies failed. The same held true for Mrs. Keech's movement which had a Dr. Armstrong, a separant go-getter who organized most of the proselytizing in the movement.

The Biased Consistency

The most common technique to achieve consonance following an exposure to a dissonant message is to twist the latter so that it fits the previous cognitive stance.[41] This also has a "boomerang effect", in so far as ego's rejection of the dissonant message entrenches him deeper into his original cognitive anchor.[42] If ego's cognitive anchor stance is very firm he tends to argue *ad hominem* against the author of the dissonant view, and not only against the view itself. There is some inconclusive empirical evidence that ego's tendency to expose himself selectively to dissonant messages increases with the magnitude of dissonance caused by the incoming information and decreases with ego's greater confidence in his opinion. These are in line with the much quoted findings that United Nations information campaigns were mostly watched on television by people who were favorable to the United Nations to begin with. Eighty percent of subjects in a given study selected advertisement for cars which they had already bought, and mothers selected lectures on the nature vs. nurture controversy, which supported their firmly held views.[43]

A very common technique of biased congruity is the one used by lawyers, theologians and Marxists. They "differentiate" the dissenting judgment. By making an edict or decree from the existing precedents, dogma and official party line, they find a niche in the total scholastic maze without losing any of its material dissonant qualities, and yet display a consonant front.

Once we have made a decision we tend to avoid, distort and be selectively exposed to messages which are dissonant with our decision.[44] In a similar vein, if we have chosen one employee out of many candidates we shall tend to be relatively blind, for a while at least, even to his most glaring shortcomings. Also, if a group has ostracized one of their members or knowingly treated him badly they will be particularly active in rejecting good opinions of him and inflating the bad ones.

If ego has suffered badly in a certain place, he will have to justify to himself and to others his having stayed there and reject advice that he leaves it. There is much to recommend, at least from the cognitive dissonance point of view, in some of the Zionist propaganda for prospective immigrants to Israel that states it is not a land of milk and honey but of blood, sweat and tears. The author remembers the awful time he had in a certain academic institution and yet he vehemently rejected the urging of his friends that he leave it. The followers of Mrs. Keech were loyal to their new creed because they invested in it greatly by resigning from their jobs and joining the movement. The harsher the initiation rites in a certain group, the dearer it is to the initiates' heart .

A whole series of studies has shown that the more tedious a task, the more ardently the subjects defended its performance. Also, if they were paid meagerly to spread the word that the task was interesting, they tended more to believe their own statements than if they were paid more reasonably.[45] Similarly, children who were threatened with a mild punishment for playing with a desired toy decreased their liking for the toy to a greater extent than children who were severely threatened not to play with it.[46] A mild punishment did not constitute a strong enough incentive to refrain from playing with the toy so the toy itself had to be devalued. In the same vein, if ego is engaged in a task for which he does not have enough motivation, he will search for more reasons to justify it. Also, new converts to a creed are its best missionaries because they have to justify to themselves and to others their radical change of creed. However alter, who does not undergo similar cognitive dissonance experiences, will not be able to understand ego's behavior or his motivation for it.

The author has recently experienced the effects of cognitive dissonance when he found himself defending even the most obscure (and hardly defensible) passages of Heidegger's *Sein Und Zeit*. A quick introspection convinced him that he spent so much time and effort to understand this most profound yet hopelessly opaque work that he felt the need to defend even its most incomprehensible passages. There are numerous examples for these biased consonances. A fellow whose car gives him a lot of trouble develops an attachment to it to justify his investments in it. The chores of correcting term papers pushes some academicians to see themselves as hard pressed pioneers struggling to achieve the lofty goals of higher education, and a colleague of the author who was engaged for six months in the thankless task of organizing a scientific congress developed a theory that congresses are a major vehicle for the dissemination of knowledge.

This aspect of the cognitive dissonance theory may receive in the present work a deeper existentialistic meaning in so far as it may fit into the wider matrix of the Camusean Sisyphus – finding meaning in his daily drudgeries and a measure of happiness in his painful interaction with his burden-stone.

The "refutation treatment" of the dissonant message is a point-by-point counter attack to dissarm the onslaught of the contradictory views or information, whereas the derogation of the source of the dissonant message diminishes its impact.[47] Finally, the "denial treatment" used and misused by politicians since time immemorial is more or less in the form of, "the prime minister/first secretary of the Party/Chairman of the Council has been misquoted by the press as saying . . . whereas in reality he said . . . " This denial strategy might reduce the cognitive dissonance of the politician, but more often than not it confounds the issue farther and blurs the message in the time-honored tradition of the politicians, that the public must never be too clear about the intentions of its leaders.

Petrification

Medusa's Stare

In the present work we are concerned with the mode of human alienation, which results from Man's frustrated efforts to reach a level of encounter with his fellow men that is meaningful to himself. This mode of alienation will be denoted as petrification, which is used in this text as a different sense than related concepts such as reification or fetishism, in Marxist as well as in Western behavioral and social science literature.[1] Petrification is a process that starts with ego seeking an intersubjective communication with alter. When this proves to be impossible, ego may experience his encounter with alter as objectifying and stultifying various components and attributes of his own cognitive processes. Petrification is not a necessary sequel to ego's breakdown of communication with his surroundings, but a possible one. In this chapter, we shall try to discuss how petrification may be avoided or rather evaded. Petrification is also not a static condition but a dynamic process; it may be slight, acute or chronic, and like a mood it may be fleeting or over-poweringly morbid.

Jean Paul Sartre, probably more than any other Existentialist thinker, has dealt with various aspects of petrification in a vein similar to ours. Sartre's basic postulate underlying his subsequent analysis is that intersubjective communication is impossible:

> For the only consciousness which can appear to me in its own temporalisation is mine, and it can do so only by renouncing all objectivity. In short the for-itself as for-itself cannot be known by the Other. The object which I apprehend under the name of the Other appears to me in a radically other form. The Other is not a for-itself as he appears to me; I do not appear to myself as I am for-the-Other. I am incapable of apprehending for myself the self which I am for the Other, just as I am

incapable of apprehending on the basis of the Other-as-object which appears to me, what the Other is for himself.[2]

Consequently, ego can but be an object to alter and vice versa. When ego is alone in his garden surrounded by lawns and trees, everything is perceived and experienced subjectively by him. But then alter enters (the other), and ego knows by inference that alter also perceives the same garden and trees and experiences them subjectively. This rearranges ego's experience of his surroundings since he has been forced to share it with alter. Sartre claims:

> There exists necessarily a relation between the Other and the statue which stands on a pedestal in the middle of the lawn, and a relation beteween the Other and the big chestnut trees which border the walk: there is a total space which is grouped around the Other, and this space is made with my space; there is a regrouping in which I take part but which escapes me, a regrouping of all the objects which people my universe.[3]

Alter thus encroaches on ego's cognitions of his surroundings, which before his appearance were a system in balance with ego as center. After alter's appearance, ego's personal space is, so to speak, diverted and cathected around alter. The result is that ego is dethroned from his uniqueness by the appearance of alter, and the ontological exclusiveness of ego is usurped by the centrifugal flow of ontological space from ego to alter, who is now installed as a partner to ego's cognitions of his surroundings. When alter looks at ego he perceives him as an object. Ego infers this from the fact known to him that he also can perceive alter only as an object. The result is that if before alter's appearance ego experienced his surroundings with himself as subject, alter's look makes ego an object to alter (i.e. objectifies him). Sartre says:

> . . . the person is presented to consciousness in so far as the person is an object for the Other. This means that all of a sudden I am conscious of myself as escaping myself, not in that I am the foundation of my nothingness but in that I have my foundation outside myself. I am for myself only as I am a pure reference to the Other.[4]

We denote this as external petrification. Furthermore, the fact that alter sees ego as an object becomes part of ego's cognition (i.e. part of himself), so that ego internalizes an objectifying alter as part of his subjectivity, which is transformed into an object.[5] This is ego's internal petrification which supplements his external petrification and starts the process of turning him into a reified object both to others and to himself. This is dramatically portrayed in Sartre's play *No Exit*, where each of the three characters not only objectify the others with his external trespassing on their ever shrinking subjectivity, but also with their ultimate and inevitable acceptance of the other's petrifying messages and internalizing them into their private hell.

Sartre sees the mutual Medusa's stare of ego and alter as petrifying each other's subjectivity. Sartre's dictum of "either the other looks at me and alienates my liberty or I assimilate and seize the liberty of the other", indicates that he envisages a world populated with separant types only where ego ever aims to overpower alter and petrify him and vice versa. We, however, wish to add the participant dimension and the submissive alter who is a willing victim to ego's petrifying communications. In this case the model is Beckett's *Endgame* where Hamm, the blind paralyzed master, subjugates and vilifies his crippled servant Clov who is a willing accomplice to his own petrification. Between Sartre's separate mutual petrification in *No Exit*, Beckett's separant–participant dyad in *Endgame* and the additional dimension of external and internal petrification, the range of the varieties and dynamics of petrification are vast indeed.

It is interesting to note that the same expression is used in Hebrew for being stared at and for being frustrated, as well as being deranged and dumb.[6] Whatever the value of this linguistic comparison, it is quite intriguing that the connotation of staring in this context means a piercing concentrated stare and not just a look giving an additional hue of a Sartrean petrifying stare. A folkloristic variation on the theme of the petrifying stare is the "evil eye". Exline says, "Others have pointed to the more fearful properties of the look". Elworthy documented the opinion that belief in the evil eye is one of the most ancient superstitions of the human race, being referred to in the literature of ancient Eygpt, Babylonia, Greece and Rome. Tomkins called our attention to contemporary news reports to the effect that English country folk attribute the wildness of pigs to the evil eye and that an American businessman hired an expert to keep employees at work by "glaring at them".[7] On a more sophisticated level, we have Hegel's assertion that to perceive is to transform.[8] By the act of attention we statify the Bergsonian flowing *durée* and the expected future is contracted over a fleeting "eye-blink" present into the oblivion of the past.[9] The Gorgon queen staring through ego's eyes not only petrifies but also annihilates.

The need to take account of others looking at ego limits his freedom. In flight the author very often leaves his shoes on his tired feet for fear that if he took them off his socks might have a hole in them, which would be noticed by the passing hostess, who thus limited the range of his possible action yet was a total stranger to him. The presence of another person in the house, even if he is a beloved friend or a welcome guest, limits the hosts' range of possible behavior and induces him to choose a course of action that he might not otherwise have taken. This presence narrows the hosts' personal freedom and petrifies various extents of his possibilities and potentialities. If this guest does not wish to bother the host and refuses in all sincerity offers of help or convenience, or apologizes profusely for every real or imaginary inconvenience he has caused the host and his family, he actually becomes bothersome and eventually is more of a nuisance than if he would have cared less about the welfare of his host. Conversely, if ego hates alter or he made him angry by an overt or covert provocation, ego is petrified by alter's presence because ego's mental energies are invested into his hatred of alter and not much is left for anything else. Also, the energy ego has to muster in order to initiate communication with alter involves varying amounts of effort depending on ego's personality type and *ad hoc* mood. Usually ego expends mental energies and attention in initiating an encounter with alter according to his expectations from the encounter, which are bound to be different from alter's expectations from it, so that the ensuing inevitable mutual frustrations lead to a joint resentment and disconnection of the encounter. Consequently, ego's attention to sensitivity towards and involvement with alter is liable to lead to ego's dependency or subjugation to alter's petrification and vice versa. Again, the Least Interest Principle reigns supreme. The more involved ego is in the encounter and the more he expects from it, the more he is liable to be dependent on the encounter with alter and the higher the chances of alter's petrification and alienation from ego. It seems that the inevitable gap between ego and alter's expectations of their encounter constitutes the built-in programming for the disruption of the encounter and the frustration of the quest for dialogue.

Ego petrifies alter if he makes him an instrument, a means to achieve his own egotistical ends. This is Buber's *I–It* relationship manifested in Sade and Casanova's manipulation of their sexual objects, and the landlady in Genet's play *The Maids*, who loves her domestic help "as she loves her arm chair. Not even that much; like her bidet, rather. Like her pink enamel lavatory seat".[10] Basically, the separant activist ego tends to impose himself on others and hence radiates external petrification, whereas the more submissive participant ego tends to introject the petrifying messages and be internally petrified. Indeed, the participant is more of a loser in his interaction with the separant go-getter. The former aims at a deeper level of encounter than the separant is willing or able to be involved in. The participant ego is, therefore, more easily frustrated in his interpersonal relations by his inner expectations that are not fulfilled and by the separant's shallow communications which are dissatisfying to him, and hence stultifying and petrifying. If both ego and alter are participants, they may initially have a better chance for a mutually satisfying encounter, but their quest for a deeper encounter makes them more sensitive to the minutest emotional nuances in each other. Every difference of opinion, emotion or attitude is augmented disproportionally and the encounter very soon lands into an especially painful mutual petrification. The separant, on the other hand, hops from one social encounter to another, full of small talk and shallow camaraderie. He usually does not expect more than the routine interaction of daily discourse from his encounter. However, in rare moments of truth the separant busybody realizes that he has spent his life in petty meanderings and inconsequential manipulations and that there is more to life than going through its routine motions. If he does not achieve the insight and rebellious stamina of a Camusean Sisyphus he is liable to burst into shrieks of agony *à la* Tolstoy's Ivan Ilitch, which will indeed curdle the blood of everyone within hearing distance.

One of the major petrifying agents is the "generalized other", also known as the "man-about-town", the "everybody says so", the *tout Paris*, and the Heideggerean *Das Man*. This is the abstraction of all the alters who demand a share in ego's existence and compliance to the rule of "one should behave like this and one should not behave like that". The generalized other embodies the normative system of the group and upholds the central measures of the mean, mode and median. It levels down the protruding irregularities and nourishes the cult of mediocrity. The generalized other is an abstraction of a delusive pseudo community, yet it exerts a tremendous pressure on ego to conform to what he defines as the generalized others' decrees as to the "proper" behavior, the *comme il faut* manners and the "comportment befitting an officer and a gentleman". This generalized other fills ego with amiety and fear, yet he does not have any real existence. Ego may not pay any attention to the real concrete others like the milkman, the grocer and the bank teller, yet the generalized other who is their abstraction exerts on him an enormous pressure. Not even ego's relevant others like his boss or his father, who have a direct bearing on his day to day existence, are as powerful and engulfing in their demands from ego as this generalized other. The latter is an omnipresent partner in ego's encounters with concrete alters. He "sits on ego's back" and pressurizes him to pay constant attention to him, to his mandates and proscriptions. He is the ever present tyrant who combines forces with the concrete alters to deprive ego of layer after layer of his subjective authenticity and subject him to a progressive external and internal petrification. Ego succumbs to the petrifying processes when he tends to evaluate his behavior according to how it seems to the generalized other, and whether it is approved or disapproved by him. This anaesthetizes ego's *Ani* (inner-self core) and lets the interactive *Atzmi* dominate the whole personality. This makes him fit for routine daily discourse and encounters but his inner sensitivities, insights and creativity are being numbed, stifled and stultified. The petrified ego is so engrossed by the generalized other that he feels transparent, and he feels that whatever goes on within his psyche (his intentions and motives) is intelligible to the others around him. *In extremis* this is portrayed by Orwell's "Big Brother", petrifying ego with his probing gadgets and thought police. However, the generalized other being a construct, an abstraction, is far removed from the concrete alters who are also different from one another, so that the generalized other dominated ego may find himself in constant conflict in his daily encounters with the concrete others, who do not conform to the images and mandates of the generalized other as internalized by ego. These conflicts are exacerbated by an *Ani*-skewed personality, which is anchored on the inner self. Ego feels that most of the concrete others are not even "scratching the surface" of his psyche. Their discourse seems shallow to him and their message bland and pointless. In extreme cases this *Ani*-skewed self caught in the web of the total strangeness of his surroundings and estrangement from all the people around him, culminates in the syndrome of the outsider so masterfully portrayed by Albert Camus' novel *The Stranger*.

It should be pointed out that ego's petrification by the generalized other has very much in common with Riesman's conceptualization of "other directedness", except that *The Lonely Crowd* deals with "other directedness" in a cultural and social context, whereas petrification by the generalized other is an existential process on the individual level of ego losing his ontological authenticity.[11]

The Inauthentic Moods

The petrified ego moves around with his feelers of empathy and tries to convey to alter what he thinks or feels alter wishes to hear. On the other hand ego, in an authentic mood, talks, preaches and even screams his inner truths in a Kierkegaardean manner irrespective of whether alter is interested in listening to ego's truths or able to understand them. Ego, alas, may soon realize as Kierkegaard did, that trying to force-feed alter his pearls of wisdom may alienate, dismay or revolt him. Kierkegaard was undaunted by his audience's reluctance to listen to his revelations, but lesser individuals might be traumatized and petrified further by their unsuccessful attempts to communicate their inner truths to misunderstanding, non-responsive, indifferent or hostile relevant others.

Another mode of external petrification is the reification of creative individuals by covetous hords of manipulators, who try and many times succeed in exploiting them to their own ends. These are the art dealers who recognize the greatness of budding and struggling painters yet buy their masterpieces for peanuts, the publishers who regard authors as burdensome instruments for their money making, and the lackeys and campfollowers of performing artists who slobber over them their fake love and flattery, so long as they can suck money and favors out of them like parasitic leeches. The author witnessed recently how pompous officials, fat society matrons and self-styled art connoisseurs descended like a cloud of locusts on the octogenarian Marc Chagall, when he visited Israel. Most of them were pushing one another to reach the old painter to ask him to sign Chagall posters and lithographs in order to raise their value manifoldly. Chagall took the only logical course to avoid being lynched by the petrifying crowd in which every individual was sweating to snatch a part of the painter for himself – the old man fled, ran into a cab, and spent the whole afternoon at the sea shore sipping tea and basking in the Mediterranean sun. He left the dignitaries, art critics and tabloid gossips waiting for him in vain and bemoaning in righteous indignation the behavior of their prey who escaped their petrifying clutches.

The Lost Opportunities

Petrification also entails a feeling of missed possibilities. Ego's elegiac complaint is that "if only he had been bolder" in an encounter with alter he might have had his way. But at the crucial moment he couldn't think and he couldn't move. He was paralyzed by alter's presence or by the context of the encounter. The post-encounter staircase arguers belong to this category, who become very bold after the meeting and recite to themselves the good points they could have raised in the meeting itself, which ended in their disfavor. Lost opportunities are also related to the similar expectations of ego and alter from their encounters, which were entertained by each one of them separately in different times, different places and different encounters. These are exemplified by the stale reunions of old friends, old flames and sweethearts who hardly have anything to say to each other or the ageing spinsters who try pathetically to recapture their waning luck with their suitors whom they refused in their young prime.

If alter hurts ego's feelings of choice and uniqueness and alter is important enough to ego to be hurt by him, ego will be petrified in so far as he will spend an unduly large proportion of his mental energies in contemplating revenge on alter or brooding in self-pity over his injured ego.

Ego may petrify alter by manipulating and controlling him through lavish gifts and favors, thus making him literally or emotionally indebted and dependent on him. This is the Heideggerean *Zuhandene* of alter by ego, making him an objectified instrument, a utensil to achieve his egotistical ends.[12] In a similar vein, ego may manipulate alter's guilt feelings in order to control him in the proverbial tradition of the Yiddishe Mama who controls (and petrifies) her family through emotional blackmail.

Another instance of petrification occurs at the outset when ego limits his encounter with alter to a specific level or segmented area. An Ayn Rand ego(ist) may decide – in line with his creed that his encounter with alter will be conducted rationally – without recourse to emotion on his part and with a total disregard of any show of emotion by alter. When alter does use emotions and empathy in his discourse with ego, who seems to ignore them, alter may feel rejected and dejected or decide to disrupt the encounter with ego who behaves like a mechanical zombie operating by some rules of logic without feelings.

A very common instance of petrification is when alter trustingly "opens up" to ego, brushing aside all reservations and defenses only to be slyly exploited by ego as an instrument and means to achieve his ends. As an interim conclusion we observe that the barriers and distortions of communication between ego and alter constitute a major basis for ego's objectifying loss of his own petrification of alter. Paradoxically, the more ego strives to communicate with alter the greater are the chances of their mutual petrification. Emerson has aptly summarized this premise when he said, "Man is insular and cannot be touched. Every man is an infinitely repellent orb".[13]

The petrified individual has been doing what the generalized other or his relevant others expected him to do. When later (usually in middle age or after) he wants to cast off their stultifying spell and "do his own thing" it is usually too late or impossible. Ego, on his way to petrification, marries someone of whom his parents, family, friends and acquaintances approve. He is very happy and proud that they look very well together when they strut to and fro on the village green. The boys are envious of his fiancee's good looks, that she is from a "good family", and that they will be well received by the pillars of the community. The fact that his fiancee is not so good in bed and that they really don't have much to say to each other when they are alone, is either selectively misperceived by ego or dismissed by him with an optimism he hardly believes in, that "things are going to improve in the future". Her other assets so valued by his family and friends are overwhelmingly important for the separant *Atzmi* bound ego on his way to his petrification by matrimony. When the time comes and ego realizes that he married his wife because his relevant others liked him to be married to her, and his sense of choice and worth was reinforced by the liking, he is usually stuck with a frigid, boring chatterbox, and it is usually too late or pointless to change anything.

When ego works in a given job or profession because his relevant others have influenced him to choose it, and not because he himself has chosen it, he will be petrified by his work irrespective of the regime he lives in. This is the major fallacy in Marxist and neo-Marxist reliance on the alienation of labor and hence the reification of the laborer in capitalist societies.[14] It is not so much the worker controlling or not controlling the means of production that is linked to his petrification, but his being subject to the choice and control of others in the type of his occupation and in the manner it has to be carried out. Ching Chiang Ho, who has to collect so many crates of dead sparrows, do calisthenics and read the sayings of Chairman Mao while he is burning with desire to be a chef in a Cantonese restaurant, or Yuri Alianshvili, who was sent by the Central Georgian Soviet Commission on Higher Education to study dam engineering while he has the talent for playing the violin, are as equally petrified by their work as Tom Smith who works in his father's stockbroker firm in Manhattan, while his real passion lies in studying the reptiles of the Arizona desert.

The Emperor's New Clothes

Ego is very often petrified by the generalized other in his leisure time and cultural activities, such as, "one should enjoy very much sailing on a boat", "it is fun to ride horses", or "it is a must to listen to the whole winter series of concerts of the Israel Philharmonic Orchestra". The author vividly remembers his first visit to the circus with his elementary school class. The teacher spoke almost incessantly for a whole week prior to the visit how wonderful the *jongleurs* of the circus were, how funny the clowns would be, and how delightful the dancing animals would be. At the actual performance the ten-year-old author thought that the clowns looked pitiful and their jokes were silly, that the animals looked sad having to perform their unnatural acts under the cruel cracking of the trainers' whips. The *jongleurs* looked pathetic as they endangered themselves to give the yelling crowd some cheap thrills. Yet, the author thought that something must be wrong with him if he did not enjoy the circus performance that *everybody* should and apparently does enjoy so much. This petrification element seems to be a basic component in Man's interpersonal relations. It is apparent in the Asch and Crutchfield type conformity studies, where the separant *Atzmi* bound ego tends to accept the erroneous consensus of others and not the dissenting yet true perception of ego's senses.[15] On a tragicomic yet very realistic level Anderson's story *The Emperor's New Clothes* has a whole crowd petrified by the anxiety to look and sound foolish, for "the whole public cannot possibly be wrong".

Programming Against Dialogue

The petrifying pressures on the generalized other are especially hard on the *Ani* bound participant ego. He finds it nauseating to smile all the time with sticky flattery to his superiors, to invite the boys from the office for dinner and to complement their wives' dresses and hair-dos. The separant manipulator, on the other hand, has no qualms about flattery or the *manus manum lavat* of power politics. Friends for him are those with whom he can exchange favors or with whom he has common enemies. The author has watched from close quarters some extreme separant egotists whose cool manipulation of others verged on perfection. These institutionalized psychopaths – high ranking army officers, government officials and academic administrators – had either no feelings at all towards others, or they trained themselves to suppress these feelings. They seemed to operate with the conviction that any affective attachment to others, both positive and negative, impedes the achievement of their manipulative aims. These extreme egotists, who are fortunately quite rare, yield an enormous power over people because their affective detachment from others makes them invulnerable to petrification and allows them to manipulate people in disinterested efficiency as if they were so many crates of soap. Hannah Arendt described the "banality of evil" of some of the top Nazi murderers as a corollary of their ability to deal with people with a total lack of affective involvement.[10] The author was present at Eichman's trial, all too aware of the fact that for Eichman, the Jews to be gassed at Auschwitz were regarded as petrified objects who had no human attributes and hence had no right to be treated as human.

Petrification is a function of involvement. The more emotionally involved ego is with alter the more dependent he is on him, and the more vulnerable he is to be petrified by alter. Generally, if ego is more involved with alter, alter has power over ego and ego is, therefore, more vulnerable to petrification by alter. A separant ego trying to overpower alter may easily do so if alter is dependent materially or emotionally on him. However, if the participant alter is not involved with ego then ego's attempts to overpower, possess and dominate alter are bound to boomerang back to ego. The evasive alter then has the trump cards vis-à-vis ego, who will be engrossed and preoccupied with his failure to dominate and control alter. Consequently, ego ends up being petrified by alter both externally and internally. Again we reach one of our main theses in our present work from another direction, as if all paths lead to it. If ego is involved with alter and seeks an encounter with him on a deeper level than alter is willing or able to reach, his chances of being petrified by alter, irrespective of whether he is a separant go-getter or a self-effacing participant, are higher with resultant higher chances of an inauthentic discourse and a disruption of the encounter altogether. The approach–avoidance programming against dialogue seems to be universal. If ego craves an encounter with alter it seems to recede like a fata Morgana, but if he is not interested in it alter virtually forces himself into ego's reluctant lap.

Other petrifying agents are guilt and shame, which have some overlapping areas with the Heideggerean notions of anxiety and fear which constitute the main characteristics of Man's "being-in-the-world". We also regard fear, anxiety, guilt and shame as some of the attributes of Man's deprivational interaction with objects and other people. However, shame is more separant, in so far as ego is ashamed of the possible reactions of the generalized other to his behavior, whereas guilt is more participant as it is felt by ego when he behaves contrary to the intuitive revelations and insights of his inner self. If ego feels – rightly or wrongly – guilt or shame towards alter, it could launch their relationship into a petrifying positive feedback cycle. Ego would refrain from meeting alter and his not coming to see him or not phoning him would further augment his guilt and shame so that more estrangement will ensue de capo. When ego and alter finally have a rendezvous intentionally or by accident, they may spend most of their time explaining or over-explaining the causes of the initial stultification of their encounter. Also, a timid participant ego may try to overcome his guilt with a violent reaction–formation show of courage and engage in a staccato effort to regain the heart or friendship of alter. The latter may be dismayed by ego's frantic reinvolvement in their encounter and clam up or back into his shell in anxious petrification. Worse still, a separant ego would project his shame on alter and accuse him of the sole responsibility for creating "bad blood" between them, so that the encounter is liable to be terminated in mutual bitterness.

Notes

Introduction – The Breakdown of Meaningful Interaction

1 E. Durkheim, *The Division of Labor in Society* (Illinois: Free Press, 1964), p. 38.

2 A. W. Gouldner, "Anti-Minotaur: The Myth of Value-Free Sociology" in *Social Problems* (1962): p. 199.

3 G. Nettler, "A Measure of Alienation" in *American Sociological Review* (1957): Vol. 22.

4 E. A. Tiryakian, *Sociologism and Existentialism* (New Jersey, 1965), p. 674.

5 E. A. Tiryakian, "Existential Phenomenology and the Sociological Tradition" in *American Sociological Review* (1965): Vol. 30, p. 962.

6 J. P. Sartre, *Being and Nothingness* (New York: Citadel Press, 1965), p. 398.

7 Ibid.

8 Ibid., p. 38.

9 K. Jaspers, *Man in the Modern Age* (London: Routledge & Kegan Paul, 1966), p. 81.

10 J. L. Simmons and B. Winograd, It's Happening: A Portrait of the Youth Scene Today (California: Marc-Laird Publications, 1968).

I Accidia and the Absurd – A Conceptual Discussion

1 E. Durkheim, *Suicide, A Study in Sociology* (Illinois: Free Press, 1951), pp. 131–60.

2 R. K. Merton, "Anomie, Anomia and Social Interaction, Contexts of Deviant Behavior" in M. B. Glinard, *Anomie and Deviant Behavior* (Illinois: Free Press, 1964).

3 Ibid., p. 213.

4 We have used the form of "accidia" and not "accidie" to resemble the personalized "anomi" and not group-based "amonie."

5 L. Srole, "Social Integration and Certain Corollaries, An Exploratory Study" in *American Journal of Sociology* (1956): pp. 709–16.

6 H. Seeman, "On the Meaning of Alienation" in *American Sociological Review* (1959): Dec. 1959.

7 M. Rosner, *Hitnakrut: Alienation – A Comprehensive Analysis of the Marxist Exposition of Alienation* (Hadera: Givat Haviva, 1967).

8 G. Lukács, *Existentialism and Marxism* (Tel Aviv: Hakibbutz HaMeuchad, 1950).

9 J. P. Sartre, *Being and Nothingness*, Part III.

10 E. Durkheim, *Encyclopedia of Religion and Ethics* ed. J. Hastings (New York: T &T Clark, 1951), pp. 65–6.

11 A. Camus, *The Myth of Sisyphus* (New York: Vintage Books, 1955), p. 23.

12 For a pioneering and penetrating treatment of scientific accidia see Hans L. Zetterberg, "Scientific Acedia" in *Soc. Focus* (1967): Vol. 1.

13 Durkheim, *Encyclopedia*, pp. 65–6.

14 F. Tannenbaum, *Crime and the Community* (New York: Columbia University Press, 1938).

15 E. M. Lemert, "Social Structure, Social Control and Deviation" in M. B. Glinard, *Anomie and Deviant Behavior* (Illinois: Free Press, 1964).

16 E. H. Sutherland and D. R. Cressey, *Principles of Criminology* (Philadelphia: Lippincott, 1970), chap. IV.

17 J.P. Sartre, *Nausea* (New York: New Directions, 1964).

18 Camus, *The Myth of Sisyphus*, p. 16.

19 Ibid., p. 17.

20 Durkheim, *Encyclopedia*, 1951, pp. 65–6.

21 Lemert, *Social Structure, Social Control and Deviation*, p. 68.

22 R. K. Merton, *Social Theory and Social Structure* (Illinois: Free Press, 1964), p. 189.

23 Ibid., pp. 153, 189.

24 A. Camus, *The Stranger* (New York: Vintage Books, 1954), p. 62.

25 Ibid., p. 74.

26 A. Camus, *The Fall* (New York: Vintage Books, 1956), p. 86.

27 Camus, *The Stranger*, pp. 13, 27.

28 Merton, *Social Theory and Social Structure*, p. 153.

29 J. Alexander and H. Stub, *The Criminal, The Judge and the Public* (Illinois: Free Press, 1957), p. 215.

30 Camus, *The Fall*, pp. 56–7.

31 Camus, *The Stranger*, p. 24.

32 Ibid., p. 44.

33 Ibid., p. 53.

34 W. A. Kaufman, *Existentialism* (New York: Meridian Books, 1958), p. 259.

35 Camus, *The Fall*, p. 84

36 K. Horne, "Culture and Neurosis" in *American Sociological Review* (1936): p. 227.

37 Camus, *The Fall*, p. 133.

38 Srole, *Social Integration and Certain Corollaries*.

39 Seeman, *On the Meaning of Alienation*, p. 534.

40 Camus, *The Stranger*, p. 103.

41 Ibid., p. 105.

42 Camus, *The Fall*, p. 87.

43 Camus, *The Myth of Sisyphus*, p. 91.

44 T. Parsons, *Essays in Sociological Theory* (Illinois: Free Press, 1954), p. 55.

45 Ibid., p. 125.

46 T. Parsons, *The Social System* (Illinois: Free Press, 1964), p. 38.

47 L. Fewer, *What is Alienation? The Career of a Concept in Sociology on Trial* (New Jersey: Prentice-Hall, 1963), p. 143.

48 Merton, *Social Theory and Social Structure*, p. 133.

49 M. R. Cohen, *Reason and Nature* (Illinois: Free Press, 1964), p. 349.

50 M. Heidegger, *Being and Time* (Oxford: Blackwell, 1967), sec. 22–8.

51 W. A. Kaufmann, *Critique of Religion and Philosophy* (New York: Harper & Brothers, 1958), p. 259.

52 H. Miller, *Plexus* (Paris: Olympia Press), p. 497.
53 Camus, *The Myth of Sisyphus*.
54 S. Freud, *An Outline of Psychoanalysis* (New York: Norton Press, 1949), p. 8.
55 Heidegger, *Being and Time*, p. 311.
56 Sartre, *Being and Nothingness*, chap. 1.
57 Kaufmann, *Existentialism*, pp. 415–16.
58 Camus, *The Myth of Sisyphus*, p. 5.
59 Kaufmann, *Existentialism*, p. 211.
60 Ibid., p. 535.
61 A. Camus, *The Rebel* (London: Hamish Hamilton, 1953), pp. 31, 51.
62 Camus, *The Myth of Sisyphus*, p. 16.

2 The Congruity Principle

1 Camus, *The Myth of Sisyphus*, p. 13.
2 A. Kuhn, *The Study of Society* (London: Social Science Paperbacks, 1966).
3 D. Krech, R. S. Crutchfeld and E. L. Ballachey, *Individual in Society* (New York: McGraw Hill, 1962), p. 504.
4 M. F. Muller, trans., *Vedic Hymns* (New York: P. F. Collier, 1950), pp. 1–48.
5 Ibid.
6 G. G. Scholem, *Major Trends in Jewish Mysticism* (New York: Schocken Books, 1941), p. 245.
7 B. Spinoza, *Spinoza's Ethics and On the Correlation of the Understanding* (London: Dent, Everyman's Library, 1959), p. 230.
8 L. Lévy-Bruhl, *La Mentalité Primitive* (Paris: Presses Universitaires de France, 1960).
9 F. Nietzsche, *The Genealogy of Morals* (New York: Modern Library, 1927).
10 H. L. Bergson, *Creative Evolution* (London: Macmillan, 1954), p. 160.
11 Any standard text of Social Psychology would contain numerous references to the basic research findings of this context.
12 T. J. Scheff, "Towards a Sociological Model of Consensus" in *American Sociological Review* (1967): pp. 32–46.
13 R. W. Brown, *Social Psychology* (Illinois: Free Press, 1965), p. 606.
14 N. F. Miller, "Comments on Theoretical Models illustrated by the Development of a Theory of Conflict Behavior" in *Journal of Personality* (1960): pp. 82–100.
15 R. S. Lind, *Knowledge for What?* (NJ: Princeton University Press, 1939), pp. 60–2.
16 G. C. Wynne-Edwards, *Animal Disposition in Relation to Social Behavior* (New York: Hafner Pub. Co., 1962).
17 Brown, *Social Psychology*, pp. 7–8.
18 A. Artaud, *Les Temps Modernes* (Paris, Feb. 1949).
19 Camus, *The Rebel*, p. 30.
20 Plotinus, *The Philosophy of Plotinus – A Representative Book from the Enneads* (New York: Appleton-Century-Crofts, 1950).
21 Ibid.
22 B. Russell, *History of Western Philosophy and its Connection with Political and Social Circumstances from the Earliest Times to the Present Day* (London: Allen & Unwin, 1946), pp. 62–3.

23 S. Freud, *The Collected Papers* (London: Hogarth Press, 1924,) p. 107.

24 Kaufmann, *Critique of Religion and Philosophy*, p. 420.

25 S. Freud, *Totem and Taboo* (London: Penguin Books, 1938).

26 Camus, *The Myth of Sisyphus*, p. 91.

27 L. Festinger, *When Prophecy Fails* (Minneapolis: University of Minnesota Press, 1956).

28 Scholem, "Mitzva Haha'ah be Avera" in *Knesset* (*Hebrew*) (1937): p. 359.

29 Ibid., p. 379.

30 Musset, "La Nuit du Mai" in Mario Praz, *The Romantic Agony* (New York: Meridian Books, 1956), p. 28.

31 W. R. Lange, *The Philosophy of Plotinus*, Vol. II (London: Green & Co., 1948), p. 62.

32 G. Sholem, *Major Trends in Jewish Mysticism* (New York: Schocken Books, 1961).

33 *The Dao De Ching*, chap. 22.

34 G. W. Leibniz, *Monadolgie: Vermunst Prinzipien der Natur und der Gnade* (Hamburg, F. Meiner, 1956), pp. 14–17.

35 Plotinus, *The Philosophy of Plotinus – A Representative Book from the Enneads.*

3   The Broken Image and the Absurd – A Theoretical Analysis

1 Heidegger, *Being and Time.*

2 R. C. Wylie, *The Self-Concept, a Critical Survey of Pertinent Research Literature* (Nebraska: Lincoln University of Nebraska Press, 1961), pp. 319–20.

3 J. C. Diggory, "The Components of Personal Despair" in E. S. Schneidman, *Essays in Self-Destruction* (New York: Science House, 1967), pp. 300–23.

4 E. Husserl, *Ideas: General Introduction to Pure Phenomenology* (London: Allen & Unwin, 1931).

5 O. W. R. Ritchie and M. R. Koller, *Sociology of Childhood* (New York: Appleton-Century-Crofts, 1964), p. 130.

6 T. G. Di Lampedusa, *The Leopard* (New York: Pantheon, 1960), p. 212.

7 Brown, *Social Psychology*, p. 657.

8 R. Tagiuri and L. Petrullo, *Person Perception and Interpersonal Behavior* (California: Stanford University Press, 1962), pp. 86–94.

9 Ibid., 63–83.

10 M. Merleau-Ponty, *Phenomenologie de la Perception* (Paris: Gallimard, 1945), p. 406.

11 Tagiuri and Petrullo, *Person Perception and Interpersonal Behavior*, pp. 54–61.

12 Ibid., pp. 258–75.

13 Brown, *Social Psychology*, p. 647.

14 E. Goffman, *Interactional Ritual* (Chicago: Aldine Pub. Co., 1967).

15 W. James, *Essays in Pragmatism* (New York: Hafner Pub. Co., 1966), p. 147.

16 S. F. Miyamoto and S. Dornbusch, "A Test of Interactionist Hypothesis of Self-Conception" in *American Journal of Sociology* (1956): pp. 399–403.

17 J. S. Adams, "Iniquity in Social Exchange" in *Advances in Experimental and Social Psychology* (New York: Academic Press, 1965), p. 293.

18 W. Buchanan and H. Cantril, *How Nations See Each Other* (Illinois: Urbana University Press, 1953).

19 S. A. Star and H. M. Hughs, "Report on an Educational Campaign" in *American Journal of Sociology* (1950).

20 Adams, *Iniquity in Social Exchange.*

21 Ibid., pp. 271–320.

22 M. Bogdanoff et al., "The Modifying Effect of Conforming Behavior" in *Clinical Review* (1961): p. 135.

23 Brown, *Social Psychology*, pp. 678–9.

24 Krech, Crutchfeld and Ballachey, *Individual in Society*, pp. 525–6.

25 T. W. Brehm and A. R. Cohen, *Explorations in Cognitive Dissonance* (New York: Wiley & Sons), 1962.

26 Adams, *Iniquity in Social Exchange*, p. 158.

27 H. K. Kelley and M.S. Shapiro, "An Experiment on Conformity to Group Norms" in *American Sociological Review.* (1954): 667–77.

28 J. W. Thibaut and H. M. Kelley, *The Social Psychology of Groups* (New York: Wiley & Sons, 1959), p. 239.

29 V.L. Allen, "Situational Factors in Conformity", in *Advances in Experimental Social Psychology*, 2 (1965).

30 D. Bell, *The End of Ideology* (Illinois: Free Press, 1968), pp. 573–94.

31 S. G. Shoham, *The Mark of Cain* (Jerusalem: Israel University Press, 1970), pp. 71–128.

32 N. W. Bell and E. F. Vogel, *A Modern Introduction to the Family* (Illinois: Free Press, 1968), p. 450.

33 Ibid., pp. 521–37.

34 Ibid., pp. 499–509.

35 Ibid., pp. 510–20.

36 Thubut and Kelley, *The Social Psychology of Groups.*

37 Bell and Vogel, *A Modern Introduction to the Family*, pp. 538–43.

38 C. S. Chilman, *Growing up Poor* (Washington, DC: US Dept. of H.E.W.), 1966.

39 J. Aronfreed, *Conduct and Conscience* (New York: The Academic Press, 1968), p. 305.

40 Ibid., p. 203.

41 W. McCord, J. McCord and A. Howard, "Familial Correlates of Aggression in Nondelinquent Male Children" in *Journal of Abnormal and Soc. Psychology* (1961).

42 A. Bandura and R. H. Walters, *Social Learning and Personality Development* (New York: Holt, Rinehart and Winston, 1959).

43 L. Kohlberg, "Development of Moral Character and Moral Ideology" in L. Hoffman and M. Hoffman, eds., *Review of Child Development Research* (1964), pp. 383–433.

44 Aronfreed, *Conduct and Conscience*, 1968, p. 316.

45 L. B. Fester and T. B. Appel, "Punishment of S-Responding in Matching to Sample by Time-Out from Positive Reinforcement" in *Journal of the Experimental Analysis of Behavior* (1961): pp. 45–6.

46 *Conduct and Conscience*, p. 318.

47 E. H. Sutherland, *The Professional Thief* (Chicago: University of Chicago Press, 1937).

48 E. H. Sutherland, *White Collar Crime* (New York: Rinehart & Winston, 1961).

49 Ibid., pp. 97, 55.

50 Brown, *Social Psychology.*

51 E. H. Sutherland and D. R. Cressey, *Principles of Criminology* (Philadelphia: Lippincott, 1970).

52   Bandura and Walters, *Social Learning and Personality Development*.

53   R. M. Chisholm, *Theory of Knowledge* (New Jersey: Prentice-Hall, 1966), p. 11.

54   Ecclesiastes 1:18.

55   S. G. Shoham, "Culture Conflict as a Frame of Reference for Research in Criminology and Social Deviance" in M. E. Wolfgang, *Crime and Culture Essays in Honor of T. Sellin* (New York: Wiley & Sons, 1968), pp. 76–8.

56   Adams, *Iniquity in Social Exchange*, pp. 271–320.

57   Brown, *Social Psychology*, p. 348.

58   G. H. Mead, *Mind, Self and Society* (Chicago: University of Chicago Press, 1934).

59   Plotinus, *The Philosophy of Plotinus – A Representative Book from the Enneads*.

60   Krech, Crutchfeld and Ballachey, *Individual in Society*.

61   Camus, *The Rebel*, p. 53.

62   A. Koestler, *The Act of Creation* (London: Hutchinson, 1964), p. 351.

63   D. C. McClelland, *Studies in Motivation* (New York: Appleton-Century-Crofts, 1953), Fig. 4.1.

64   Kaufmann, *Critique of Religion and Philosophy*, pp. 423–4.

65   Cohen, *Reason and Nature*, p. x.

66   Merton, *Anomie, Anomia and Social Interaction, Contexts in Deviant Behavior*, p. 140.

67   W. J .H Sprott, *Human Groups* (London: Pelican Books, 1958), pp. 28–35.

68   S. Rosenzweig, "The Experimental Measurements of Types of Reaction to Frustration" in H. A. Murray, ed., *Explorations in Personality* (Oxford: Oxford University Press, 1962).

69   P. J. Lazarsfeld and M. Rosenberg, *The Language of Social Research* (Illinois: Free Press, 1955), p. 53.

70   Merton, *Anomie, Anomia and Social Interaction, Contexts in Deviant Behavior*.

71   This has been demonstrated, *inter alia*, by the studies of the *Centre National de Recherche Sociologique* in Paris, on the Pieds-Noirs.

72   Scholem, *Major Trends in Jewish Mysticism*.

73   Camus, *The Myth of Sisyphus*, p. 11.

74   V. Van Gogh, *The Letters* (London: Collins, 1963), pp. 154, 166–7.

75   Ibid., p. 236.

76   Ibid., p. 340.

77   A. Koestler, *The Yogi and the Commissar* (London: Cape, 1945), p. 18.

78   Camus, *The Myth of Sisyphus*, p. 11.

79   M. Buber, *I and Thou* (New York: Charles Scribner & Sons, 1958), p. 11.

80   Ibid., pp. 16–7.

81   M. Buber, *Between Man and Man* (London: Routledge & Kegan Paul, 1949), p. 160.

82   T. F. O'Dea, *The Sociology of Religion* (New Jersey: Prentice-Hall, 1966), p. 10.

83   Scholem, *Major Trends in Jewish Mysticism*, p. 245.

84   L. Neuman, *A Hassidic Anthology* (New York: Schocken Books, 1963), p. 427.

85   A. W. Watts, *Myth and Ritual in Christianity* (London: Thames & Hudson, 1954), p. 134.

86   Scholem, *Major Trends in Jewish Mysticism*, p. 246.

87   Ibid., p. 246.

88   Ibid., p. 317.

89   Ibid., p. 318.

90 The late Chief Rabbi Kook expounded this doctrine.
91 S. Freud, *The Future of and Illusion* (New York: H. Liveright, 1949), pp. 29–9.
92 S. A. Kierkegaard, *The Present Age and the Difference Between a Genius and an Apostle* (New York: Harper & Row, 1962).
93 Heidegger, *Being and Time*, sec. 27.
94 K. Jaspers, *Man in the Modern Age* (London: Routledge & Kegan Paul, 1966), p. 41.
95 D. Bell, *The End of Ideology* (Illinois: Free Press 1960), p. 301.
96 McClellan, *Studies in Motivation*, 1955.
97 Ibid.
98 R. R. Dines, A. C. Clarke and S. Dintz, "Levels of Occupational Aspiration: Some Aspects of Family Experience as a Variable" in *Americn Sociological Review* (1956): pp. 212–15.
99 Durkheim, *The Division of Labor in Society.*
100 R. K. Merton, *Social Structure and Anomie in Social Theory and Social Structure* (Illinois: Free Press, 1957).
101 Shoham, *The Mark of Cain*, chap. 13.
102 M. Scheller, *Ressentiment* (Illinois: Free Press, 196).
103 Camus, *The Myth of Sisyphus.*

4 The Absurd Revisited

1 Camus, *The Myth of Sisyphus*, p. 16.
2 S. G. Shoham, *The Myth of Tantalus,* 2nd revised edition (Brighton & Portland: Sussex Academic Press, 2005).
3 E. Ericson, "The Problem of Identity" in *Journal of American Psychoanalysis. Ass.4* (1956): 56–121.
4 Shoham, *The Myth of Tantalus.*
5 Shoham, *The Myth of Tantalus*, chapter 2.
6 I. Kant, *Critique of Pure Reason* (Köniksberg: Akademic Ausgabe, 1787), pp. 38,40,80.
7 M. Merleau-Ponty, *Phenomenology of Perception*, p. xi.
8 G. Vesey, *Perception* (London: Macmillan, 1972), pp. 29, 30.
9 Ibid., p. 3.
10 G. S. Klein, *Perception. Motives and Personality* (New York, 1970), p. 49.
11 See ibid., pp. 49 et seq.; Z. Giora, *Psychopathology* (New York: The Gardner Press, 1975), pp. 53– 54.
12 Vesey, *Perception,* pp. 5, 14, 43–44.
13 Ibid., pp. 43–44.
14 Kant, *Critique of Pure Reason,* pp. 44, 61.
15 M. Heidegger, "Sein und Zeit" in *Jahrbuch fur Philosophie und Phanomenologische Forschung* 8 (1927); Merleau-Ponty, *Phenomenology of Perception*, p. 410.
16 Heidegger, *Sein und Zeit,* pp. 350, 373.
17 See H. Jonas, *The Gnostic Religion* (Boston: Beacon Press, 1963), p. 336.
18 H. Bergson, *The Creative Mind,* trans. M. L. Andison (New York: Philosophical Library, 1946), pp. 16 et seq.
19 Shoham, *Myth of Tantalus,* chapter 1.
20 Ibid., chapters 5, 6, 7.

21 K. Wolff, *The Sociology of Georg Simmel* (New York: The Free Press of Glencoe, 1964). p. 122.

22 Shoham, *Myth of Tantalus,* chapters 5, 6, 7.

23 Ibid., chapters 5, 6.

24 We shall later link our present premise to Petri's "augmentation" and "reduction", as well as Klein and Holzman's "leveling" and "sharpening". See A. Petrie, *Individuality in Pain and Suffering: The Reducer and Augmenter* (Chicago: University of Chicago Press, 1967), pp. 138–140; and G. S. Klein, and P. S. Holzman, "The Schematizing Process: Perpetual Attitudes and Personality Qualities in Sensitivity to Change" in *American Psychologist* 5 (1950): p. 312.

25 See L. Festinger, H. W. Ricken and S. Schachter, *When Prophecy Fails* (New York: Harper & Row, 1964).

26 Shoham, *Myth of Tantalus,* chapters 5, 6, 7.

27 S. H. Bergman, *Dialogical Philosophy from Kierkegaard to Buber* (Jerusalem: The Bialik Institute, 1974, Hebrew).

28 Sartre, *Being and Nothingness,* pp. 340 et seq.

29 A. Camus, *The Misunderstanding* (New York: Vintage Books, 1962).

30 Sartre, *Being and Nothingness.*

31 J. Genet, *Deathwatch* (London: Faber & Faber,) 1961.

5 The Cognitions of Dialogue

1 See R. D. Laing, *Self and Others* (Harmondsworth: Penguin Books, 1975), pp. 44 et seq.

2 Shoham, *The Myth of Tantalus.*

3 Krech, Crutchfield and Ballachey, *Individual in Society,* pp. 30 et seq.

4 Shoham, *The Mark of Cain.*

5 Shoham, *The Myth of Tantalus,* chapter 3.

6 For a recent analysis of the cognitive processes see Zvi Giora, *Psychopathology: A Cognitive View* (New York: The Gardner Press, 1975).

7 R. R. Blake and G. V. Ramsey, *Perception: An Approach to Personality* (New York: The Ronald Press, 1951), p. 271.

8 Krech, Crutchfield and Ballachey, *Individual in Society,* pp. 17, 20.

9 G. A. Kelly, *The Psychology of Personal Constructs* (New York: W. W. Morton & Co., 1955), pp. 40, 55.

10 This is not unlike Kelly's "anticipations" in ibid.

11 See F. Barron, M. Jarvik and S. Bunnell Jr., "The Hallucinogenic Drugs in Altered States of Awareness" in *Scientific American* (San Francisco: W. H. Freeman & Co., 1972) pp. 99 et seq.

12 H. J. Eyesenck, *The Biological Basis of Personality* (Springfield, Ill: Charles C. Thomas, 1967), p. 76.

13 Rosenzweig, *Types of Reaction to Frustration.*

14 C. G. Jung, *Psychological Types* (London: Kegan Paul, 1944), p. 567.

15 Eyesenck, *The Biological Basis of Personality,* pp. 36–37.

16 A. Petrie, *Individuality in Pain and Suffering: The Reducer and Augmenter* (Chicago: University of Chicago Press, 1967), pp. 138–40.

17 H. A. Witkin et al., *Psychological Differentiation* (New York: Wiley, 1962).

18   See G. S. Klein and H. J. Schlesinger, "Perceptual Attitudes, Toward Instability" in *Journal of Personality*, 19 (1951): 289 and G. S. Klein, "The Personal World Through Perception" in *Perception: An Approach to Personality*, ed. R. R. Blake and G. V. Ramsey (New York: The Ronald Press, 1951).

19   Krech, Crutchfield and Ballachey, *Individual in Society*, p. 21.

20   J. B. Deregowski, "Effect of Cultural Valve of Time upon Recall" in *British Journal of Social and Clinical Psychology* 9 (1970): pp. 37–41.

21   Shoham, *Myth of Tantalus*, chapters 2, 3.

22   A. W. Watts, *The Way of Zen* (New York: Mentor Books, 1957), p. 63.

23   Seyyed Hossein Nasr, *Sufi Essays* (London: Allen & Unwin, 1972), p. 37.

24   Cited by Max Weber, *The Protestant Ethic and the Spirit of Capitalism* (New York: Scribner, 1958), p. 48.

25   Shoham, *Myth of Tantalus*, chapter 4.

26   Blake and Ramsey, *Perception*, p. 267.

27   R. E. Ornstein, *On the Experience of Time* (New York: Pelican Books, 1975), pp. 29–36, 29.

28   Ibid., chapters 2, 3.

29   M. Guyau, *La Genese de l'idee de temps* (Paris, 1890), cited in ibid., p. 37.

30   M. Frankenhaeuser, *Estimation of Time, An Experimental Study* (Stockholm: Almgvist & Wiksell, 1959).

31   J. Ortega y Gasset, *Man and People* (New York: W. W. Norton & Co.), pp. 29–30.

32   Shoham, *Myth of Tantalus*, pp. 20–22.

33   Ibid., pp. 10–12.

34   F. Heider, *The Psychology of Interpersonal Relations* (New York: John Wiley & Sons, 1964), chapter 4.

35   E. E. Jones and G. R. Goethals, "Order Effects in Impression Formation: Attribution Context and the Nature of the Entity" in *Attribution; Perceiving the Causes of Behavior,* ed. by E. E. Jones and D. E. Kanouse (USA and Canada: General Learning Press, 1971).

36   R. E. Nisbett and S. Valins, "Perceiving the Causes of One's Own Behavior", in ibid.

37   D. E. Kanouse, "Language, Labeling and Attribution", in ibid.

38   Kelly, *Psychology of Personal Constructs*, pp. 8–9.

39   G. A. Kelly, "A Summary Statement of a Cognitively-oriented Comprehensive Theory of Behavior" in *Readings for a Cognitive Theory of Personality* ed. J. C. Mancuso (New York: Holt,) Winehart & Winston, 1970), p. 39.

40   C. G. Jung, "Synchronicity: An Acausal Connecting Principle" in *The Nature of Human Consciousness,* ed. R. E. Ornstein (San Francisco: W. H. Freeman & Co.), pp. 445–7.

41   Krech, Crutchfield and Ballachey, *Individual in Society*, p. 28.

42   A. Michotte, *La Perception de la Causalite* (Louvain: Publication Universitaires de Louvain, 1954).

43   H. H. Kelley, *Attribution in Social Interaction* (New York: General Learning Press, 1977), p. 8.

44   George Klein, *Perception, Motives and Personality* (New York: Alfred Knopf, 1970).

45   A. H. Hastorf, D. S. Schneider and S. Polefks, *Person Perception* (Reading, Mass.: Addison & Wesley Pub., 1970).

46   B. Von Haller Gilmer, *Psychology* (New York: Harper & Row, 1970), p. 178.

47 H. Cantril, "Perception and Interpersonal Relations" in *Journal of Psychology* 114 (1957): p. 119.

48 S. Fisher, "Sex Difference in Body Perception" in *Psychological Monographs* 78 (1964): p. 14.

49 See J. S. Bruner, "Personality Dynamics and the Process of Perceiving", in Blake and Ramsey, *Perception, An Approach to Personality*, pp. 121 et seq.

50 N. Cameron, "Perceptual Organization and Behavior Pathology", in ibid., pp. 283 et seq.

51 J. S. Bruner and L. Postman, "Emotional Selectivity in Perception and Reaction" in *Journal of Personology* (1947): pp. 16, 69.

52 H. S. Sullivan, *Psychoanalysis and Interpersonal Psychiatry* (New York: Science House, 1970).

53 W. N. Dember, "The New Look in Motivation" in *Readings for a Cognitive Theory of Personality*.

54 W. Fuchs, "Completion Phenomena in Hemianopic Vision" in *The Eye*, ed. J. M. Heaton (London: Tavistock, 1968), p. 93.

55 S. M. Lurie, "The Effect of Body Position of Meridional Variations in Scotopic Acuity" in *Journal of American Psychology* 76 (1963): p. 598.

56 R. Hilgard, "The Role of Learning in Perception' in Blake and Ramsey" in *Perceptions: An Approach to Personality*, p. 100.

57 W. R. Garner, "To Perceive is to Know" in *Readings for a Cognitive Theory of Personality*, pp. 302–11.

58 G. M. Stratton, "Some Preliminary Experiments in Vision without Inversion of the Retinal Image" in *Psychological Review* 3 (1896): p. 611.

59 I. Kohler, "The Formation and Transformation of the Perceptual World" in *Psychological Issues* 4 (1964): p. 12.

60 Hastorf, Scheinder and Polefks, *Person Perception*, p. 43.

61 Blake and Ramsey, *Perception: An Approach to Personality*, p. 10.

62 E. Frenkel-Brunswick, "Intolerance of Ambiguity as an Emotional and Perceptual Personality Variable" in *Journal of Personology* 18 (1949): p. 108.

63 J. M. Heaton, ed. *The Eye* (London: Tavistock, 1968), p. 64.

64 Ibid., p. 63.

65 Ibid., p. 37.

66 J. S. Bruner and C. C. Goodman "Value and Need as Organizing Factors in Perception" in *Journal of Abnormal Social Psychology* 42 (1947): p. 33.

67 D. C. McClelland and J. W. Atkinson, "The Projective Expression of Needs: The Effects of Different Intensities of the Hunger Drive on Perception" in *Jour. of Psychology* 25 (1948): p. 205.

68 J. C. Franklin et al., "Observations of Human Behavior in Experimental Semistarvation and Rehabilitation" in *Journal of Clinical Psychology* 4 (1948): pp. 28–45.

69 Heaton, *The Eye*, p. 61.

70 D. C. McClelland, *Personality* (New York: Holt, Rinehart & Winston, 1951).

71 J. Piaget, *The Psychology of Intelligence* (New York: Harcourt Brace, 1950), pp. 75–76.

72 C. Turnbull, *The Forest People* (London: Chatto & Windus, 1961).

73 See Shoham, *Myth of Tantalus,* chapter 1, as to the age related changes in *Weltanschauung.*

74 B. Von Haller Gilmer, *Psychology* (New York: Harper & Row, 1970) p. 172.

75 See Heaton, *The Eye,* pp. 40–41 for other criteria of perceptual grouping.

76 Heider, *Psychology of Interpersonal Relations,* pp. 182 et seq.

77 M. Sherif, D. Taub, C. I. Howland, "Assimilation and Contrast Effects of Anchoring Stimuli on Judgments" in *Journal of Experimental Psychology* 55 (1958): pp. 150–5.

78 A. S. Luchins, "Primacy – Recency in Impression Formation" in *The Order of Presentation in Persuasion,* ed. Howland (New York: Yale University Press, 1957).

79 S. E. Asch, "Forming Impressions of Personality" in *Journal of Abnormal and Soc. Psychology* 41 (1946): pp. 271–2.

80 E. E. Jones, "Order Effects in Impression Formation: Attribution Context and the Nature of the Entity" in *Attribution; Perceiving the Causes of Behavior,* p. 42–3.

81 See G. J. W. and G. S. Klein, "Subliminal Effects of Verbal Stimuli" in *Journal of Abnormal and Soc. Psychology* 59 (1959): 167; see also other references in Blake and Ramsey, *Perception, an Approach to Personality,* pp. 270–1.

82 Heaton, *The Eye,* pp. 188, 189.

83 S. C. Mclaughlin, "Visual Perception in Strabismus and Amblyopia" in *Psychological Monographs* 78 (1964): p. 12.

84 W. Johnson, *People in Quandaries* (New York: Harper, 1946).

85 Heaton, *The Eye,* pp. 99, 100, 105, 117.

86 S. Arieti, "The Microgeny of Thought and Perception" in *Archives of General Psychology* 6 (1962): p. 454.

87 T. E. Wechowic, "Shape Constancy in Schizophrenic Patients" in *Journal of Abnormal and Soc. Psychology* 68 (1964): p. 177.

88 J. Chapman, "The Early Symptoms of Schizophrenia" in *British Journal of Psychiatry* 112 (1966): p. 225.

89 L. Bender, *A Visual Motor Gestalt Test and Its Clinical Use* (New York: The American Orthopsychiatric Ass., 1938).

90 W. Mayer-Gross, "Experimental Psychoses and other Mental Abnormalities Produced by Drugs" in *British Medical Journal* 2 (1951): 317.

91 See W. Dennis, "Cultural and Developmental Factors in Perception" in Blake and Ramsey, *Perception: An Approach to Personality,* p. 148.

92 R. E. L. Masters and J. Houston, *The Varieties of Psychedelic Experience* (New York: Dell, 1966).

93 For some cultural factors in misperception see Heider, *The Psychology of Interpersonal Relations,* pp. 53 et seq.

94 Blake and Ramsey, *Perception: An Approach to Personality,* p. 5.

95 Hastorf, Schneider and Polefks, *Person Perception,* p. 39.

96 Asch, *Forming Impressions of Personality.*

97 J. Wishner, "Reanalysis of Impressions of Personality" in *Psychological Review* 67 (1960): pp. 96–112.

98 Shoham, *The Mark of Cain.*

99 Jones and Kanouse, eds., *Attribution: Perceiving the Causes of Behavior,* p. 9.

100 Ibid.

101 See J. Piaget, *The Child's Conception of the World* (New York: Humanities Press, 1951); Piaget, *The Moral Judgement of the Child* (New York: The Free Press, 1948).

102 For references to the theoretical formulation and empirical evidence for this

premise see D. O'Donovan, "Rating Extremity: Pathology or Meaningfulness", in *Readings for a Cognitive Theory of Personality*, p. 326.

103 Hastorf, Schneider and Polefks, *Person Perception*, pp. 16–17.

104 Jones and Kanouse, eds., *Attribution: Perceiving the Causes of Behavior*, p. 86.

105 J. Bieri, "Cognitive Complexity, Simplicity and Predictive Behavior" in *Readings for a Cognitive Theory of Personality*, p. 277.

106 Ibid.

107 D. Byrne, "Interpersonal Attraction as a Function of Affiliation, Need and Attitude Similarity", in *Readings for a Cognitive Theory of Personality*, pp. 548 et seq.

108 Jones and Kanouse, *Attribution: Perceiving the Causes of Behavior*; E. E. Jones and R. E. Nisbett, *The Actor and the Observer: Divergent Perceptions of Causes of Behavior* (New York: General Learning Press, 1971), p. 85.

109 Ibid.

110 D. J. Bern, "Self Perception Theory" in *Advances in Experimental Social Psychology*, ed. L. Berkowitz (New York: Academic Press, 1965).

111 S. Valins, "Cognitive Effects of False Heart Rate Feedback" in *Journal of Personology and Social Psychology* (1966): pp. 400–8.

112 G. C. Davison and S. Valins, "Maintenance of Self-Observation and Response to Aversive Stimulation" in *Journal of Personology and Social Psychology* 16 (1970): pp. 1–4.

113 R. V. Exline, "Visual Interaction: The Glances of Power and Preference" in *Nebraska Symposium on Motivation* (1971), p. 185.

114 P. Ekman and W. V. Frieser, "Non-Verbal Leakage and Clues to Deception" in *Social Encounters*, ed. M. Argyle (Harmondsworth: Pelican Books, 1973), pp. 132 et seq.

115 See E. E. Jones and K. E. Davis, "From Acts to Disposition" in *Advances in Experimental Social Psychology*, p. 219.

116 For the primacy and recency effects on person perception see A. S. Luchins, "Primacy-Recency in Impression Formation" in Howland, *The Order of Presentation in Persuasion* (New York: Yale University Press).

117 J. Mills and J. M. Jellison, "Effect on Opinion Change of How Desirable the Communication is to the Audience the Communicator Addressed" in *Journal of Personality and Social Psychology* 6 (1967): pp. 98–101.

118 E. E. Jones, K. J. Gergen and R. G. Jones, "Tactics of Ingratiation Among Leaders and Subordinates in a Status Hierarchy" in *Psychological Monographs* 77 (1963): p. 566.

119 A. Pepitone, "Motivational Effects in Social Perception" in *Human Relations* 1 (1950): pp. 57–76.

120 Hastorf, Schneider and Polefks, *Person Perception*, p. 51.

121 Allen, *Situational Factors in Conformity*, p. 113.

122 E. E. Jones and K. E. Davis "From Acts to Dispositions", in ibid., p. 222.

123 S. Schachter and J. E. Singer, "Cognitive, Social and Physiological Determinants of Emotional States" in *Psychological Review* 69 (1962): 379–9.

124 P. Ekman, "Universals and Cultural Differences in Facial Expressions of Emotions" in *Nebraska Symposium on Motivation* (1970), pp. 207 et seq.

125 W. LaBarre, "The Cultural Basis of Emotions and Gestures" in *Journal of Personality* 16 (1947): p. 55.

126 R. L. Birdwhistell, "The Kinetic Level in the Investigation of Emotions" in *Expression of the Emotions in Man*, ed. P. H. Knapp (New York: International University Press, 1963), p. 126.

127 Laing, *Self and Others*.

128 See M. Argyle and J. Dean, "Eye Contact, Distance and Affiliation" in *Sociometry* 28 (1965): pp. 289–304.

129 M. D. Reimer, "Abnormalities of the Gaze, A Classification" in *Psychiatric Quarterly* 29: 659–72.

130 G. Simmel, "Sociology of the Senses: Visual Interaction" in *Introduction to the Science of Sociology*, ed. R. E. Park and E. W. Burgess (Chicago: University of Chicago Press, 1924), p. 358.

131 R. D. Laing, H. Phillipson and A. R. Lee, *Interpersonal Perception* (New York: Harper & Row, 1966).

6 The Errant Ego and Its Errands

1 *Talmud Sanhedrin*, chapter 4.

2 M. Buber, *Tales of the Hassidim: The Early Masters* (New York: Schocken Books, 1968), p. 251.

3 Heider, *The Psychology of Interpersonal Relations*, p. 156-7.

4 J. P. Sartre, "An Explication of The Stranger" in *Camus*, ed. Germaine (Englewood Cliffs, 1962), p. 109.

5 A. Camus, *Notebooks* (New York: The Modern Library, 1965), p. 52.

6 Heider, *The Psychology of Interpersonal Relations*, p. 35-7.

7 E. Frenkel-Brunswick, "Personality Theory and Perception" in *Perception: An Approach to Personality*, eds. R. R. Blake and G. V. Ramsey (New York: The Ronald Press, 1951), p. 376.

8 M. Nordau, *The Conventional Lies of Our Civilization* (Tel Aviv: Mitzpah Publishing Co., 1930), p. 99.

9 Shoham, *The Myth of Tantalus*, chapter 2.

10 D. E. Kanouse and L. R. Henson Jr., "Negativity in Evaluations" in *Attribution: Perceiving the Causes of Behavior*, eds. E. E. Jones and D. E. Kanouse (USA and Canada: General Learning Press, 1971), pp. 49, 52.

11 Ibid., p. 56.

12 G. S. Klein, "The Personal World Through Perception" in *Perception*, eds. Blake and Ramsey, p. 333.

13 R. C. Oldfield, "Memory Mechanisms and the Theory of Schemata" in *Readings for A Cognitive Theory of Personality*, ed. J. C. Mancuso (New York: Holt, Rinehart and Winston, 1970).

14 See J. G. Miller "Unconscious Processes and Perception" in *Perception*, eds. Blake and Ramsey, pp. 272 et seq.

15 S. Schachter and J. E. Singer, "Cognitive, Social and Physiological Determinants of Emotional States" in *Psychological Review* 69 (1962): pp. 373–99.

16 R. E. Nisbett and S. Valins, "Perceiving the Causes of One's Own Behavior" in *Attribution: Perceiving the Causes of Behavior*, eds. Jones and Kanouse.

17 Schachter and Singer, *Cognitive, Social and Physiological Determinants of Emotional State*.

18   J. London, *Martin Eden* (New York: Penguin Books, 1936), p. 342.

7   Involvement and Interaction

1   S. G. Shoham, *Salvation Through the Gutters* (Washington: Hemisphere Publications, 1979).
2   Camus, *The Misunderstanding*, pp. 91–2.
3   Ibid., p. 92.
4   Ibid., p. 96.
5   Ibid., p. 132.
6   Laing, *Self and Others*, p. 87.
7   Ibid., p. 85.
8   Compare G. Ichheiser, *Misunderstandings in Human Relations* (Chicago: University of Chicago Press, 1949), pp. 18, 37.
9   L. R. Houseman and G. Levine, "Incremental Exchange Theory: A Formal Model for Progression in Dyadic Social Interaction" in *Advances in Experimental Soc. Psych*. Vol. 9, ed. L. Berkowitz (New York: Academic Press, 1954), pp. 191–229.
10   M. Buber, "Distance and Relations" in *Psychiatry* 20 (1957).
11   Laing, *Self and Others*.
12   M. Merleau-Ponty, *Phenomenology of Perception*, p. 43.
13   Shoham, *The Myth of Tantalus*, chapter 2.
14   See M. Klein, *Contributions to Psychoanalysis* (London: Hogarth Press, 1948), p. 27.
15   See Heider, *The Psychology of Interpersonal Relations*, p. 194–5.
16   S. Freud, *New Introductory Lectures in Psychoanalysis* (New York: W. W. Norton & Co., 1933), and p. 91.
17   J. S. Bruner, "Review of G. A. Kelly's 'The Psychology of Personal Constructs'" in *Contemporary Psychology* 1 (1956): pp. 355–7.
18   M. Sherif, D. Taub and I. Holland, "Assimilation and Contrast Effects of Anchoring Stimuli on Judgments" in *Journal of Experimental Psychology* 55 (1958): 150–5.
19   Freud, *New Introductory Lectures*, p. 91.
20   W. C. Schutz, *FIRO: A Three-Dimensional Theory of Interpersonal Behavior* (New York: Holt, Rinehart & Winston, 1958).
21   The basic work on this subject that served as a basis for numerous replications and developments is D. C. McClelland, J. W. Atkinson and E. L. Lowell, *The Achievement Motive* (New York: Appleton-Century-Crofts, 1953).
22   S. Schachter, "Experimental Studies of the Sources of Gregariousness" in *The Psychology of Affiliation* (California: Stanford University Press, 1965).
23   R. V. Exline, "Visual Interaction: The Glances of Power and Preference" in *Nebraska Symposium on Motivation* (1971): p. 167.
24   N. Mailer, *Armies of the Night* (New York: Dial Press, 1964), pp. 160–3.
25   H. H. Kelly, *Attribution in Social Interaction* (New York: General Learning Press, 1971), p. 8.
26   Laing, *Self and Others*, p. 108, et seq.
27   Merleau-Ponty, *Phenomenology of Perception*, Preface, p. xiii.
28   Exline, *Visual Interaction*, p. 189.
29   Sullivan, *Psychoanalysis and Interpersonal Psychiatry*.
30   Shoham, *Myth of Tantalus*, chapters 1, 2.

31   See E. E. Jones and D. E. Kanouse, eds., *Attribution: Perceiving the Causes of Behavior* (Morristown, N.J., General Learning Press, 1972).

32   S. Freud, *An Autobiographical Study* (London: Hogarth Press and Institute of Psychoanalysis, 1946), pp. 75–6.

33   Amos Elon, *Herzl* (Tel Aviv: Am Oved Pub. House, 1976), p. 314.

34   See Heider, *The Psychology of Interpersonal Relations,* p. 193.

35   F. Nietzsche, *The Birth of Tragedy* (New York: Random House, 1927), p. 951.

36   For a full exposition of the Tantalus Ratio see Shoham, *Myth of Tantalus.*

37   E. R. Leach, "Michelangelo's Genesis" in *Times Literary Supplement,* March 18, 1977.

38   C. Lévi-Strauss, *The Savage Mind* (Chicago: Chicago University Press, 1966), pp. 23 et seq.

39   F. Nietzsche, *Thus Spake Zarathustra* (New York: The Modern Library, 1937), p. 3.

8   Personality Type – The Medium Controlling the Message

1   Laing, *Self and Others,* pp. 44 et seq.

2   Ibid., pp. 48–49.

3   Ibid., pp. 112–13.

4   P. Ekman and W. V. Friesen, "Non Verbal Leakage and Clues to Deception" in *Psychiatry* 32 (1969): pp. 88–105.

5   E. Goffman, *The Presentation of Self in Everyday Life* (Edinburgh: Edinburgh University Press, 1956).

6   H. C. Triandis, "Cultural Influences Upon Cognitive Processes" in *Advances in Experimental Social Psychology,* ed. L. Berkowitz (New York: Academic Press, 1964), pp. 1–41.

7   Cited in R. R. Blake and G. V. Ramsey eds., *Perception: An Approach to Personality* (New York: The Ronald Press, 1951), p. 15.

8   See M. Cole and S. Scribner, *Culture and Thought* (New York: Wiley, 1974), p. 87.

9   Ibid., p. 71

10   J. W. Berry, "Ecology and Socialization as Factors in Figural Assimilation and the Resolution of Binocular Rivalry" in *International Journal of Psychology* 4 (1969): pp. 271–80.

11   M. H. Segall, D. T. Campbell and M. J. Herskovitz, *The Influence of Culture on Visual Perception* (Chicago: Bobbs-Merrill, 1966).

12   Ibid.

13   M. Wober, "Distinguishing Centri-Cultural from Cross-Cultural Tests and Research" in *Perception and Motor Skills* 28 (1969): p. 488.

14   Shoham, *Myth of Tantalus,* chapter 2.

15   E. G. French, "Effects of Interaction of Motivation and Feedback on Task Performance" in *Readings for a Cognitive Theory of Personality,* ed. J. C. Mancuso (New York: Holt, Rinehart and Winston, 1970), p. 399.

16   E. T. Hall, "A System of Notation of Proxemic Behavior" in *American Anthropologist* 65 (1963): pp. 1003–26.

17   O. M. Watson and T. D. Graves, "Quantitative Research in Proxemic Behavior" in *American Anthropologist* 68 (1966): pp. 971–85.

18   P. Ekman, "Universals and Cultural Differences in Facial Expressions of Emotion" in *Nebraska Symposium on Motivation* (1971), pp. 207–83.

19 Ibid., p. 216.

20 Ibid., p. 225.

21 Ibid., p. 257.

22 M. Cole and S. Scribner, *Culture and Thought* (New York: Wiley, 1974), p. 184.

23 E. E. Evans-Pritchard, *Essays in Social Anthropology* (New York: The Free Press of Glencoe, 1963), p. 211.

24 Ibid., p. 228.

25 Shoham, *The Mark of Cain.*

26 H. Garfinkel, "Conditions of Successful Degradation Ceremonies" in *American Journal of Sociology* 61 (1956): pp. 421–2.

27 J. L. Simmons and H. Chambers, "Public Stereotypes of Deviants" in *Social Problems* 13 (1965).

28 Shoham, *Mark of Cain,* p. 111.

29 T. J. Scheff, ed., *Mental Illness and Social Processes* (New York: Harper & Row, 1967).

30 T. J. Scheff, *Being Mentally Ill* (Chicago: Aldine, 1966), pp. 33–4.

31 T. J. Scheff, *Labeling Madness* (Englewood Cliffs: Prentice-Hall, 1975), p. 5.

32 J. Nunnally, *Popular Conceptions of Mental Health* (New York: Holt, Rinehart & Winston, 1961), p. 233.

33 See Shoham, *Mark of Cain,* chapter 9.

34 M. K. Temerlin, "Suggestion Effects in Psychiatric Diagnosis" in *Journal of Nervous and Mental Disease* 147 (1968): pp. 349–58.

35 D. L. Rosenham, "On Being Sane in Insane Places" in *Science* 179 (1973): pp. 250–8.

36 W. R. Gove, "Societal Reaction, an Explanation of Mental Illness: An Evaluation" in *American Sociological Review* 35 (1970): pp. 874–84. Cited in T. S. Szasz, *The Manufacture of Madness* (St. Albans: Paladin, 1973), p. 354.

38 W. Wickleburgh and D. W. Porritt, "Transforming Theory into Legislation" in *Focusing* on *Madness,* eds. E. Bates and P. R. Wilson (Brisbane: University of Queensland Press, 1978).

39 N. N. Kittrie, *The Right to be Different* (Baltimore: The Johns Hopkins Press, 1971).

40 S. Bloch and P. Reddaway, *Psychiatric Terror: How Soviet Psychiatry is Used to Suppress Dissent* (New York: Basic Books, 1977).

41 *Time Magazine,* September 12, 1977.

42 Cited in Carl Solomon "Report from the Asylum" in *Protest,* eds. G. Feldman and M. Gartenberg (London: Panther, 1960), pp. 139–40.

43 A. Janik and S. Toulmin, *Wittgenstein's Vienna* (New York: Simon and Schuster, 1973), pp. 61–2.

44 R. Greenly, "Alternative Views of the Psychiatric Role" in Scheff, *Labeling Madness,* pp. 41–2.

9   Defenses, Rituals and Slanted Congruity

1 S. Freud, *Inhibitions, Symptoms and Anxiety* (London: The Hogarth Press, 1959), p. 20.

2 Shoham, *The Myth of Tantalus,* chapters 6 and 7.

3 P. R. Singer, "A Cognitive View of Rationalized Projection" in *Journal of Projective Techniques and Personality Assessment* 27 (1963): pp. 235–43.

4 J. Piaget, "Principal Factors Determining Intellectual Evolution from Childhood to Adult Life" in *Factors Determining Human Behavior* (Cambridge, Mass.: Harvard University Press, 1937).

5   G. Ichheiser, "Misunderstandings in Human Relations: A Study in False Social Perception" in supplement to the 1949 issue of *American Journal of Sociology*, p. 51.

6   E. Goffman, *The Presentation of Self in Everyday Life* (Edinburgh: Edinburgh University Press, 1956).

7   Ibid., p. 24.

8   R. R. Blake and G. V. Ramsey, *Perception: An Approach to Personality* (New York: The Ronald Press, 1951), p. 164.

9   These are the classic F scale and Rokeach's measure of open and closed mindedness. See T. W. Adorno, E. Frenkel-Brunswick, D. J. Kevinson, and R. N. Sanford, *The Authoritarian Personality* (New York: Harper & Row, 1950); M. Rokeach, *The Open and Closed Mind* (New York: Basic Books, 1960).

10   E. E. Jones and D. E. Kanouse, *Attribution: Perceiving the Causes of Behavior* (Morristown, New Jersey: General Learning Press, 1972).

11   H. Levy and R. D. Dugan, "A Factorial Study of Personal Constructs" in *Readings for a Cognitive Theory of Personality*, ed. J. C. Mancuso (New York: Holt, Rinehart and Winston, 1970).

12   Janik and Toulmin, *Wittgenstein's Vienna*, pp. 61–2.

13   Goffman, *Presentation of Self in Everyday Life*, pp. 66, 14.

14   Ibid., pp. 50, 52, 53.

15   Ibid., p. 77.

16   Ibid., p. 142.

17   Ibid., p. 29.

18   Shoham, *The Mark of Cain*, chap. 4.

19   Ibid., chap. 6.

20   Goffman, *Presentation of Self in Everyday Life*, p. 42.

21   Ibid.

22   Ibid., p. 75.

23   P. M. Blau and W. R. Scott, "Processes of Communication in Formal Organizations" in *Social Encounters*.

24   R. K. Merton, "Social Structure and Anomie" in *Social Theory and Social Structure* (New York: The Free Press, 1957).

25   E. A. Tiryakian, *Socialogism and Existentialism* (Englewood Cliffs: Prentice-Hall, 1962), p. 129.

26   G. B. Shaw in F. Harris, *Oscar Wilde* (New York: Dell, 1960), p. 355.

27   Goffman, *Presentation of Self in Everyday Life*, chap. 1.

28   E. Aronson, "The Theory of Cognitive Dissonance" in *Advances in Experimental Social Psychology*, Vol. IV, ed. L. Berkovitz (New York: Academic Press, 1969).

29   For other instances of defense mechanisms to reduce cognitive dissonance see P. R. Singer, "A Cognitive View of Rationalized Projection" in *Journal of Projective Techniques and Personality Assessment* 27 (1963): pp. 235–43.

30   L. Festinger, *A Theory of Cognitive Dissonance* (Stanford: Stanford University Press, 1957), p. 137.

31   J. L. Freedman and D. O. Sears, "Selective Exposure" in *Advances in Experimental Social Psychology*, pp. 58–60.

32   Ibid., p. 69.

33   Krech, Crutchfield and Ballachey, *Individual in Society*, p. 38.

34   F. Frenkel-Brunswick, "Intolerance of Ambiguity as an Emotional and Perceptual

Variable" in *Journal of Personology* 18 (1949): pp. 108–43; *The Open and Closed Mind* (New York: Basic Books, 1960).

35   Aronson, *Theory of Cognitive Dissonance.*

36   Festinger, *Theory of Cognitive Dissonance,* pp. 16–77.

37   Heider, *The Psychology of Interpersonal Relations,* p. 183.

38   O. Y. Harvey, H. H. Kelly and A. A. Shapiro, "Reaction to Unfavorable Evaluations of the Self by Other People" in *Journal of Personality* (1957): pp. 393–411.

39   Shoham, *The Myth of Tantalus.*

40   Festinger, Riecken and Schachter, *When Prophecy Fails,* p. 4.

41   Ibid., chap. 1.

42   J. L. Freedman and D. O. Sears, "Selective Exposure" in *Advances in Experimental Social Psychology* (1975): p. 58.

43   M. Sherif, O. Taub and C. I. Howland, "Assimilation and Contrast Effects of Anchoring Stimuli on Judgments" in *Journal of Experimental Psychology* 55 (1958): pp. 150–55.

44   Freedman and Sears, *Selective Exposure,* pp. 58, 77, 92, 61–3, 76–7.

45   Aronson, *Theory of Cognitive Dissonance,* p. 3.

46   L. Festinger and J. M. Carlsmith, "Cognitive Consequence of Forced Compliance" in *Journal of Abnormal Social Psychology* 58 (1959): pp. 203–10.

47   Aronson, *Theory of Cognitive Dissonance,* p. 5.

10   Petrification

1   See R. F. Geyer and D. R. Schweitzer, *Theories of Alienation* (Leiden: Nijhoff 1976); R. Schacht, *Alienation* (New York: Doubleday Anchor, 1971); J. Israel, *Alienation* (Boston: Alyn and Bacon, 1971).

2   Sartre, *Being and Nothingness,* p. 218.

3   Ibid., p. 231.

4   Ibid., p. 236.

5   Ibid., pp. 241, 245, 248, 261, 265.

6   Eliezer Ben Yehuda, *Thesaurus Totius Hebraitatis,* Vol. VIII, p. 4046.

7   Exline, *Visual Interaction: The Glances of Power and Preference,* p. 167.

8   Schacht, *Alienation,* p. 40.

9   See Merleau-Ponty, *Phenomenology of Perception,* p.40.

10   J. Genet, *The Maids* (London: Faber and Faber, 1959), p. 16.

11   D. Reisman et al., *The Lonely Crowd* (New Haven: Yale University Press, 1961).

12   M. Heidegger, *Existence and Being* (Chicago: Regnery, 1949), p. 29.

13   R. W. Emerson, *Selections* (Boston: Houghton Mifflin Co., 1960), p. 61.

14   Israel, *Alienation,* chapters 3 and 4.

15   S. E. Asch, *Social Psychology* (Englewood Cliffs: Prentice-Hall, 1961).

16   H. Arendt, *Eichman in Jerusalem* (London: Faber and Faber, 1963).

Index

Note: This is an index of concepts, not persons. The persons mentioned in the text are (with exceptions that have been included in the index *in passim*) illustrative examples or authorities.

Index